INDUSTRIAL RELATIONS LAW

INDUSTRIAL RELATIONS LAW IN THE UK

Pascale LORBER
Tonia NOVITZ

intersentia

Cambridge – Antwerp – Portland

Intersentia Publishing Ltd.
Trinity House | Cambridge Business Park | Cowley Road
Cambridge | CB4 0WZ | United Kingdom
Tel.: +44 1223 393 753 | Email: mail@intersentia.co.uk

Distribution for the UK:
Hart Publishing Ltd.
16C Worcester Place
Oxford OX1 2JW
UK
Tel.: +44 1865 517 530
Email: mail@hartpub.co.uk

Distribution for the USA and Canada:
International Specialized Book Services
920 NE 58th Ave. Suite 300
Portland, OR 97213
USA
Tel.: +1 800 944 6190 (toll free)
Email: info@isbs.com

Distribution for Austria:
Neuer Wissenschaftlicher Verlag
Argentinierstraße 42/6
1040 Wien
Austria
Tel.: +43 1 535 61 03 24
Email: office@nwv.at

Distribution for other countries:
Intersentia Publishing nv
Groenstraat 31
2640 Mortsel
Belgium
Tel.: +32 3 680 15 50
Email: mail@intersentia.be

Industrial Relations Law in the UK
Pascale Lorber and Tonia Novitz

© 2012 Intersentia
Cambridge – Antwerp – Portland
www.intersentia.com | www.intersentia.co.uk

ISBN 978-90-5095-959-9
NUR 828

British Library Cataloguing in Publication Data. A catalogue record for this book is available from the British Library.

PREFACE

'Industrial Relations' is not a phrase that is often used today. It may appear to be something of the past, reminiscent of times when trade unions were strong and significantly influential. It corresponds to an era where employment relations were primarily 'regulated' or determined by collective actors, on a national, sectoral or plant level. In those times, law played a relatively minor role and it was regarded by the relevant actors as unnecessary. The Industrial Relations Act 1971 was a first attempt to regulate the industrial actors comprehensively. Yet, it was unsuccessful as unions did not cooperate with what the legal framework required. Referring to 'industrial relations law' was perhaps very pertinent under the successive Conservative governments of the 1980s and the 1990s as trade unions became subject to a raft of measures designed to limit their powers and influence. Is industrial relations law still relevant today? While the title of this book was chosen by the author of the Belgian volume who had started commissioning a series of manuscripts on this subject,[1] it appears very pertinent to consider this area of law at a time when the concept of industrial relations is at a crossroads. In this book, industrial relations law is understood broadly as covering the law applicable to collective actors.[2] These are primarily trade unions and the book therefore follows a relatively traditional approach of considering the relationship between trade unions and employers and between trade unions and their members. However, two factors make it important to re-consider the traditional approach and to take a slightly different view on industrial relations. Firstly, the strength of the unions seems to be consistently declining as membership decreases and the coverage of collective bargaining diminishes. Secondly, another type of collective voice has emerged. Mainly introduced by European Community (now Union) law, employee representatives can be involved in decision making via information and consultation mechanisms. For this purpose, a dual channel of representation was created and non-union representation is increasing. This picture is explained by a number of factors ranging from economic developments to political and regulatory choices. The outcome is a worrying yet potentially interesting future. The negative assessment

---

[1]   M. RIGAUX and P. HUMBLET, *Belgian Industrial Relations Law*, Intersentia EWL, Antwerp 2005.
[2]   Although it is rightfully more largely defined as an area of social relations and an academic subject that analyses the world of work in L. CLARKE, E. DONNELLY, R. HYMAN, J. KELLY, S. MCKAY and S. MOORE, 'What's the Point of Industrial Relations?' (2011) 27 *International Journal of Comparative Labour Law and Industrial Relations* 239.

results from the lack of legal initiatives that would truly reform and invigorate the traditional role and functions of trade unions (collective bargaining and industrial action), despite constant criticism by transnational bodies that uphold human rights and fundamental freedoms. The positive outlook is inspired by the potential that instruments such as the Information and Consultation of Employees Regulations can create for trade unions and non-trade union representatives. These topics have been considered through six chapters. Firstly, 'Industrial Relations and the Law' looks at the current picture created by successive governmental policies. Actors and the tools available to them to exercise their roles are examined, highlighting new functions and how the law is dealing with the category of non-union representatives. The second chapter tackles freedom of association and how governments seem to have taken very little notice of its application in the UK. Thirdly, the trade union's principal function of collective bargaining is analysed, assessing the legacy of the statutory recognition procedure. In the fourth chapter, relationships between members and their unions are examined, demonstrating that internal union affairs have been unduly interfered with by the law. The subject of industrial action follows in the fifth chapter. Finally, chapter 6 considers the statutory obligation to inform and consult workers via representatives.

Many people have helped with the production of this book. Firstly, we are most grateful to Intersentia and Tom Scheirs and Ann-Christin Maak in particular, for their patience and understanding. Pascale thanks her co-author Tonia Novitz for agreeing to work with her and for her extraordinary assistance and input during the long life of this project. Pascale is also thankful to the University of Leicester for granting study leaves to write and complete this book. She benefitted from much support from her colleagues at the law school, with special thanks going to Mark Bell and David Antill. Working with the University College Union (UCU) on a local level has also contributed to some of Pascale's reflections. Thanks go to Sue Davis and Julie Cooper for their insight. Finally, on a personal level, writing this book would not have been possible without an incredibly supportive family. Pascale *remercie chaleureusement ses parents*. She also dedicates this book to Oliver Woolhouse and to Theo and Hugo Woolhouse-Lorber who are always a great source of joy. Tonia likewise owes many thanks to her co-author for including her in this exciting project. She owes thanks to the University of Bristol for study leave which has helped to complete this book. She has benefitted tremendously from the assistance of colleagues there and institutions elsewhere, especially Charlotte Villiers, Lydia Hayes, Alan Bogg, and Shae McCrystal. As always, Tonia thanks Phil Syrpis for his ongoing support and is very grateful to Alex and Kris Syrpis for their continued ability to distract her from the world of work.

Pascale Lorber and Tonia Novitz, March 2012

CONTENTS

LIST OF ABBREVIATIONS

ACAS	Advisory, Conciliation and Arbitration Service
BIS	Department for Business, Innovation and Skills
BJIR	British Journal of Industrial Relations
CAC	Central Arbitration Committee
CBI	Confederation of British Industry
CEACR	ILO Committee of Experts on the Application of Conventions and Recommendations
CFA	ILO Governing Body Committee on Freedom of Association
CJEU	Court of Justice of the European Union (used for all cases including for those decided prior to the change of name from European Court of Justice to the current CJEU)
CO	Certification Officer
EA	Employment Act
ECHR	European Convention on Human Rights
ECtHR	European Court of Human Rights
ECR	European Court Reports
EPA	Employment Protection Act
ERA	Employment Rights Act
ERelA	Employment Relations Act
ESC	European Social Charter
ETUC	European Trade Union Confederation
EU	European Union
EUCFR	European Union Charter of Fundamental Rights
EWC	European Works Council
FTER	Fixed Term Employees (Prevention of Less Favourable Treatment) Regulations
HRA	Human Rights Act
HRC	Human Rights Committee
ICCPR	International Covenant on Civil and Political Rights
ICER	Information and Consultation of Employees Regulations
ICESCR	International Covenant on Economic, Social and Cultural Rights
IJCLLIR	International Journal of Comparative Labour Law and Industrial Relations
ILO	International Labour Organisation
ILJ	Industrial Law Journal

IRA	Industrial Relations Act
IRJ	Industrial Relations Journal
IRLR	Industrial Relations Law Reports
MLR	Modern Law Review
SI	Statutory Instrument
TUC	Trades Union Congress
TICER	Transnational Information and Consultation of Employees Regulations
TULRCA	Trade Union and Labour Relations (Consolidation) Act
TUPE	Transfer of Undertakings (Protection of Employment) Regulations
UDHR	Universal Declaration on Human Rights
UN	United Nations

CHAPTER 1

INDUSTRIAL RELATIONS
AND THE LAW

1. INTRODUCTION – THE STATE OF INDUSTRIAL RELATIONS

Today's industrial relations landscape is difficult to paint in all its complexity. It is a landscape that has evolved over time but in a fashion which suggests a change in the role of collective actors and a potential weakening of their significance. Despite a brief stasis, from 1997–2010, generally membership of trade unions and employers associations is in decline.[1] Trade union membership was at 7.3 million in 2010–11 compared with a peak 13.2 in 1979.[2] Union density was 27% in 2010 compared with 50% in 1980.[3] As a result, the coverage of collective bargaining is also shrinking.[4] As workplace representatives become a rarer breed, there are growing concerns regarding a 'representation gap', namely the gap between the number of people who want some form of collective representation and those who actually enjoy this.[5]

The factors explaining the fall in the number of people joining unions and those represented by unions are varied but taken together, they explain the current state of affairs. Changes in the economic environment in which undertakings operate reduce the opportunities for union presence: for example manufacturing and public sectors, which have been traditional strongholds for unions, are shrinking; outsourcing is growing and the varieties of atypical employment relationship make it more difficult for unions to recruit and organise. Additionally, and of importance for this book, the law has imposed restrictions on unions to exercise their traditional functions (for example by outlawing the

---

[1] Certification Officer, Annual Report 2010–11, p. 2.
[2] Certification Officer, Annual Report 2010–11, para. 4.6.
[3] C.F. WRIGHT, 'What role for trade unions in future workplace relations' (ACAS Future of Workplace Relations discussion paper series, September 2011), p. 2.
[4] See chapter 3.
[5] See for example, DTI, *Workplace Representatives: a Review of their Facilities, Government Response to Public Consultation*, November 2007, reported in M. WYNN and G. PITT, 'The Revised Acas Code of Practice 2010 on Time Off for Trade Union Duties and Activities: Another Missed Opportunity' (2010) 39 *ILJ (Industrial Law Journal)* 209.

closed shop, encouraging direct communication with individuals, and limiting the ability to take industrial action). Some positive developments do provide a counterbalance to this rather bleak picture. Unions have merged, as have employers' associations, to become stronger actors. The number of days lost because of labour disputes is increasing in the light of public sector cuts, showing that collective action is still seen as effective by some workers and their unions.[6] Other collective voices are developing to supplement and sometimes replace trade unions. Representatives have acquired new statutory functions which still support workers, but in novel ways.

The purpose of this chapter is to establish how the current landscape has emerged, focussing on the role of the law in the industrial relations picture. The first section will consider how public policy and judicial interventions have shaped the law currently applicable to collective actors. Secondly, the current legal status, roles and protection granted to such actors will be examined. Thirdly, the institutions that certify the existence of the collective organisations and intervene in times of conflict are scrutinised. Finally, questions are asked about the future of traditional stakeholders considering the economic and political climate.

2. POLICY HISTORY AND COLLECTIVE LABOUR LAW

There have been a number of important stages in the history of labour law which shape today's regulation of collective relations. Only a brief chronological analysis is provided below, as other commentators have written extensively on this issue.[7] While originally the courts attempted to limit the development of a collective voice for workers, parliament aided trade unions to establish themselves as lawful organisations, entitled to protect workers' interests within certain parameters when organising collective action. After a period of 'abstinence' from legal intervention and a growth of trade unions' influence, legislation has acted as a pendulum for and against trade unions, either trying to limit its powers or encouraging the exercising of its traditional functions, depending on the political ethos governing the country.

---

[6]   Labour Disputes, Labour Market Statistics, December 2011 available from Office of National Statistics, <www.ons.gov.uk/ons/rel/lms/labour-market-statistics/december-2011/statistical-bulletin.html#tab-Labour-disputes--not-seasonally-adjusted-> accessed 16.12.2011.

[7]   For example, P. DAVIES and M. FREEDLAND, *Labour Legislation and Public Policy*, Clarendon Press, Oxford 1993, and *Towards a Flexible Labour Market: Labour Legislation and Regulations since the 1990s*, Oxford University Press, Oxford 2007.

2.1. TRADE UNIONS AND THE COMMON LAW

In the 18th and 19th centuries, in an environment of industrial revolution, attempts by workers' organisations to bargain with employers to increase wages and improve conditions of employment, or to strike, were unlawful either under criminal or tort law. The Combination Acts 1799 and 1800 made collective organisations of workers illegal. Trade unions could also be accused of criminal conspiracy at common law. Interference with wages or any of the prerogatives of the employer were deemed unacceptable. Common law was therefore hostile to collectivist values.

Nevertheless, from the late 19th century onwards, Britain started decriminalising combinations of workers. The 1871 Trade Union Act recognised trade unions as lawful organisations that could defend workers' rights and that should be free from legal intervention in their internal affairs. Employers reacted by seeking to use civil law and tort, in particular, to limit the role of trade unions in shaping terms and conditions of employment and in using strikes. For example, trade unions that called workers out on strike would be accused by employers of committing the tort of inducing breach of contract. Judges were sympathetic to employers' arguments and the House of Lords decided that trade unions could be sued in their own names for damages and could therefore face bankruptcy.[8] Parliament responded to judicial creativity by enacting the Trade Dispute Act 1906 giving immunities to trade unions against some torts such as inducing breach of contract and conspiracy when they were organising industrial action. The immunities would only be triggered however, if certain conditions were met; in particular, the industrial action had to take place '*in contemplation or furtherance of a trade dispute*'. In this event, the trade union had a blanket immunity from being sued for tortious liability. For over half a century this Act was going to protect industrial actions from the interference of the courts.

2.2. *LAISSEZ FAIRE* AND THE DONOVAN REPORT

For the larger part of the 20th century, at least until the 1960s, the role of the law was limited in collective employment relations. The period was labelled as *laissez faire* because workers' and employers' organisations were best left to negotiate terms and conditions in workplaces through collective bargaining. Governments did not regulate the establishment of a bargaining system either.[9] The result was

---

[8]   *Taff Vale Railway Co v Amalgamated Society of Railway Servants* [1901] AC 426.
[9]   P. DAVIES and M. FREEDLAND, *Labour Legislation and Public Policy*, Clarendon Press, Oxford 1993, pp. 8–24.

the presence of strong trade unions on a national, sectoral and workplace level to bargain with employers.

By the 1960s, there was a perception that the industrial decline in the UK was due to the increasing role and powers of trade unions, in particular of their shop stewards. There were a growing number of unofficial 'wildcat' strikes.[10] The courts had tried to deal with this by limiting the protection given to trade unions through their interpretation of the immunity system,[11] but this was not deemed sufficient. As a result, a Royal Commission on Trade Unions and Employers' Associations, lead by Lord Donovan was appointed in 1965. Its task was to *'consider relations between management and employees and the role of trade unions and employers' associations in promoting the interests of their members and in accelerating the social and economic advance of the nation'*. The final report of 1968 found a trend of decline in the traditional industry-wide collective bargaining and a growth of chaotic arrangements at plant level. The conclusions led to a number of reforms. From then on, the idea of 'taming' trade unions and their powers were championed by successive Conservative governments, using different methods, while Labour tried first to restore some of the unions' freedom before modestly trying to repair some of the worst damage inflicted on unions by the Thatcher –Major era of the 1980–90s.

2.3. CONSERVATIVE v LABOUR: REGULATING TRADE UNIONS AFFAIRS AND ACTIVITIES

The Heath government elected in 1970 wanted to draw some lessons from the Donovan Report and enacted the 1971 Industrial Relations Act (IRA). It was radical because it went further than the Donovan Report and tried to import American and continental concepts of labour law. This was particularly the case with regard to the powers and organisational capacity of the trade unions. The new legislation tried to use the law to regulate trade unions affairs and collective bargaining. This was a fundamental change of culture, since the abstentionist stance previously applied was reversed. Nevertheless, this interventionist attitude continued to operate on the premise that collective bargaining was the best method to administer employment relations. The model promoted by Heath ultimately failed, as the trade union movement refused to participate or support the new legislation.[12] The resistance to the changes were further evidenced by the repeal of the IRA 1971 by the subsequent Labour government.

---

[10]   Ibid. pp. 239–240.
[11]   See for example *Rookes v Barnard* [1964] AC 1129 where the tort of intimidation was applied to industrial action.
[12]   P. DAVIES and M. FREEDLAND, above n. 9, chapter 7.

The 1974 new administration had entered a social contract with the trade union movement. The Labour party had agreed to repeal the 1971 Act, to improve individual protection and to strengthen collective bargaining. This was in exchange for trade unions 'restraint'; in other words, there was an understanding that trade unions would not use industrial action to push for higher wages in what was already an inflationary economic climate. On the collective side, this pact was translated into a review of the immunity available to trade unions and individuals in trade disputes. Very significantly, the Advisory, Conciliation and Arbitration Service (ACAS) was constituted with the express mission to encourage the extension of collective bargaining. The law was therefore used to promote and support collective bargaining and collective organisations.[13] However, this pro-employee and trade union stance came to an end relatively quickly.

Following the 'Winter of Discontent', a series of strikes which seriously disrupted the country, Margaret Thatcher's Conservative party came to power. A new era began to dawn for employment law, as the Prime Minister's social and economic philosophy led to serious changes. The views of Hayek, an economist who argued that the decline of the British economy was due to the power of trade unions, influenced the shaping of public policy significantly. He advocated that market forces should be free from any intervention, either by the state, in the form of regulations, or from trade unions' collective bargaining and strikes.[14] The practical consequences were the enactment of numerous statutes seeking to restrict the powers of the unions.[15] They subjected trade unions to very detailed procedures for their internal organisation[16] and limited the cases in which strikes were legal.[17] This was done in the name of democratisation of trade unions and in order to prevent the abuse of union power. The democratic argument was very appealing and difficult to argue against, although the Conservatives understood democracy in a fashion that has been criticised for being individualistic and simplistic.[18] As will be seen in subsequent chapters (4 and 5 for example) this legislative change had serious negative effects on the ability of the unions to operate on behalf of their members.

---

[13] Ibid., chapter 8.

[14] LORD WEDDERBURN, 'Change, Struggle and Ideology in British Labour Law' in LORD WEDDERBURN, *Labour Law and Freedom: Further Essays in Labour Law* Lawrence and Wishart, 1995.

[15] The following Acts were enacted: the Employment Acts 1980, 1982, 1988 and 1990; the Trade Union Act 1984; the Trade Union and Labour Relations (Consolidation) Act 1992 and the Trade Union Reform and Employment Rights Act 1993.

[16] See chapter 4.

[17] See chapter 5.

[18] S. FREDMAN, 'The New Rights: Labour Law and Ideology in the Thatcher Years' (1992) 12 *OJLS (Oxford Journal of Legal Studies)* 24; and M. FORD, 'Citizenship and Democracy in Industrial Relations: The Agenda for the 1990's' (1992) 55 *MLR (Modern Law Review)* 241.

After an era of state abstentionism, followed by positive support toward collective organisation, the Conservative period was characterised by its hostility towards collective relations. The return of a Labour government in 1997 came, however, with high expectations that Conservative policies would be reversed and that trade unions would regain their powers. The government's plan was laid out in 'Fairness at Work'.[19]

With regard to the spirit of the overall policy, *Fairness at Work* immediately signalled that there was no return to the situation of the 1970s, i.e. the giving back of powers to the trade unions, but that the previous Conservative policy was not acceptable either.[20] A Third Way was envisaged. It supported the idea that the labour market needs flexibility but not at the expense of security for workers.[21] The aim was said to be the replacement of the old model of conflict between management, workers and their representatives by a culture of 'partnership'.[22] As a result, trade unions were the beneficiaries of new measures, notably when it came to their role as workers' representatives. Most significantly, the Employment Relations Act 1999 re-introduced a statutory procedure for the recognition of trade unions for the purpose of collective bargaining, thus compelling employers to bargain with trade unions (although, notably, not to reach any collective agreement).[23] Further, individual employees taking part in lawful industrial actions were given enhanced statutory protection against dismissal.[24] Nevertheless, important aspects introduced by the Conservative administration were left untouched by the government. For example, the rules governing internal regulations of trade unions were not amended.[25] The majority of the very restrictive laws on industrial action was not altered, despite constant findings of breach by supervisory bodies within the International Labour Organization, as regards treatment of secondary action and the arbitrarily limited scope of protection from dismissal.[26]

---

[19] Cm 3968. On the Labour government treatment of collective rights, see T. NOVITZ and P. SKIDMORE, *Fairness at Work – A Critical Analysis of the Employment Relations Act 1999 and its Treatment of Collective Rights*, Hart, 2001; P. DAVIES and M. FREEDLAND, *Towards a Flexible Labour Market – Labour legislation and regulations since the 1990s*, Oxford University Press, Oxford 2007, chapter 3.

[20] 'The White paper [...] seeks to draw a line under the issue of industrial relations law. There will be no going back. The days of strikes without ballot, mass picketing, closed shop and secondary actions are over'. *Fairness at Work* Foreword by the Prime Minister.

[21] For further insights in the concept in relation to Labour Law, see for example H. COLLINS, 'Is there a Third Way in Labour Law' in J. CONAGHAN, R.M. FISCHL, K. KLARE (eds.) *Labour Law in an era of Globalisation – Transformative Practices and possibilities,* Oxford University Press, Oxford 2002, p. 449.

[22] See for example *Fairness at Work*, para. 1.7 or 2.8 or 4.7.

[23] TULRCA, schedule A1.

[24] TULRCA, s. 238A.

[25] See chapter 4 for more details.

[26] From the International Labour Organisation or the Committee of Experts monitoring the European Social Charter – See chapters 2 and 5.

Ultimately, a review of the Labour government actions towards collective labour law led some authors to argue that it had accepted the neoliberal underpinnings of the previous Conservative administrations,[27] and had done very little to increase collectivist values.[28]

2.4. THE COALITION AGENDA

The Conservative and Liberal Democrat coalition government formed after the 2010 General Election laid out its programme in those terms: '*We will review employment and workplace laws, for employers and employees, to ensure they maximize flexibility for both parties while protecting fairness and providing the competitive environment required for enterprise to thrive*.'[29] As an immediate consequence, the 'Employment Law Review 2010–2015' was launched.[30] The aim of the Review is clearly stated as '*to make it as easy as possible for businesses to take people on*.'[31] While job creation is clearly a worthy goal, the language used suggests that this may be at the cost of employment protection. As the review is intended to take place over the life of the current parliamentary period, there are ongoing projects. Most of the work so far has focused on individual employment law and more significantly individual dispute resolution, for example with the re-introduction of a two-year qualifying period to claim unfair dismissal[32] and proposals to introduce fees to access employment tribunals.[33] An Employer's Charter was also enacted focusing on the rights of employers and what they are entitled to do to manage their staff.[34] These measures certainly seem to confirm the more business and employer-friendly ethos of the current government. Other initiatives are also having an impact on employment law and feed into the Employment Law Review. A Growth Review aims '*to create the right conditions for business to flourish*' notably by '*removing barriers preventing them from performing to their full potential*.'[35] As a result, employment law measures such as the right to request time off for training has been removed from the statute book for employees when the company's workforce is less than 250. Similarly,

---

[27]   See P. SMITH, 'New Labour and the commonsense of neoliberalism: trade unionism, collective bargaining and workers' rights' (2009) 40 *IRJ (Industrial Relations Journal)* 337.

[28]   A. BOGG, 'Employment Relations Act 2004: Another False Dawn for Collectivism' (2005) 34 *ILJ* 72.

[29]   *The Coalition: our Programme for Government*, (HM Government: 401238 / 0510, May 2010) p. 10.

[30]   See   <www.bis.gov.uk/policies/employment-matters/employment-law-review>   accessed 16.12.2011.

[31]   Ibid.

[32]   Ibid.

[33]   See   <www.justice.gov.uk/consultations/et-fee-charging-regime-cp22–2011.htm>   accessed 16.12.2012.

[34]   URN 11/680.

[35]   <www.bis.gov.uk/policies/growth/growth-review accessed> 16.12.2011.

the 'Red Tape Challenge', which runs from April 2011 until 2013, aims to review all regulations that have an impact on business. Members of the public, businesses and representative bodies are invited to give their views on legislation by theme, allowing them '*to feed in views directly to the Government on new priorities for reform*'.[36] Employment law, with its 160 regulations, was open to discussion in October 2011 and covered again mainly individual aspects of recruiting, managing staff, letting them go and enforcement of rights. The exercise was underpinned by a discussion document, setting out the government's approach. In *Flexible, Effective, Fair: promoting economic growth through a strong and efficient labour market*, there is hardly any mention of collective labour law or actors, except as agents supporting the enforcement of rights.[37] The implicit understanding would seem to be that employers and employees should negotiate their relationship with minimal intervention from the government and that employers should communicate directly with their workforce.[38] The message appears to be very similar to the language of the 1980s: less intervention from the state in labour relations. The government itself recognises that the UK is one of the least regulated labour markets, giving it a competitive advantage.[39] It is therefore questionable whether less protection is still necessary, although the aim is clear:

> A core of fundamental employment protections is needed: to safeguard employees from unscrupulous businesses and to ensure that good employers are competing on a level playing field, not undercut by unscrupulous competitors. This set of fundamental protections should be limited to the minimum necessary; it should also be simple, straightforward and easy to understand.[40]

Finally, the government has also made clear that it would stop 'gold plating' European Directives,[41] which is seen as a practice of going beyond the minimum required by the European Union (EU) legislation, certainly when it comes to social policy measures. The Employment Law Review intends to re-consider the issues of transfer of undertakings and collective redundancy consultation.[42] Both sets of rules involve employee representatives being informed and consulted

---

[36] BIS, Department for Business, Innovation and Skills, *Flexible, Effective, Fair: promoting economic growth through a strong and efficient labour market* (URN 11/1308, October 2011) para. 5.

[37] Ibid. para. 8.

[38] Ibid. para. 6.

[39] Ibid. para. 4.

[40] Ibid. para. 9.

[41] *The Coalition: our Programme for Government*, (HM Government: 401238 / 0510, May 2010) p. 10.

[42] As announced in May 2011 and see the publication of BIS, 'Call for Evidence on Redundancy Consultation Rules' (URN 11/1371, November 2011) and 'Call for Evidence: Effectiveness of Transfer of Undertakings (Protection of Employees) Regulations 2006' (URN 11/1376, November 2011).

on specific matters. The Review could therefore lead to amendments of these well-established principles, with a potential impact on the role and powers of collective actors.[43]

The more traditional areas of collective labour law such as collective bargaining or industrial action have not been mentioned as yet, although the public sector strikes of the last twelve months encouraged the CBI (Confederation of British Industry) [44] and Conservative politicians to threaten review of the current rules to make them even more stringent.[45] The lack of interest in collective labour law may suggest that the legal framework is 'weak' enough and would therefore not interfere with the current government aims of minimising interference with business.

This historical background and explanation of different UK governments' philosophies concerning employment law should assist in understanding the current state of the law. In addition to national political philosophies, the influence of the European Community, now the European Union, has also led to important modifications in the collective field of labour relations.

3. ACTORS

The traditional actors of the industrial relations landscape are trade unions and employers' associations. The former developed as combinations to give voice to workers in order to counter the economic and social power of employers. Today, while the number of trade union members is declining, trade unions remain present at undertaking level, as well as sectorally and nationally. The Trade Union Congress (TUC) represents 58 affiliated unions and lobbies for its members at national and European levels. Employers' associations were created as a response to the proliferation of trade unions. They intended to increase employers' bargaining strength and ensure co-operation in the face of growing pressure from worker voice.[46] The Confederation of British Industry (CBI) represents employers' associations, advising its members and fulfilling the same role as the TUC in national and European instances. In addition to the traditional parties, the number and significance of workers' representatives

---

[43] See chapter 6.

[44] B. GROOM and E. RIGBY, CBI chief calls for tougher strike laws, *Financial Times – Business*, 17.05.2011.

[45] See Parliamentary debates of 30.11.2011 following the general public sector strike on pension. Some MPs requested changes in the law requiring a minimum turn out for balloting union members (also suggested by the CBI) as figures showed that less than half union members had voted in favour of the strike; the minister indicated that this is not currently envisaged; see <http://services.parliament.uk/hansard/Commons/bydate/20111130/mainchamberdebates/part002.html> accessed 16.12.2011.

[46] S. DEAKIN and G.S. MORRIS, *Labour Law*, 5th ed., Hart, Oxford 2009, pp. 671–675.

who are non-union representatives are increasing significantly, following management initiatives and changes in the law. This section will consider how collective actors are defined, their traditional roles and the protection they are granted when undertaking their activities. The emphasis of this section will be on workers' representatives.

3.1. DEFINITIONS

Statutes define trade unions and employers' associations. Employee representatives who are non-union are not separately categorised or defined as such in statutes, but have emerged as a growing form of collective voice, through transposing measures of European Union Directives.

3.1.1. Trade unions

Section 1 of TULRCA 1992 defines a trade union as *'an organization [...] which consists wholly or mainly of workers of one or more descriptions and whose principal purposes include the regulation of relations between workers of that description or those descriptions and employers or employers' associations'*. The existence of a trade union is therefore dependent on its membership and its main role, the regulation of employment relations, either with one employer or an employers' association. An organisation needs to have been approved by the Certification Officer (CO) as fulfilling the above definition to be listed as a trade union.[47] Listing however is voluntary and the CO keeps records of bodies which fulfil the definition of trade unions but do not request to be listed by the CO.[48] Listing is not automatic. The CO recently reported that some organisations wish to be listed as trade unions to qualify to represent workers in grievance and disciplinary situations as allowed by statutes. However, such organisations have been reported as demanding fees from individuals to play a representative role. The CO has been mindful of this development and has monitored, case by case, whether the organisation would fulfill the statutory definition.[49] The latest CO's annual report records 177 listed trade unions compared to 502 in 1983.[50] The main reasons for the decline are the mergers of numerous unions, rather than necessarily declining trade union strength, although declining membership numbers would suggest that is also the case.

---

[47] TULRCA, s. 2(4).
[48] Certification Officer, Annual Report 2010–11, para. 1.7. The CO indicates that it is aware of 15 unions which are not listed but would fulfil the statutory definition. However, it recognises that it is therefore difficult to establish how many unions are in existence at any one time.
[49] Ibid. p. 2.
[50] Ibid. A list of all existing trade unions is found in the Annex, pp. 44–48.

Being listed is a pre-condition for trade unions to obtain a certificate of independence.[51] Only independent trade unions may have access to statutory rights, such as recognition for collective bargaining or consultation in redundancy situations. The certificate of independence is granted by the CO where the union conforms to section 5 of TULRCA 1992 which states:

> '"independent trade union" means a trade union which –
> (a) is not under the domination or control of an employer or group of employers or of one or more employers' associations, and
> (b) is not liable to interference by an employer or any such group or association (arising out of the provision of financial or material support or by any other means whatsoever) tending towards such control.'

The criteria used by the CO are history, membership base, organisation and structure, finance, employer-provided facilities and negotiating record.[52] The refusal to list a union or issue a certificate of independence or their withdrawal can be appealed before the Employment Appeal Tribunal (EAT) on a point of law.[53] The independence of a trade union is also essential in order for the trade union to make an application under the statutory recognition procedure[54] and have access to a number of rights, such as time off for trade union duties and activities.

3.1.2. Employers' associations

Employers' associations are defined in statute in an analogous manner to trade unions as an organisation which consists wholly or mainly of employers or individual owners of undertakings of one or more descriptions and whose principal purposes include the regulation of relations between employers of that description or those descriptions and workers or trade unions.[55] The CO is the relevant authority for the listing of employers' associations, following a similar procedure to that of trade unions. There are currently 62 employers' associations.[56]

3.1.3. Other collective voice

Traditionally, statute had only envisaged trade unions as collective representative of the workforce. Collective bargaining could only occur with a recognised trade

---

51 TULRCA, s. 6.
52 Certification Officer, Annual Report 2010–11, para. 2.7. These criteria were established by case law, *Blue Circle Staff Association v Certification Officer* [1977] IRLR *(Industrial Relations Law Report)* 20.
53 TULRCA, s. 9.
54 See chapter 3 for developments on recognition.
55 TULRCA, s. 122.
56 Certification Officer, Annual Report 2010–11, para. 1.7.

union[57] and when European Directives started requiring the involvement of employee representatives, UK law translated such requirement by empowering the same recognised trade unions.[58] However, employee participation and voice has always been valued by many employers who see the productivity benefit of engaging with the workforce. Outside the law, communication with the workforce has therefore taken many forms. Employers have involved the workforce directly in different ways (through quality circles for example) or through representatives who are either union members, stand-alone representatives, or a mix of the two (for example through consultative committees).[59] The use of non-union voice has increased sharply over the last 25 years while the use of union voice only has decreased. Instances of dual representation (union and non union) have diminished, but not as significantly.[60] It is estimated that over half of worker representatives are non-union.[61] This change could partly be explained by legal influence. Firstly, the use of recognised unions as the only employee voice for information and consultation obligations was judged in breach of European Directives because employees were left without a voice in instances where unions were not recognised.[62] Statutes therefore had to provide for a dual channel of representatives in those instances (originally for collective redundancies and transfer of undertakings), but this change effectively opened the way to a statutory recognition of non-union representatives.[63] However, trade unions remained the priority channel if they were recognised. Secondly, subsequent transposition of Directives on information and consultation[64] did not offer that 'special' place to trade unions but privileged the election of representatives, thus undermining the status of unions.[65] Finally, regulations even permitted direct communication with the workforce instead of dialogue with representatives, potentially in breach of the

---

[57] TULRCA, s. 178.

[58] For example through the obligation to inform and consult workers' representatives in transfer of undertaking or collective redundancies situations respectively in TUPE 2001, regs. 10–12 and EPA 1975, s. 99.

[59] B. Kersley, C. Alpin, J. Forth, A. Bryson, H. Bewley, G. Dix, S. Oxenbridge, *Inside the Workplace: Findings from the 2004 Workplace Employment Relations Survey*, Routledge, London 2006, p.132.

[60] C. F. Wright, above n. 3, p. 4.

[61] ACAS booklet, *Non union representation* (October 2009) p. 1.

[62] Case C-383/92 (collective redundancies) *Commission v UK* [1994] ECR I-2479.

[63] See for example P. Davies, 'A Challenge to Single Channel' 23 (1994) *ILJ* 272.

[64] Council Directive 97/74/EC extending, to the United Kingdom of Great Britain and Northern Ireland, Directive 95/45/EC on the establishment of a European Works Council or a procedure in Community-scale undertakings and Community-scale groups of undertakings for the purposes of informing and consulting employees [1997] OJ L10/22 and Council Directive 02/14/EC of the European Parliament and of the Council of 11 March 2002, establishing a general framework for informing and consulting employees in the European Community [2002] OJ L80/29. See chapter 6 for details.

[65] P. Davies and C. Kilpatrick, 'UK Worker Representation After Single Channel' (2004) 33 *ILJ* 121.

European Directive.[66] While employers have continued to involve the workforce, it seems therefore that there is a trend towards more direct communication, and where a collective voice is proposed or required, the consultation or negotiation happens less through trade unions than in the past. Research also shows that employers set up consultation or dialogue mechanisms but the motivation is not necessarily compliance with the law or value of collective voice but a way in which employers seek to secure more control over the workforce.[67] Against this changing background, there is still significant evidence that union involvement is the most effective representation mechanism for the defence of workers' interests.[68]

3.2. ROLE OF TRADE UNIONS

'Trade unions play a significant role in directly shaping people's working lives in Britain today.'[69] Union tasks are varied. They change in response to evolving circumstances, but clearly remain crucial. Ewing identified five principal functions which he labelled as service, representation, regulatory, government and public administration. They are illustrated in this section.[70]

Originally the trade union collective voice was needed to counteract economic power of employers. Workers' interests were defended by negotiating terms and conditions through collective bargaining and by using industrial action.[71] Collective bargaining is less prominent today and is not expressly supported by the State as a means of regulating working conditions. Legislative measures have increasingly guaranteed some minimum protection but the State is not delegating the regulations of terms and conditions to industrial actors.[72] Despite this state of play, it is still evident that where trade unions are present, wages are higher,[73] employees assert their rights more easily and working conditions have improved beyond the statutory minimum.[74]

---

[66]   See Information and Consultation of Employees Regulations 2004 (transposing the 2002 Directive, above at n. 64), reg. 16(1)(f).
[67]   C.F. Wright, above n. 3, p. 4.
[68]   Ibid.
[69]   Ibid. p. 2.
[70]   K.D. Ewing, 'The Function of Trade Unions' (2005) 34 *ILJ* 1.
[71]   See chapters 3 and 5.
[72]   K.D. Ewing, above n. 70, pp. 14–15.
[73]   C.F. Wright, above n. 3, p. 6.
[74]   T. Colling, 'What space for unions on the floor of rights? Trade Unions and the enforcement of statutory individual employment rights' (2006) 35 *ILJ* 140, 160.

Subsequently, unions have gained the statutory role to be informed and consulted on matters that affect the workforce. Originally specific situations such as redundancies required unions' involvement[75], but later on they also had the possibility to be part of forums that discuss the economic, social and financial situation of the undertaking, whether at local or transnational level.[76]

While unions interact with employers on behalf of their members, they also provide crucial support and individual representation in the workplace. In situations of disciplinary processes, unions' role was enshrined in statute under the previous Labour governments, as all employees have a right to be accompanied to formal grievance or disciplinary hearings.[77] Research shows that union representatives significantly protect workers' interests and contribute positively to dispute resolution while non-union companions have no substantive impact on the dispute outcome.[78] Trade unions also provide additional benefits, such as insurance or legal advice. These 'advantages' are identified as 'the service function' of the unions according to EWING.[79]

New competence has also been given to unions in the field of learning and development. Under the recent Labour government, 'union learning representatives' (ULRs) were given time off to undertake their duties.[80] The position involves identifying training needs of the members, providing information on learning and training matters and arranging training and learning. This new function has been very successful in several ways. It has helped to promote personal and professional development for members. Unions have been considered more positively in the workplace, as there is less antagonism and more cooperation on matters such as training. Managers report that they value the work of the representatives and the impact on the skills gap.[81] The measure has also enabled recruitment of new members and as of 2010, 25,000 ULRs had been trained.[82]

---

75   TULRCA, s. 188.
76   Through the Information and Consultation of Employees Regulations (ICER) SI 2004/3426 and the Transnational Information and Consultation of Employees Regulations (TICER) SI 1999/3323, see further in chapter 6.
77   Employment Relations Act (ERelA) 1999, s. 10.
78   R. SAUNDRY, C. JONES and C. ANTICLIFF, 'Discipline, representation and dispute resolution – exploring the role of trade unions and employee companions in workplace discipline' (2011) 42 *IRJ* 195.
79   K.D. EWING, above n. 70, p. 3.
80   Through the Employment Act (EA) 2002, inserting s.168A in TULRCA.
81   C.F. WRIGHT, above n. 3, pp. 11–12.
82   B. CLOUGH, *The Origins, Role and Impact of Union Learning Representatives in the UK and other Countries*, Working Paper No 1 Revised August 2010, Unionlearn, TUC.

Finally, outside the workplace, trade unions engage in political lobbying. The governmental and public administration function of the union involves influencing government 'in order to secure legislation that will enable them to perform their other functions'.[83] As trade unions have traditionally been close to the Labour party[84], examples of participation in the elaboration or implementation of policy or legislation include the 'Social Contract' that was entered by the TUC and the Labour government of 1974, leading to the repeal of the Industrial Relations Act 1971. More recently, trade unions representatives, but also employers' representatives, were appointed to the Low Pay Commission following the decision to introduce a statutory minimum wage in 1997.[85] Both TUC and CBI also signed agreements on the implementation of European Directives.[86]

3.3. RIGHTS AND PROTECTION OF WORKERS' REPRESENTATIVES

This section will consider how workers' representatives are given the relevant 'tools' to perform their tasks and how they are protected if they are subject to detrimental treatment by employers by reason of the functions that they undertake. Some of the safeguards granted to union representatives apply to union members in general. This is because the detriment occurs due to union membership as well as union activities. In this regard, it will be shown that the law does not always discriminate between the reasons for the protection. However, this section will highlight that some of the rights given to union representatives are not always available to non-union representatives. This is explained by the fact that some of the worker representative functions are still only entrusted to unions, but even where the law offers the possibility to have union representation or non-union representation, for example in the field of information and consultation, the law is not always coherent.

3.3.1. Time off for duties and activities

In order to represent workers, collectively and individually, representatives must have the necessary time to be trained, to prepare and attend meetings with their own union officials or other representatives, with management and with their

---

83 K.D. EWING, above n. 70, p. 4.
84 See chapter 4.
85 D. METCALF, 'The British National Minimum Wage' (1999) 37 *BJIR* (*British Journal of Industrial Relations*) 171, 173.
86 For example in relation to Council Directive 02/14/EC (above n. 64): see M. HALL, 'Assessing the Information and Consultation of Employees Regulations 2004' (2005) 35 *ILJ* 103, 104 or K.D. EWING, above n. 70, p. 19.

members or fellow workers. This was originally recognised in statute[87] and in a separate ACAS Code of Practice, *Time off for trade union duties and activities*, which was recently revised.[88] The picture however has become more complex because, as has been pointed out in previous sections, non-union representatives exercise some of the functions that used to belong solely to trade unions. The inflation of statutory provisions that require the involvement of employee representatives, such as for example the Information and Consultation of Employees Regulations (ICER) 2004,[89] has lead to more individual pieces of legislation providing for facility time. The combination of hard and soft law is consequently patchy and indeed relatively skeletal. Arguably, this demonstrates the slow response of law to current changes in the employee representation field. ACAS recently produced two new guides to accompany the original ACAS code of practice: they both deal with managing time off, training and facilities but one is directed to trade union representatives while the other is for non-union representation.[90]

Considering trade unions first, it should be noted that only *recognised* trade unions are entitled to the rights discussed below, evidencing the crucial importance of such status. TULRCA allows trade union representatives to request time off from their work to undertake *duties* and *activities*. *Duties* cover functions '*related to or connected with*' the subjects of collective bargaining, including therefore the topics listed in section 178 of TULRCA (for example, terms and conditions of employment or allocation of work, etc.)[91] *Duties* further include information and consultation for redundancy and transfer matters and training for the exercise of such duties.[92] *Activities* are not specifically defined but there is reference to '*activities of the unions or any activities in relation to which the employee is acting as a representative of the union*'.[93] The ACAS Code further provides that activities can be undertaken by trade union representatives but also union members when they take part in union meetings for example, or consult one of their officers.[94] A crucial difference between duties and activities is pay. While time off is available for both, payment is only authorised by statutes for union duties.[95] The ACAS Code however indicates that employers should consider payment in some circumstances, such as to ensure that workplace

---

87   TULRCA, ss. 168–173.
88   Code of Practice 3 – January 2010 – for an analysis, see M. WYNN and G. PITT, above n. 5.
89   SI 2004/3426.
90   ACAS booklet, *Non union representation* (October 2009) and ACAS booklet, *Trade Union Representation in the Workplace* (October 2009).
91   ACAS Code of Practice, *Time off for trade union duties and activities*, para. 12.
92   TULRCA, s. 168.
93   TULRCA, s. 170.
94   ACAS Code of Practice, above n. 88, para. 37.
95   TULRCA, s. 169.

meetings are fully representative.[96] Union learning representatives (ULRs) are dealt with in a separate section, although the personal scope and rights are the same; simply the matters on which they can take time off are clearly specific to their function.[97] Similarly, health and safety representatives have always had their own generic statutory rights,[98] as well as specific codes and guidance.[99] The ACAS code, however, refers to all three types of representatives.

Non-union representatives constitute an eclectic category. They are creatures of statute, each piece of relevant legislation granting some rights to such a representative. ACAS usefully lists the type of representatives concerned and the rights attached to them.[100] They can be divided into three subcategories according to the amount of support they are entitled to. Firstly, some non-union representatives have the corollary rights to recognised union representatives because they were created as a result of European law which required dual representation for effective application of Directives.[101] In situations of collective redundancy, transfer of undertakings and health and safety, if recognised trade unions are not present, non-union representatives can be informed and consulted. Representatives and candidates for elections all have reasonable paid time off for the performance of their duties and for training.[102] Secondly, a group of employee representatives created by ICER 2004 or the Transnational Information and Consultation of Employees Regulations 1999 (TICER)[103] have access to paid time off to carry out their duties.[104] TICER employee representatives did not used to have a statutory right to training but the regulations have been amended to include such a right,[105] following a recast of the European Directive[106]. As a result, there is now a statutory discrepancy between employee representatives depending on whether they exercise their function for a multinational or a national undertaking. Finally, some elected non-union employee representatives can 'negotiate' workforce agreements. Such

---

[96]   ACAS Code of Practice, above n. 88, para. 41.

[97]   TULRCA, s. 168A.

[98]   Safety Representatives and Safety Committees Regulations 1977 (SI 1977/500), regs. 4(2) and 4A(2).

[99]   HSE, *Consulting Employees on Health and Safety – a brief Guide to the Law* (2008) <www.hse. gov.uk/pubns/indg232.pdf> accessed 14.12.2011, pp. 5–6.

[100]   ACAS booklet, *Non union representation* (October 2009) pp. 3–4.

[101]   Case C-383/92 (collective redundancies) *Commission v UK* [1994] ECR I-2479, mentioned in 3.1.3 above and discussed in chapter 6.

[102]   Employment Rights Act (ERA) 1996, s. 61 for redundancy and transfer representatives for example.

[103]   TICER 1999, SI 1999/3323.

[104]   ICER, regs. 27–29 and TICER 1999, regs. 25–27.

[105]   TICER 1999, reg. 25(1A) inserted by TICE (Amendment) R 2010, SI 2010/1088 reg. 16.

[106]   Directive 2009/38/EC of the European Parliament and of the Council of 6 May 2009 on the establishment of a European Works Council or a procedure in Community-scale undertakings and Community-scale groups of undertakings for the purposes of informing and consulting employees (Recast) [2009] OJ L122/28.

agreements are allowed by specific regulations which transpose European Directives. Like collective agreements they can derogate from statutory standards in working time,[107] or use of fixed term contracts,[108] for example. However, the relevant regulations do not provide the elected representatives negotiating such agreements with time off to exercise their duties or to go on training. This is in sharp contrast with the rights granted to trade unions when they exercise duties relating to collective bargaining. For non-union representatives, who potentially had less access to training and are less experienced in negotiation, in particular in areas where the law permits derogations from statutory standards, it would have been appropriate to allow for such facilities.

3.3.2. Protection against detriment and dismissal

Under the fundamental entitlement to freedom of association,[109] all trade union members are protected against dismissal and detriment simply because they belong to a trade union or because they perform activities for a trade union.[110] In this section, the focus will be on the protection granted to employee representatives when they undertake such activities. Regardless of the type of representatives concerned (trade union or non-union), all relevant legislation protects against detriment and dismissal. The rules applicable to union representatives will first be considered before assessing the patchy protection granted to non-union representatives.

3.3.2.1. Trade union representatives

Trade unions representatives, like union members, are protected in three ways, following the life of an employment contract. They cannot be refused employment, suffer detriment while employed or be dismissed by reason of their union activities. While the first limb of protection has only recently been added to the portfolio of measures through the Blacklisting Regulations 2010,[111] the other rights came from the Industrial Relations Act 1971 before being more precisely defined under the successive Thatcher governments.[112] The intervention of the European Court of Human Rights led to further refinement of statutory entitlements as UK law was deemed to be in breach of Article 11 of the European Convention of Human Rights when employers tried to induce employees not to

---

[107] Rules relating to night work and rests in Working Time Regulations 1998, sched. 1.
[108] Fixed Term Employees (Prevention of Less Favourable Treatment) Regulations (FTER) 2002, SI 2002/2034, sched. 1.
[109] Analysed at length in chapter 2.
[110] TULRCA, Part III, Rights in relation to union membership and activities, ss. 137–177.
[111] SI 2010/493 and fuller discussion below.
[112] S. DEAKIN and G.S. MORRIS, above n. 46, p. 710.

be represented by unions for the purpose of collective bargaining.[113] The word *activities* is not defined in law but it is presumed to have similar meaning to the same word in the context of time off and may include some union duties, as discussed above.

Starting with protection against dismissal, if trade union representatives can establish that their employment was terminated because they took part or proposed to take part in union activities at an appropriate time, the dismissal is automatically unfair.[114] Trade union activity is therefore one of the grounds which does not require a minimum qualifying period before an employee is able to take matters to an employment tribunal. This may constitute a considerable advantage when the qualifying period increases to two years on 6 April 2012.[115] Furthermore, a representative who acts swiftly may obtain interim relief preventing the employer from dismissing him until the hearing if he can show that the dismissal is likely to be for union activities.[116] However, the special protection given to trade union representatives is not as beneficial as it might appear. Firstly, the activities must be at an appropriate time. The activities must take place outside working hours or during working hours, but as authorised by the employer. This leaves the door open to litigation about what has or has not been authorised.[117] Secondly, the burden of proof lies with the employee. Establishing that, but for her trade union activities, the employee would not have been dismissed is a difficult undertaking, especially as employers will usually attach a capacity or discipline tag to the dismissal.[118]

Similar limitations apply to the protection against detriment short of dismissal on grounds of trade union activities. According to TULRCA section 146(1) (b): '*A worker has the right not to be subjected to any detriment as an individual by any act, or any deliberate failure to act, by his employer if the act or failure takes place for the sole or main purpose of [...] (b) preventing or deterring him from taking part in the activities of an independent trade union at an appropriate time, or penalizing him for doing so*'. The personal scope of the protection is wider as 'workers' can claim detriment while only an 'employee' can use section 152

---

[113] *Wilson and NUJ v UK, Palmer, Wyeth and RMT v UK, Doolan and others v UK* [2002] IRLR 568.

[114] TULRCA, s. 152(1)(b). This also includes the situation where a trade union representatives is selected for redundancy, TULRCA, s. 153.

[115] Change announced by BIS on 23 November 2011, see < www.bis.gov.uk/policies/employment-matters/employment-law-review/latest-developments> accessed 17.12.2011.

[116] TULRCA, ss. 161–166.

[117] For an example of dispute on whether employer could refuse time off for union activities, see K.D. EWING, *Fighting Back: resisting 'union busting' and 'strike breaking' in the BA dispute,* Institute of Employment Rights 2011, p. 20–23.

[118] In the BA dispute, a union representative claimed unsuccessfully unfair dismissal because of trade union activities see K.D. EWING (2011) above n. 117.

against unfair dismissal.[119] As a consequence, 'workers' whose contracts are terminated on grounds of trade union activities, can resort to section 146 as dismissal is a detriment.

The material scope of section 146 is complex because it has been extended to include failure to act, since the original legislation only covered 'actions' and not omissions. Such lacuna was exploited by the House of Lords in *Associated Newspapers Ltd v Wilson, Associated British Ports v Palmer,* which adopted a very literal interpretation of the word 'action' short of dismissal, such that it was not being able to include 'omission'.[120] The word detriment would potentially cover situations such as not granting a promotion or a pay increase. Another difficulty arises with the requirement that the act or failure to act must have been for the main or sole purpose of preventing the worker from taking part in union activities. Cases show that where trade union representatives apply for promotion and are refused on the basis that they have to undertake some activities instead of union duties to obtain the pay increase or promotion, establishing that such criteria are for the sole purpose of deterring from undertaking union activities is a significant hurdle for the representative.[121] This is true even though it is for the employer to demonstrate the sole or main purpose for which that employer acted or failed to act.[122] Other acts of detriment could include a final warning because of trade union activities. In *Gayle v Sandwell and West Birmingham Hospitals NHS Trust,*[123] the claimant had refused to attend meetings with her manager to discuss time off for trade union duties and was issued with a final warning. For the Court of Appeal, section 146 had not been breached, as the sole purpose of the final warning was not to prevent or deter her from undertaking her activities but was the result of a disciplinary procedure following refusal to follow management instructions. If a complaint for detriment is successful, an employment tribunal can make a declaration to that effect and award compensation that is considered as just and equitable in the circumstances, having regard to the infringement complained about and to any loss sustained by the complainant.[124] The courts have included non-pecuniary loss which is more beneficial than representatives making a claim under section 152 for unfair

---

[119] Only employees are entitled to claim unfair dismissal under s. 94 Employment Rights Act 1996.

[120] *Associated Newspapers Ltd v Wilson, Associated British Ports v Palmer* [1995] IRLR 258.

[121] See *Gallacher v Department of Transport* [1994] IRLR 231 where the trade union representative was unsuccessful and contrast with *Southwark London Borough Council v Whillier* [2001] ICR 1016.

[122] TULRCA, s. 148(1).

[123] [2011] IRLR 810 (a case perhaps more famous for LJ Mummery's views on the criticisms of procedural fairness and efficiency in the Employment Tribunals).

[124] TULRCA, s. 149.

dismissal.[125] The compensation under section 146 is akin to remedies available under anti-discrimination law in this respect as there is no cap on compensation. As a result, and paradoxically, *workers* who are dismissed for reasons of trade union activities might be better off than employees claiming for automatic unfair dismissals.

Following the European Court of Human Rights judgment of *Wilson* and *Palmer*,[126] the Employment Relations Act 2004 amended TULRCA 1992 to insert a new category of protection against inducement relating to union membership and activities.[127] For the purpose of this section, an employer is prohibited from making an offer to a worker if the sole or main purpose is to induce the worker not to take part, at an appropriate time, in the activities of an independent trade union. The scenario envisaged is that money or other 'sweeteners' are given to the union representative to stop him or her from taking part in union activities. While the formula is similar to the other rights discussed above, the remedies consist of a declaration by the employment tribunal and fixed amount to be paid individually to the complainant.[128]

Finally, trade union members cannot be refused access to employment because of their membership to a trade union.[129] However, this right originally did not extend to trade union activities. Consequently, if an employer was made aware of an applicant's past union activities and refused the job on that basis, the applicant had no recourse despite being a clear discriminatory practice. The Labour government had tried to remedy the situation giving the Secretary of State power to prohibit blacklists, a practice that consist of compiling lists of trade union activists to sell them to interested employers.[130] However, such power was not used in the absence of evidence of this practice. In 2009, the construction industry blacklist was exposed.[131] As a result the Employment Relations Act 1999 (Blacklists) Regulations 2010[132] provide that it is unlawful to compile, supply, sell or use a prohibited list.[133] The latter would contain details of trade union members or past and present activities and would be used with a view to discriminate in relation to recruitment or treatment of workers.[134] Remedies

---

[125] *Brassington v Cauldon Wholesale Ltd* [1978] ICR 405 and *London Borough of Hackney v Adams* [2003] IRLR 402.

[126] Above n. 113.

[127] ERelA 2004, s. 29 inserted s.145A-F in TULRCA.

[128] £3,300 at the time of writing, TULRCA, s. 145E.

[129] TULRCA, s. 137.

[130] ERelA 1999, s. 3.

[131] See K.D. EWING, *Ruined Lives Blacklisting in the UK Construction Industry, A Report for UCATT*, Institute of Employment Rights, London 2009.

[132] SI 2010/493. For an analysis of the regulations see, C. BARROW, 'The Employment Relations Act 1999 (Blacklists) Regulations 2010, SI 2010 no 493' (2010) 30 *ILJ* 300.

[133] Reg. 3(2).

[134] Reg. 3(2)(b).

against an employer include an order to pay compensation,[135] currently not less than £5,000[136] and a recommendation to take action within a specified period 'for the purpose of obviating or reducing the adverse effect on the complainant of any conduct to which the complaint relates.'[137] Non-compliance with a recommendation can lead to the tribunal increasing compensation to a maximum of £65,000.[138] Such compensation can also include injury to feelings.[139]

3.3.2.2. Non-union representatives

It has already been established that the law requires the intervention of representatives in situations such as health and safety, information and consultation bodies or to negotiate workforce agreements. In such cases, trade unions can be elected or appointed, but where they are not, protection against dismissal and detriment for other representatives exists to an extent. The rights concerned are found in the relevant pieces of legislation and are not considered generically, as for trade unions. It is not intended to cover each type of representative in this section but to illustrate with some examples the extent of their protection. A general comparison between trade union and non-union representatives shows that the differences of treatment are relatively minimal, as illustrated below. The protection granted to trade unions representatives by the blacklisting regulations and the rules regarding inducement not to take part in union activities, however, have not been extended to non-trade union representatives. The omissions may be explained by the relatively recent changes in those two domains. It can nevertheless be envisaged that a non-union representative is not chosen for a post because the recruiting employer has been informed that he (or she) had been a militant voice in a consultation forum.

Firstly, redundancy and transfer representatives are protected against dismissal. Section 103 of the Employment Rights Act 1996 renders a dismissal automatically unfair if the principal reason is being a representative or a candidate or for performing the functions of a representative. There is no mention of the timing of the activities compared to the rule applied to union representatives. The protection against detriment is very similar to the one available to union representatives and is found in section 47. The enforcement of the rights can be exercised before an employment tribunal which can award compensation which is just and equitable in the circumstances, having regard to the infringement and any loss attributable to the employer's act or failure.[140]

---

135   Reg. 8(1)(a).
136   Reg. 8(3).
137   Reg. 8(1)(b).
138   Reg. 8(7).
139   Reg. 8(2).
140   ERA 1996, s. 49.

Secondly, under ICER 2004 and TICER 1999, similar rights exist. In ICER, dismissal will be automatically unfair if the reason for termination (or if several reasons, the principal reason) is one of the reasons listed.[141] They are varied and encompassing as they effectively cover most aspects of exercising or intending to exercise the function of a representative, a candidate to be a representative or a negotiator.[142] They include taking time off to perform representatives' duties, making a complaint to a tribunal for enforcing a right, expressing views about whether employees should vote in favour of a negotiated agreement or express doubts about whether a ballot had been adequately conducted.[143] This protection also applies if the representative is selected for redundancy for these reasons.[144] Similarly detriment is prohibited if the less favourable detriment is explained by the same reasons cited above.[145] TICER 1999[146] which apply to multinationals, have very similar protection for negotiating representatives, candidates and information and consultation representatives.[147] The provisions for ICER and TICER representatives appear to be more detailed and prescriptive than the rules applicable to trade unions representatives.

Thirdly, elected workers' representatives who negotiate workforce agreements are protected against dismissals and detriment when they exercise their functions.[148] The scope of the protection is very similar to the one granted to non-union representatives elected for the purpose of redundancy and transfer of undertakings discussed above.

4. THE INSTITUTIONAL SAFEGUARDS

Just as industrial relations were significantly outside the realm of the law for a large period of time, the regulation of collective actors and their relationships have been entrusted to bodies which do not belong to the traditional justice system. The office of the Certification Officer (CO) was created to keep records of collective organisations and deal with members' complaints. The Central Arbitration Committee (CAC) arbitrates disputes over the main functions of

---

[141] ICER 2004, reg. 30.
[142] In ICER, employee representatives are either elected or appointed to be the recipient of information and consultation or to negotiate an information and consultation agreement. They can undertake both or either function.
[143] ICER, reg. 30 (3) and (6).
[144] ICER, reg. 31.
[145] ICER, reg. 32.
[146] SI 1999/3323. See chapter 6 for a full discussion of the instrument.
[147] TICER, regs. 28–30.
[148] For example, Working Time Regulations 1998, regs. 31–32 or Fixed Term Employees (Prevention of Less Favourable Treatment) Regulations (FTER) 2002, reg. 6.

employee representatives: collective bargaining and information and consultation. The Advisory, Conciliation and Arbitration Service (ACAS) was formed originally to promote collective bargaining and help resolve collective conflicts. These three bodies are permanent, independent and have statutory powers. Their functioning and administration is also governed by statute.[149]

There are exceptions to the less legalistic approach to collective relations disputes. Firstly, what is perceived as an individual right, such as the protection against discrimination on grounds of trade union activities, is enforced by employment tribunals. Similarly, when industrial conflicts escalate and the legality of strikes or other actions are tested, parties reach to the judicial system, such as the High Court, for specific remedies, such as injunctions.[150] Finally, decisions of two of the three bodies mentioned above (CO and CAC) can be appealed before the Employment Appeal Tribunals.

The remainder of this section considers in more detail the specific functions of these institutions. Future reforms may however soon occur. Following the Coalition government's wish to review all public bodies, the Public Bodies Act 2011 now provides ministers with an express power to merge the CO and the CAC.[151]

4.1. CERTIFICATION OFFICER (CO)[152]

The office of the Certification Officer found its origin in the 1975 Employment Protection Act. Its tasks are listed in statute, now under the relevant sections of TULRCA 1992. Firstly, it determines the status of trade unions and employers' associations and is therefore the gateway to accessing rights of collective bargaining, for example.[153] The CO keeps records of all trade unions and employers' associations. Secondly, the internal administration of these organisations also form part of the CO's portfolio. Annual returns must be sent to him[154] and he can investigate financial affairs.[155] Trade union members may complain to the CO if access to financial records are refused.[156] The CO also approves the establishment and continuance of political funds and deals with complaints of individual members in relation to that fund.[157] Adjudication on

---

[149] TULRCA, part VI.
[150] See chapter 5 on industrial conflict.
[151] S 2 and Sched. 2.
[152] For a more detailed analysis, see D. COCKBURN, 'The Certification Officer' in L. DICKENS and A.C. NEAL (eds.) *The Changing Institutional Face of British Employment Relations,* Kluwer Law International, The Netherlands 2006, p. 91.
[153] See section 3.1.1. and 3.1.2 above.
[154] TULRCA, s. 32 and 131.
[155] TULRCA, s. 37A.
[156] TULRCA, s. 30.
[157] TULRCA, s. 73 and see chapter 4.

matters concerning election of officers within the union is an additional duty.[158] Finally, where a member considers that the union is in breach of the union rules, it can complain to the CO.[159]

4.2. CENTRAL ARBITRATION COMMITTEE (CAC)[160]

The CAC was also formally established in 1975. Its main function is to arbitrate, either by voluntary agreement or through adjudication when necessary. Originally, it dealt primarily with issues concerning the disclosure of information for the purpose of collective bargaining.[161] However, its remit has significantly broadened since 1999. Firstly, it was entrusted with the application for and disputes about the statutory trade union recognition and de-recognition procedures.[162] Secondly, the regulations that require information and consultation of employees at national (ICER 2004) or transnational level (TICER 1999)[163] give the CAC the powers to arbitrate on the establishment and operation of the information and consultation bodies.[164] The majority of its work is devoted to the statutory recognition procedure, but an increasing number of cases are testing the ICE Regulations.[165] The CAC usually sits with a chairman and two representatives of employers and workers.

4.3. THE ADVISORY, CONCILIATION AND ARBITRATION SERVICE (ACAS)[166]

ACAS is an organisation that has a varied portfolio and whose main role has been modified over the years. While it traces its origin to the end of the 19th century when the government set up a voluntary conciliation and arbitration service,[167] it became a statutory body with the Employment Protection Act 1975. Today it has numerous functions which are for the benefit of individuals as well

---

158 TULRCA, s. 55 and see chapter 4.
159 TULRCA, s. 108A, and see chapter 4.
160 For a more detailed analysis, see S. GOULDSTONE and G. MORRIS, 'The Central Arbitration Committee' in L. DICKENS and A.C. NEAL (eds.), above n. 152, p.79.
161 EPA 1975, ss. 19–21.
162 TULRCA, sched. A1 and see chapter 3.
163 As well as Regulations enacting legislation relating to European companies (The European Public Limited-Liability Company Regulations 2004, SI 2004/2326), cooperative societies (The European Cooperative Society Regulations 2006, SI 2006/2078) and cross-border mergers (The Companies (Cross-Border Mergers) Regulations 2007, SI 2007/2974).
164 See chapter 6.
165 See CAC annual reports, available on its website at < www.cac.gov.uk> accessed 15.12.2011.
166 For a more detailed analysis, see K. SISSON and J. TAYLOR, 'The Advisory, Conciliation and Arbitration Services' in L. DICKENS and A.C. NEAL (eds.), above n. 152, p. 25.
167 See 'our history' on ACAS website (<www.acas.org.uk/index.aspx?articleid=1400> accessed 16.12.2011).

as trade unions and employers' associations. Its overall duty is spelt out in statute as promoting the improvement of industrial relations.[168] It used to encourage *'the extension of collective bargaining'*, but this part of ACAS role was deleted by the Conservative government in 1993, in line with its objective of limiting the role of collective regulation of employment relations. ACAS functions are both individual and collective. The former now primarily focus on advice through help line and arbitration on unfair dismissal cases, topics which are outside the remit of this manual. On the collective front, ACAS fulfils three functions. Firstly, it provides advice to collective organisations in the same way that it may do for individuals, on matters which affect industrial relations.[169] Secondly, ACAS can offer conciliation to parties in a trade dispute, either at their request or of its own volition. Collective conciliation takes place by the appointment of an officer who will seek to help parties reach a settlement.[170] Research shows that collective conciliation is used by small and larger workplaces, both in private and public sectors. It is regarded as a successful way to resolve potential trade disputes and ACAS is often drafted into procedures which deal with resolving collective disputes.[171] Finally, if conciliation fails, ACAS can arbitrate disputes at the request of one of the parties but only if all parties consent.[172] Arbitration will only be considered if existing dispute resolution procedures (found for example in collective agreements) have been exhausted, or if a special reason justifies arbitration in ACAS' view. Arbitration is the most formal form of intervention as the parties agree to be bound by the arbitrator's decision, after the arbitrator has questioned the parties involved. ACAS may, for example, be called in when a dispute has arisen between trade union and employers about the extent of a pay increase when the parties have failed to reach a resolution.

5. THE FUTURE OF COLLECTIVE VOICE

The remaining chapters of this volume will show that the future for trade unions seems challenging. The traditional role of bargaining collectively is declining despite the existence of the statutory recognition procedure. Statutory regulation of internal affairs and industrial action remain burdensome. A new non-union voice, potentially collective but often individual, is emerging, taken up and promoted by employers, whilst acknowledged and permitted by law. The role of the union representative is altering, moving from negotiator to being a source of support for individual grievance and dispute or for training needs. These challenges are examined in the following chapters of this book.

---

[168]   TULRCA, s. 209.
[169]   TULRCA, s. 213.
[170]   TULRCA, s. 210.
[171]   See A. DAWE and F. NEATHEY, *ACAS Conciliation in collective employment disputes*, Ref: 05/08, ACAS Research Paper, August 2008.
[172]   TULRCA, s. 212.

CHAPTER 2
FREEDOM OF ASSOCIATION

1. INTRODUCTION

There is no straightforward constitutional recognition of freedom of association in the United Kingdom (UK), since there is no single written constitutional source. Domestic legal protection of 'freedom of association' arises by virtue of the Human Rights Act 1998 (HRA), which incorporates into UK domestic law 'Convention rights' set out in the Convention for the Protection of Human Rights and Fundamental Freedoms 1950 (also known as the European Convention on Human Rights or ECHR). Article 11 of the ECHR makes provision for protection of freedom of association, as follows:

> 1. Everyone has the right to freedom of peaceful assembly and to freedom of association with others, including the right to form and to join trade unions for the protection of his interests.

> 2. No restrictions shall be placed on the exercise of these rights other than such as are prescribed by law and are necessary in a democratic society in the interests of national security or public safety, for the prevention of disorder or crime, for the protection of health or morals or for the protection of the rights and freedoms of others. This article shall not prevent the imposition of lawful restrictions on the exercise of these rights by members of the armed forces, of the police or of the administration of the State.

By virtue of section 2 of the HRA, the findings of the European Court of Human Rights (and past decisions of the European Commission on Human Rights) must be taken into account by any UK court or tribunal '*determining a question which has arisen in connection with a Convention right*'. Section 3 of the HRA provides that all domestic legislation must be interpreted '*so far as it is possible to do so*' in conformity with Convention rights.[1] Under section 6, apart from certain limited exceptions, it is unlawful for a public authority[2] to act in a way which is

---

[1]   *Ghaidan v Godin-Mendoza* [2004] 2 AC 557.
[2]   As regards what is a public authority, see s. 6(3)(b) and subsequent interpretation in *Aston Cantlow PCC v Wallbank* [2004] 1 AC 546 and *L v Birmingham City Council* [2008] 1 AC 95. This does not seem to encompass what would otherwise be public authorities while engaged

incompatible with a Convention right. However, legislation cannot be invalidated by virtue of any breach of Convention rights; instead, due to section 4, the courts can issue a *'declaration of incompatibility'* which may place pressure on the UK government to repeal or amend legislation. Article 11 might be expected, in these ways, to operate as a constraint on the content and application of all UK legislation and the development of common law. The extent to which this is indeed the case is, as shall become clear, debatable.

Only certain Convention rights derived from the ECHR have been domesticated by the HRA, as defined in that legislation.[3] Other international human rights obligations relating to freedom of association, which are set out in other international instruments, have not been incorporated into UK law. The UK has a dualist legal system, such that in the absence of formal incorporation of an international instrument into UK law via legislation, such as statute or regulation, this instrument is not binding and cannot be relied upon as a cause of action before UK courts. This means that international labour conventions or human rights treaties relating to freedom of association may only assist courts in interpreting domestic legislation, since it is presumed that the UK would act in accordance with its international obligations.[4] They may also be relevant to interpretation of Article 11 of the ECHR, given that the European Court of Human Rights has sought to adopt an approach to application of this provision which is 'integrated' with other international human right instruments and their interpretation by other UN bodies or UN agencies.[5]

It is however notable that the HRA does not encompass entitlements arising under another instrument adopted by the Council of Europe, the European Social Charter 1961 (ESC). This instrument, as its name suggests, seeks to protect socio-economic rights (as opposed to civil and political rights) and has been neglected in comparison with the ECHR.[6] The UK Government has ratified the ESC but has not ratified the Revised Social Charter or the Collective Complaints Protocol of 1991, which would subject UK labour law and practice to greater

---

in 'private' activities, such as when acting as an employer. See S. PALMER, 'Human Rights: Implications for Labour Law' (2000) 59 *Cambridge Law Journal* 168; and K.D. EWING, 'The Human Rights Act and Labour Law' (1998) 27 *ILJ* 275.

3   See Human Rights Act 1998, s.1 and Schedule 1. Omitted, for example, are Article 13 (the right to an effective remedy) as well as Protocols 4, 6, 7 and 12.

4   On monist approaches, see V. LEARY, *International Labour Conventions and National Law*, Martinus Nijhoff, The Hague 1982, pp. 165–6.

5   V. MANTOUVALOU, 'Is There a Human Right Not to be a Trade Union Member?' Labour Rights under the European Convention on Human Rights' in C. FENWICK and T. NOVITZ (eds.), *Human Rights at Work: Perspectives on Law and Regulation*, Hart, Oxford 2010, pp. 442–4.

6   On the case for incorporation of the ESC into UK law, see K.D. EWING, 'Social Rights and Constitutional Law' (1999) *Public Law* 105.

scrutiny.[7] Most importantly, the ESC has no formal status under UK domestic law, which would seem to give the UK government the capacity to disregard the findings of the European Committee of Social Rights. This Committee has stated repeatedly that the UK remains in violation of its obligations relating to the right to organise (Article 5 of the ESC) and the right to bargain collectively (Article 6 of the ESC),[8] both of which, as shall be discussed below, the European Court of Human Rights views (under its integrated approach) as implicit in freedom of association under Article 11 of the ECHR.

The UK has also ratified other key instruments which make provision for protection of freedom of association, namely ILO Conventions and the UN Covenants of 1966. The latter, once again, suffer from the acceptance by the international community of what many regard as a false dichotomy between civil and political rights and socio-economic rights, such that there is a UN International Covenant on Civil and Political Rights (ICCPR) and another separate UN International Covenant on Economic, Social and Cultural Rights (ICESCR). Nevertheless, on the basis of the content of these instruments, alongside the ESC, the case has been made for legal reform of various aspects of UK legislation regarding industrial relations.[9]

This chapter seeks to examine the source of various disagreements regarding the appropriate application of the entitlement to freedom of association. We begin by considering the theoretical basis for protection of such a freedom and, in particular, how divergence in the understanding of its theoretical underpinnings has given rise to different views as to its application to labour relations.

The chapter then proceeds to examine first the international and then European legal sources of a right to freedom of association. The relevant provisions of International Labour Organization (ILO) Conventions are addressed in some detail, alongside the jurisprudence developed by the ILO Governing Body Committee on Freedom of Association. The Universal Declaration on Human Rights 1948 (UNDHR), the ICCPR and its sister instrument, the ICESCR are also considered.

---

7   See 'The United Kingdom and the European Social Charter' Factsheet February 2011, Department of the European Social Charter, Directorate General of Human Rights and Legal Affairs.

8   European Social Charter European Committee of Social Rights Conclusions XIX-3 (2010) (UK), Articles 2, 4, 5 and 6 of the Charter, Council of Europe, Strasbourg 2010, pp. 10–15.

9   K.D. EWING and J. HENDY, *A Charter of Workers' Rights,* Institute of Employment Rights, London, 2002; T. NOVITZ, 'International Promises and Domestic Pragmatism: To What Extent will the Employment Relations Act 1999 Implement International Labour Standards Relating to Freedom of Association?' (2000) 63 *MLR* 379; and more recently, R. DUKES, 'The Statutory Recognition Procedure 1999: No Bias in Favour of Recognition?' (2008) 37 *ILJ* 236, 260 et seq.

The chapter goes on to highlight how the approach of the International Labour Organization (ILO) once differed from that adopted in respect of the Council of Europe instrument, the ECHR, but how the two have since coalesced. It will be concluded by considering what impact ECHR case law has had on the text of human rights instruments adopted within the European Union (EU), how it has affected the jurisprudence of the Court of Justice of the European Union (CJEU), and what changes may be expected in the light of recent developments.

It is suggested that international and European jurisprudence on freedom of association is relevant to at least three controversial issues which are the subject of debate in UK industrial relations. The first is the question of whether freedom of association should be regarded as positive or negative in nature, which may affect whether workers are entitled to refuse to join a trade union and trade unions to refuse to admit certain members. The second is the question whether an entitlement to participate in collective bargaining is implicit in the right to freedom of association, and the implications this may have for the legality of incentives offered by an employer to opt out of collective bargaining. The third is the potential connection between freedom of association and the right to strike. If such a connection can be made, then UK legislation which seeks to place certain limits on access to industrial action may be subject to renewed scrutiny and will potentially have to be amended. All these issues will be revisited later in this book in the context of UK industrial relations practice and legislation. It is, however, vital to appreciate that collective labour law in the UK can be shaped, not only by domestic policy, but by international and European legal norms concerning freedom of association.

2. THEORIES OF FREEDOM OF ASSOCIATION

Freedom of association, as a general principle, could have application to the workplace in a variety of ways. For example, it would appear that an employer obliged to respect freedom of association should not be able to discriminate against workers on grounds of their intimate association in personal relationships, their religious affiliations, or even their determination to assemble for the purpose of expressing their opinions. Such appears to be the view taken by the US Supreme Court, which has regarded a right to associate with others to be implied in the First Amendment.[10] However, our focus is on how the term has come to be associated with trade unions and their activities.

---

[10] A. Long, 'The Troublemaker's Friend, Retaliation against Third Parties and the Right of Association in the Workplace' (2007) 59 *Florida Law Review* 931, 937; J.M. Magrid and J.D. Prenkert, 'The Religious and Associational Freedoms of Business Owners' (2004–5) 7 *University of Pennsylvania Journal of Labour and Employment Law* 191, 210; see also *Roberts v US Jaycees*, 468 US 609 (1984).

The idea of 'freedom of association' encapsulates the liberty of an individual to make the choice freely whether or not to associate with any other individual. It is commonly understood to be derived from a liberal tradition, centred on the autonomy of individuals, as opposed to coercion by the state. Indeed, it would seem to originate from assertions of individual freedom of conscience and of speech in the context of organisations established for charitable, religious and scientific purposes. As John Stuart Mill in his essay 'On Liberty' describes the principle: *'from the liberty of each individual, follows the liberty [...] of combination among individuals; freedom to unite, for any purpose not involving harm to others [...]'*[11]

Only very gradually did this freedom come to be extended to the sphere of industrial relations.[12] For a considerable period of time, additional restrictions were placed on workers' collective organisation, not experienced by other charitable, religious and scientific associations.[13] Nevertheless, by 1927, the conclusion of an ILO survey was that governments *'which recognised the right of association and of assembly in general, could not indefinitely maintain the paradox of forbidding a certain category of citizens from combining and meeting'.*[14]

Viewed in this fashion, that is, primarily as a civil liberty to be exercised by an individual, the decision to join an organisation, such as a trade union, can be regarded as a matter of personal choice rather than collective responsibility. It is on this basis that, as LORD WEDDERBURN commented, *'those propounding individualist philosophies interpret this freedom with emphasis, like Hayek, upon the right to **disassociate**'.*[15] In other words, the freedom to join a trade union is to be equated with the freedom not to join. The two are entirely equivalent.

Moreover, such an approach places emphasis on the liberty of individuals to act, so that the state would seem to have performed its duty to protect freedom of association merely by refraining from interfering with workers' choices to join and form trade unions. It is the authors' view that it is this notion of personal freedom which has dominated individual labour law in the UK, such that the state has historically not provided any positive protection of trade unions,

---

11   J.S. MILL, 'On Liberty' in J.S. MILL, *Utilitarianism, Liberty and Representative Government,* J.M. Dent & Sons, London 1960, p. 75.
12   E. ALKEMA, 'Freedom of Associations and Civil Society' in Council of Europe, *Freedom of Association Proceedings*, Council of Europe Press, Strasbourg, 1994, pp. 58–9; and C.W. JENKS, *The International Protection of Trade Union Freedoms,* Stevens & Sons, London, 1957.
13   H. PELLING, *A History of British Trade Unionism,* Second Edition, Penguin, Harmondsworth 1963, p. 25.
14   ILO, *Freedom of Association: Report and Draft Questionnaire* (1927) ILC, 10th Session, International Labour Office, Geneva, p. 12.
15   LORD WEDDERBURN, 'Freedom of Association and Philosophies of Labour Law' (1989) 18 *ILJ* 1, 17.

collective bargaining or a right to strike, but has rather provided (limited) statutory immunities to protect those who exercise free choice to engage in such activities.[16] Indeed, the rhetoric of choice has been prominent in New Labour policy documentation.[17] More recently, emphasis has been placed on flexibility in the labour market and removing 'red tape' which obstructs effective management by employers, particularly in the context of the 'Red Tape Challenge' linked to the Conservative-Liberal Democrat Coalition Government's 'Employment Law Review'.[18]

It is, however, important to be reminded that there are alternative ways in which to approach the liberal discourse. For example, SHELDON LEADER has argued that freedom of association entails, not so much that individual choice be protected, but rather the freedom of workers '*to do collectively what they are allowed to do individually*'.[19] He phrases this claim in '*the language of equal protection*', taking the view that persons should not have less freedom as a group than they have individually.[20] Whereas others taking such a view have argued for a narrow conception of freedom of association, focussed almost entirely on the preferences of individual workers and being reluctant to contemplate consequential obligations for employers or the state,[21] LEADER has used this claim as a basis for far-reaching trade union rights. For example, he has even argued for the capacity of trade unions to place sanctions on 'free riders', namely those who take the benefit of collectively negotiated increases in pay, without contributing trade union dues or participating in industrial action, on the basis that no one should be able to benefit from the collective action without providing one's own contribution.[22] Were LEADER's arguments to be regarded generally as compelling, there might be considerable scope for arguing that wide-ranging permission should be given by the state to the pursuit of trade union activities and indeed that greater steps should be taken to make provision for legal

---

[16] For discussion of *collective laissez-faire*, see chapter 1.

[17] *Fairness at Work* Cm 3968 (London: TSO, 1998), para. 4.8; T. NOVITZ and P. SKIDMORE, *Fairness at Work: A Critical Analysis of the Employment Relations Act 1999 and its Treatment of Collective Rights,* Hart, Oxford 2001, at pp. 15–16.

[18] See <www.bis.gov.uk/policies/employment-matters/employment-law-review> accessed 31.10.2011.

[19] S. LEADER, *Freedom of Association: A Study in Labor Law and Political Theory,* Yale University Press, New Haven 1992, pp. 23 and 200. See also discussion of Leader's work in T. NOVITZ, 'Workers' Freedom of Association' in J.A. GROSS and L. COMPA, *Human Rights in Labour and Employment Relations: International and Domestic Perspectives,* Labor and Employment Labour Relations Series, University of Illinois, Champaign, Illinois 2009.

[20] Ibid., 189.

[21] B. LANGILLE, 'The Freedom of Association Mess: How we got into it and how we can get out of it' (2009) 54 *McGill Law Journal* 177.

[22] S. LEADER, above n. 19, pp. 79 and 234. This issue has been viewed by others as an intractable problem. See for example F. VON PRONDZYNSKI, *Freedom of Association and Industrial Relations: A Comparative Survey,* Mansell, London 1987, p. 127.

protection of such activities, including the ability of trade unions to discipline members who do not adhere to the terms of their membership.

One difficulty with LEADER's argument, however, is his attempt to treat with formal parity individual and collective action. Coordinated collective action, by virtue of its scale, has a much greater effect than action taken solo. Indeed, the difficulty with the application of a liberal standpoint to workers' exercise of freedom of association in trade unions is that it is, in many respects, different from the exercise of freedom to associate for other purposes. In the industrial sphere, the desire to act collectively stems from the economic circumstances and material needs of workers, and entails a challenge to the existing social order. In joining trade unions, workers seek to address long-standing inequalities of bargaining power between employer and worker. Workers appreciate that, through trade unions, they can engage in a quasi-democratic process, electing representatives to give their opinions voice. In this way, in the industrial relations context, there are subsidiary arguments for trade unions as a source of democratic representation and which link protection of freedom of association to freedom of speech. Moreover, in so doing, workers have the opportunity to argue persuasively for improved terms and conditions in collective bargaining, without being exposed personally to the ire of their employer. They may also go further and use their collective strength to organise industrial action which places pressure on an employer to agree to those terms. To this extent, trade unions can and will do 'harm' to employers in the sense that they claim for their members a share of economic wealth which would otherwise go to their employers. However, in pursuing their objectives, trade unions can offer potentially concrete material benefits to workers as well as to employers.[23] For these reasons, it has been argued that freedom of association can be regarded as not only a civil liberty, but as a political right to participation in workplace decision-making,[24] as well as a socio-economic right based on material claims to income.[25] By supplementing traditional liberal arguments with recognition of other powerful claims that workers may make, a richer conception of freedom of association is achievable.[26]

---

[23]   For a recent investigation into the material benefits which collective bargaining can offer to trade union members, see the results of the ILO study published as S. HAYTER, *The Role of Collective Bargaining in the Global Economy: Negotiating for Social Justice,* ILO/Edward Elgar, Geneva/London 2011, which provides evidence that collective bargaining can deliver both equity (in terms of reduction of wage gaps) and efficiency gains (in terms of flexible, innovative agreements boosting productivity).

[24]   See A. BOGG, *The Democratic Aspects of Trade Union Recognition,* Hart, Oxford 2009.

[25]   T. NOVITZ, *International and European Protection of the Right to Strike,* Oxford University Press, Oxford 2003, Chapter 3.

[26]   See for example C. SUMMERS, 'Book Review: Sheldon Leader, *Freedom of Association: A Study in Labor Law and Political Theory*' (1995) 16(2) *Comparative Labor Law and Policy Journal* 262, 268–9; and T. NOVITZ, above n. 19, pp. 125–8.

If the multitude of reasons for protection of freedom of association are acknowledged – specific to the context of work – which are of a political and socio-economic nature, in addition to the exercise of individual liberty, then it becomes possible also to have regard to the practical reasons for not equating positive and negative dimensions of freedom of association, but giving them different weight. For example, if (as is generally the situation in the UK) *'union-negotiated terms and conditions are available to everyone (or extended to everyone by the employer), paying and non-paying employees alike, it generally makes no sense for a self-interested, utility-maximising person to join a union and pay dues [...] If free riding becomes pervasive, union dues could rise, in principle, to an excessive level and effectively discourage anyone from joining'.*[27] Moreover, HARCOURT and LAM point to the resource problems posed for trade unions which continually have to mount organising drives to reach non-unionised workplaces.[28] It could be added that this is made all the more difficult by the ways in which property rights are relied upon to obstruct trade union access to the workplace, other than in very limited defined circumstances provided in the statutory trade union recognition procedure set out in Schedule A1 of the Trade Union and Labour Relations (Consolidation) Act 1992.[29] HARCOURT and LAM also observe that workers' freedom of contract will not lead to genuine contractual diversity, since it will be the employer which, in the absence of the correction in bargaining power offered by trade unions, will generally set terms and conditions of employment. Moreover, collective bargaining can set minimum terms and conditions above which differentiation can occur.[30] Indeed, a richer conception of freedom of association can assist in identifying what constitutes anti-union discrimination, particularly where workers experience less favourable treatment on the basis of participation in collective bargaining. It may also serve as a potential justification for the right to strike, and, as shall be discussed, this is the approach to interpretation of freedom of association adopted by supervisory bodies in the ILO and, more recently, the European Court of Human Rights.

The variety of ways in which freedom of association can be understood and applied is evident from the development of the complex matrix of international and European labour and human rights instruments discussed below. The content and interpretation of these sources of entitlement has been the subject of ongoing debate, regarding at least three discrete issues. The first is the status of the negative freedom to disassociate when compared to positive freedom of association in a trade union. The second is the nature of any link between

---

[27]   M. HARCOURT and H. LAM, 'Freedom of Association, Freedom of Contract and the Right-to-Work Debate' (2006) 18(4) *Employee Responsibilities and Rights Journal* 249, 255–6.

[28]   M. HARCOURT and H. LAM (2006) above n. 27, 254.

[29]   See chapter 3 below. See also BOGG (2009) above n. 24, pp. 186–200.

[30]   M. HARCOURT and H. LAM, above n. 27, 260.

freedom of association and collective bargaining. The third final, and possibly most controversial issue, is whether an entitlement to take industrial action is a necessary aspect of freedom of association. In relation to each of these issues, international and European legal norms reflect the tensions between grounds for protection of collective action vis-à-vis merely maintaining some scope for individual choice. However, it should be stressed that the latter individualistic interpretation of freedom of association has largely prevailed in the UK to date.

3. ILO TREATMENT OF FREEDOM OF ASSOCIATION

Given the tripartite structure of the ILO, which entails representation of workers' and employers' organisations from each ILO Member State, it was not surprising that the Preamble to the first Constitution of the International Labour Organization (ILO) in 1919 stated that freedom of association was a principle of '*special and urgent importance*' which applied for '*all lawful purposes*' to both '*the employed*' and '*employers*'. Article I of the Declaration of Philadelphia of 1944, subsequently appended to the ILO Constitution, added that '*freedom of expression and of association are essential to sustained progress*' and Article III went further in that ILO objectives were to include '*the effective recognition of the right of collective bargaining [...]*' These constitutional provisions have since been elaborated upon in a number of ILO Conventions and Recommendations, most notably through the medium of 'core' ILO Conventions No. 87 on Freedom of Association and Protection of the Right to Organise 1948 and No. 98 on the Right to Organise and Collective Bargaining 1949.

The UK was the first state to ratify both ILO Conventions No. 87 (on 27 June 1949) and No. 98 (on 30 June 1950). Nevertheless, as shall become apparent in later chapters, the UK never introduced any implementing legislation, as the then government took the view that the UK was already in compliance with the standards contained in these two instruments.[31]

Convention No. 87 establishes, by virtue of Article 2, the freedom of workers and employers to organise and, subject only to the rules of the organisations concerned, join organisations of their own choosing. This freedom includes, by virtue of Article 3, '*the right to draw up their constitutions and rules, to elect their representatives in full freedom, to organize their administration and activities and to formulate their programmes*'. This entitlement is extended, through Articles 5 and 6, to trade union and employer federations and confederations. Convention

---

31   P. Davies and M. Freedland, *Labour Legislation and Public Policy*, Oxford University Press, Oxford, 1993, pp. 42–43.

No. 87 is, thereby, concerned with the exercise of freedom to associate by workers and employers alike, without undue interference from the State. In this sense, it maps on to the liberal view of freedom of association outlined above. However, a positive obligation is to be placed on ratifying States, such as the UK, which are obliged under Article 11 to take '*all necessary and appropriate measures to ensure that workers and employers may exercise freely the right to organise*'.

ILO Convention No. 98 '*on the Right to Organise and Collective Bargaining*' provides more specifically for the conditions in which freedom of association can be realised, such as freedom from acts of anti-union discrimination (Article 1) and freedom from interference (Article 2). Article 2(2) states: '*In particular, acts which are designed to promote the establishment of workers' organisations under the domination of employers or employers' organisations, or to support workers' organisations by financial or other means, with the object of placing such organisations under the control of employers or employers' organisations, shall be deemed to constitute acts of interference within the meaning of this Article.*' Convention No. 98 also stresses the importance of collective bargaining. Article 4 lays the onus on states to ensure that: '*Measures appropriate to national conditions shall be taken, where necessary, to encourage and promote the full development and utilisation of machinery for voluntary negotiation between employers or employers' organisations and workers' organisations, with a view to the regulation of terms and conditions of employment by means of collective agreements.*' In this sense Convention No. 98 mirrors and expands upon the positive obligations placed on states by virtue of Convention No. 87.

It should be noted that the freedom to association, the right to organise and to engage in collective bargaining does not remain unqualified. Both ILO Conventions Nos. 87 and 98 exclude the armed forces and the police, who are to be covered by national law and regulation. Convention No. 98, by virtue of Article 6, '*does not deal with the position of public servants engaged in the administration of the State, nor shall it be construed as prejudicing their rights or status in any way*'. Rights to protection from anti-union discrimination and protection of public employees' organisations from '*acts of interference by a public authority*' were extended to public employees by virtue of ILO Convention No. 151 concerning Protection of the Right to Organise and Procedures for Determining Conditions of Employment in the Public Service 1978, which was ratified by the UK on 19 March 1980 (once again, without any implementing legislation). Article 8 of the latter Convention makes specific provision for the settlement of disputes in this sector, '*through negotiation between the parties or through independent and impartial machinery, such as mediation, conciliation and arbitration, established in such a manner as to ensure the confidence of the parties involved*'.

'Freedom of association and the effective recognition of the right to collective bargaining' have been recognised as 'fundamental rights' under Article 2 of the ILO Declaration on Fundamental Principles and Rights at Work 1998 and again in Part I, Article A of the ILO Declaration on Social Justice for a Fair Globalization 2008. While both declaratory instruments contain 'follow-up mechanisms' intended to encourage best practice rather than identify breach of international legal obligations,[32] the 'fundamental rights' elaborated therein have since been used as a basis for trade conditionality.[33] Moreover, ratification and effective compliance with ILO Conventions Nos. 87 and 98 provide the basis for more generous tariff access under the generalised system of preferences operated by the European Union.[34]

The bare text of these ILO instruments has been interpreted and applied by two key ILO supervisory bodies. One is the ILO Committee of Experts on the Application of Conventions and Recommendations (CEACR), which monitors state reports regarding ratified Conventions. The other is the ILO Governing Body Committee on Freedom of Association (CFA), founded in 1951, which hears complaints related to potential violations of freedom of association, and in doing so, has developed a substantial jurisprudence on the subject. The CFA views freedom of association as a constitutional principle which all ILO members are bound to protect, regardless of ratification of ILO Conventions Nos. 87 and 98.[35]

The ILO has adopted what has been described as a *'liberal interpretation of freedom of association'*,[36] which places emphasis on the free choice to join a trade union, including determination of trade union constitutions, and criticises preconditions for establishment or registration of a trade union.[37] However, notably, this has not led to ILO condemnation of the 'closed shop'. The ILO CFA

---

[32]   J. BELLACE, 'The ILO Declaration of Fundamental Principles and Rights at Work' (2001) 17 *IJCLLIR (International Journal of Comparative Labour Law and Industrial Relations)* 201.

[33]   See T. NOVITZ, 'Social Policy: Normative Power Europe at Work?' in J. ORBIE (ed.), *Europe's Global Role: External Policies of the European Union*, Ashgate, Aldershot 2008.

[34]   Council Regulation (EC) No.732/2008 of 22 July 2008 applying a scheme of generalised tariff preferences available at <http://eur-lex.europa.eu/LexUriServ/LexUriServ.do?uri=OJ:L:2008: 211:0001:0039:EN:PDF> accessed 31/10.2011.

[35]   *Case No. 102 (South Africa)*, 15th Report of the CFA (1955), para. 128; see also ILO 2006: para. 2. Although it should be noted that under ILO 2006: para. 8: 'The Committee's mandate is not linked to the 1998 ILO Declaration on Fundamental Principles and Rights at Work – which has its own built-in follow-up mechanisms – but rather stems directly from the fundamental aims and purposes set out in the ILO Constitution.'

[36]   T. CARAWAY, 'Freedom of Association: Battering ram or Trojan horse?' (2006) 13(2) *Review of International Political Economy* 210, 219.

[37]   ILO *Freedom of Association: Digest of Decisions of the Freedom of Association Committee of the Governing Body of the ILO* 5th Revised Edition, ILO, Geneva 2006 (Hereafter ILO Digest), paras. 272–334.

did not consider that workers need to be given a choice as to which trade union they would join, when collective bargaining arrangements which required them to join one recognised trade union were in their interests. This is evident from CFA conclusions reached in a case brought by a trade union, the Aeronautical Engineers' Association in Croydon, in 1954. The CFA concluded that, in circumstances where the applicant union was denied representation of members in a particular workplace, because the employer had agreed to 'closed shop' check off and bargaining arrangements with another union, *'the complainant has failed to offer sufficient proof that the refusal of the employers to recognise the complaining organisation as a bargaining agent constitutes, in the present case, an infringement of trade union rights'*, taking the view that the closed shop was not considered to lead to anti-union discrimination by virtue of ILO Convention No. 98.[38] Attempts to raise the same issue again were rejected again in 1957 and 1958.[39]

Indeed, the CFA has expressed concern *'that the emphasis on individual responsibility for bargaining [...] can be detrimental to collective bargaining'*.[40] The Committee recognises that it is important not only for employers, but also workers to have freedom of choice. It appreciates that, unless the state intervenes and introduces suitable mechanisms for the promotion of collective bargaining, workers may be unable to choose collective bargaining, given the superior bargaining power of an employer.[41]

For these reasons it would seem that the ILO CFA does not question legislation which gives the most representative trade unions certain privileges in terms of negotiating rights[42] and the collective agreements that they conclude being extended to other workers.[43] This is so as to ensure the efficacy of collective bargaining and suggests that, if the UK could perfect its statutory recognition legislation, by adequately protecting against trade union discrimination and extending trade unions' access to the workplace, the Committee would have no difficulty endorsing the introduction of compulsory recognition.[44] It is also notable that the CEACR has criticised UK legislation on the basis that there should be greater and more effective protection of dismissal for workers who

---

38   *Case No. 96 (UK)*, 13th Report of the ILO CFA at para. 138.
39   See *Case No. 162 (UK)*, 26th Report of the CFA; and *Case No. 182 (UK)*, 30th Report of the CFA.
40   *Case No. 1698 (New Zealand)* 292nd Report (1994), para. 726.
41   *Case No. 1698 (New Zealand)* 295th Report (1994), paras. 253–8.
42   ILO *Digest*, paras. 346–59.
43   *Ibid.*, paras. 1050–1053.
44   CEACR: Individual Observation concerning Right to Organise and Collective Bargaining Convention, 1949 (No. 98) United Kingdom (ratification: 1950) Published: 2009; CEACR: Individual Observation concerning Right to Organise and Collective Bargaining Convention, 1949 (No. 98) United Kingdom (ratification: 1950) Published: 2011. See also chapter 3 below.

have taken lawful industrial action.[45] Indeed, both the CFA and CEACR consider that there is a clear connection to be drawn between freedom of association and an entitlement to participate in collective bargaining[46] and between freedom of association and the right to strike.[47]

The CFA has acknowledged that certain restrictions may be placed by governments on collective bargaining and industrial action in the army, police force and other public servants.[48] However, the ILO Committee has been adamant that any restrictions placed on such a right must be proportionate to the harm potentially caused, and be accompanied by 'compensatory guarantees' such as the provision of *adequate, impartial and speedy conciliation and arbitration proceedings in which the parties concerned can take part at every stage and in which the awards, once made, are fully and promptly implemented'.*[49]

Indeed, since 1979 the CFA and CEACR have indicated that various aspects of UK law are in breach of ILO Conventions Nos. 87 and 98, which relate to the right to organise, the right to engage in collective bargaining and the right to strike. For example, the ILO CEACR has found repeatedly that lack of any legal protection for sympathy action in the UK is highly problematic,[50] but no legislative reform is contemplated by the current UK Labour Government in this regard.

In 2005, the CFA found that, in the UK, the protection of freedom of association was unduly hindered by restrictions placed on the right to strike in the prison service, insofar as such restrictions were not matched by the necessary compensatory guarantees relating to alternative effective systems of conciliation and arbitration. Moreover, they were concerned that the UK government was not prepared to articulate the scope of exceptional circumstances in which it would not comply with the findings of arbitration by the duly appointed Pay Review Body (PRB).[51]

The lack of legal status of the findings of ILO supervisory bodies is evident from the way in which CFA findings regarding prison officers were treated in a

---

45　See CEACR: Individual Observation concerning Convention No. 87, Freedom of Association and Protection of the Right to Organise, 1948 United Kingdom: 2011.

46　ILO *Digest*, para. 881: 'The right to bargain freely with employers with respect to conditions of work constitutes an essential element in freedom of association…'.

47　Ibid., para. 523.

48　Ibid., para. 572.

49　Ibid., para. 595–6.

50　ILO CEACR: Individual Observation concerning Convention No. 87 (UK): 2007; and ILO CEACR: Individual Observation concerning Convention No. 87 (UK): 2011.

51　*Case No. 2383 (UK)*, 336th Report (2005), paras. 773 and 777.

judgment of the English High Court delivered by Mr Justice Wyn Williams.[52] In that case, the Ministry of Justice sought the issue of an injunction by the Court to prevent any future industrial action by prison officers, on the basis that the strike was in breach of a Joint Industrial Relations Procedural Agreement, under which prison officers forego industrial action and agree instead that their pay be determined in response to recommendations made by an independent PRB. The union alleged that since the government had not fully implemented the findings of the PRB, the injunction should not be issued and relied on the findings of the CFA in this regard. The union argued that government was said not to have come with 'clean hands' and was not therefore entitled to the equitable remedy sought. However, the recommendations of the ILO CFA were not considered to be determinative by the High Court, because the UK government continued to assert its entitlement to depart from the findings of the Pay Review Body on the basis of 'affordability' and, in the absence of a monist legal system, government policy must prevail. The government of the time certainly did not heed the view of the CFA, but proceeded instead to introduce legislation so as to ensure that prison officers would, in the future, be under an unconditional statutory obligation not to strike.[53] ILO norms, one might therefore conclude, have relatively little weight, either in UK courts or with the UK legislature.

4. UN INSTRUMENTS

4.1. UNIVERSAL DECLARATION OF HUMAN RIGHTS 1948

The notion of negative freedom of association is not so much a feature of ILO jurisprudence, but was recognised in the foundational human rights instrument, the Universal Declaration of Human Rights (UDHR), adopted under the auspices of the United Nations in 1948. Article 20 of this instrument states that:

> '(1) Everyone has the right to freedom of peaceful assembly and association; and (2) No one may be compelled to belong to an association.'

In this context, the right to associate and the right to disassociate are placed side by side, as if they were two sides of the same coin. Notably, there is no mention in this instrument of trade unions as a manifestation of freedom of association. Instead, Article 23(4) provides independently that: *'Everyone has the right to form and to join trade unions for the protection of his interests.'*

---

52   *The Ministry of Justice v POA* [2008] EWHC 239, at para. 42.
53   Criminal Justice and Public Order Act 1994, since amended by Criminal Justice and Immigration Act 2008.

4.2. 1966 UN COVENANTS

By way of contrast, Article 22 of the 1966 International Covenant on Civil and Political Rights (ICCPR) adopted by the UN General Assembly, recognises expressly only the positive right of association, stating that: *'Everyone shall have the right to freedom of association with others, including the right to form and join trade unions for the protection of his interests.'* Article 8 of its twin instrument, the 1966 International Covenant on Economic, Social and Cultural Rights (ICESCR), contains more far-reaching provisions relating to collective worker activity, rather than freedom of association *per se.* In particular, this provision places the onus on State parties to ensure:

1. The right of everyone to form trade unions and join the trade union of his choice, subject only to the rules of the organisation concerned, for the promotion and protection of his economic and social interests. ...
2. The right of trade unions to establish national federations of confederations and the right of the latter to form or join international trade-union organisations;
3. The right of trade unions to function freely subject to no limitations other than those prescribed by law and which are necessary in a democratic society in the interests of national security or public order or for the protection of the rights and freedoms of others;
4. The right to strike, provided that it is exercised in conformity with the laws of the particular country.

Both instruments indicate, as regards freedom to associate and the right to form and join trade unions, that these entitlements may be restricted but only insofar as such restrictions are *'prescribed by law'* and *'necessary in a democratic society in the interests of national security or public order or for the protection of the rights and freedoms of others'.* Both instruments also specify that none of these entitlements extend to members of the armed forces or the police or, in the case of the ICESCR, *'the administration of the State'.*

Article 22 of the ICCPR and Article 8 of the ICESCR are also made expressly subject to the proviso that: *'Nothing in this article shall authorize States Parties to the International Labour Organisation Convention of 1948 concerning Freedom of Association and Protection of the Right to Organize to take legislative measures which would prejudice, or to apply the law in such a manner as to prejudice, the guarantees provided for in that Convention.'* One might therefore expect that ILO jurisprudence, which states that a right to strike is a vital aspect of freedom of association would influence the approach taken by the UN Human Rights Committee (HRC) to interpretation of the ICCPR. However, the HRC has been hesitant to adopt ILO jurisprudence uncritically. In 1982, a complaint was considered inadmissible by the majority of the HRC, on the basis that Article 22 of the ICCPR did not encompass a right to strike, since specific provision had been made for such a right under the ICESCR, which had not been ratified by all parties to the ICCPR.[54] Since that date, several concluding observations of the HRC on compatibility with Article 22 indicate that restriction of a right to strike under national laws may amount to a violation of that provision.[55] Yet, the artificial divide between civil and political rights on the one hand and socio-economic rights on the other, reflected in the division between the ICCPR and the ICESCR, would seem to have obstructed attempts to link freedom of association with collective action.

Once again, although the UK has ratified both instruments, it has never adopted implementing legislation. Indeed, the UK is viewed by the UN Committee on Economic, Social and Cultural Rights to be in breach of its obligations regarding collective bargaining and the right to strike,[56] not least because the latter has never been given constitutional or legislative effect in the UK, but is protected solely by means of immunity. As was observed by Lord Justice Maurice Kay in *Metrobus v Unite the Union*: '*In this country, the right to strike has never been much more than a slogan or a legal metaphor. Such a right has not been bestowed by statute.*'[57] The consequences of this omission are considered later in this book.[58]

5. THE COUNCIL OF EUROPE: THE ECHR AND THE ESC

In the Council of Europe, when deliberating whether the wording of the UDHR should be applied in a European context, the drafters of the ECHR deliberately selected a different formulation whereby, under Article 11, freedom of association was explicitly linked to the right to form and join trade unions and no mention was made of the negative freedom to disassociate.[59] The drafters did however envisage that restrictions could be placed on such an entitlement, especially in relation to members of the armed forces, police or administration of the state.

---

[54] *J.B. et al v Canada*, CCPR/C/28/D/118/1982.

[55] See e.g., Concluding Observations on Lithuania, (2004) UN doc. CCPR/CO/80/LTU, para. 17. See also Concluding Observations on Chile, (1999) UN doc. CCPR/C/79/Add. 104, para. 25. Discussed in S. JOSEPH, 'UN Covenants and Labour Rights' in C. FENWICK and T. NOVITZ above n. 5.

[56] See Concluding Observations of the UN Committee on Economic, Social and Cultural Rights 1997, para. 11; and Concluding Observations of the UN Committee on Economic, Social and Cultural Rights 2002, para. 16; and more generally, Concluding Observations of the Committee on Economic, Social and Cultural Rights 2009, para. 13.

[57] *Metrobus Ltd v Unite the Union* [2009] IRLR 851, para. 118.

[58] See Chapter 5.

[59] See T. NOVITZ, above n. 25, p. 232.

The European Social Charter, in a manner comparable to the ICESCR, sets out in detail entitlement to organise and participate in collective activities. Article 5 of the ESC sets out the right of both workers and employers to organise, so that the Contracting Parties, such as the UK *'undertake that national law shall not be such as to impair, nor shall it be so applied as to impair, this freedom'*. Whether members of the armed forces are covered by this guarantee is to be determined by national laws or regulations. Article 6 sets out in considerable detail *'the right to bargain collectively'* which imposes positive obligations on Contracting Parties:

1. to promote joint consultation between workers and employers;
2. to promote, where necessary and appropriate, machinery for voluntary negotiations between employers or employers' organisations and workers' organisations, with a view to the regulation of terms and conditions of employment by means of collective agreements;
3. to promote the establishment and use of appropriate machinery for conciliation and voluntary arbitration for the settlement of labour disputes; and recognise:
4. the right of workers and employers to collective action in cases of conflicts of interest, including the right to strike, subject to obligations that might arise out of collective agreements previously entered into.

Both the ECHR and ESC (under Article 11(2) and Article 31 respectively) state that restrictions or limitations are permissible insofar as they were *'prescribed by law and are necessary in a democratic society for the protection of the rights and freedoms of others or for the protection of public interest, national security, public health, or morals'*.[60]

The European Court of Human Rights subsequently determined (and recently reiterated) that negative freedom of association is implicit in Article 11 of the ECHR,[61] such that the efforts of the drafters of the ECHR were, in this regard, in vain. The 1979 judgment of that Court in *Young, James and Webster*[62] led to the dismantling of the 'closed shop' or compulsory trade unionism in the UK, despite the views of the ILO CFA that this practice was defensible. The principle of 'negative' freedom of association, namely that a worker is entitled to refuse to be a member of a trade union, is now a well-established feature of ECHR jurisprudence relating to Article 11. It is an approach which has subsequently been endorsed by the European Committee of Social Rights, the committee of

---

60   ECHR, Art. 11(2) and ESC, Art. 31.
61   Most recently confirmed in *Applications Nos. 52562/99 and 52620/99 Sørensen v Denmark and Rasmussen v Denmark*, judgment of the European Court of Human Rights, 11.01.2006.
62   *Young, James and Webster v UK* (1982) 4 EHRR 38.

independent experts responsible for scrutiny of compliance with the ESC and interpretation of its provisions.[63]

More recently, and controversially, the Court has applied the notion of negative freedom of association for the benefit of trade unions in the case of *ASLEF v UK*.[64] This concerned the decision taken by a British union to exclude from its membership Mr Jay Lee who was a member of the British National Party, (which advocates racist policies contrary to the constitutional objectives of the union). That exclusion was challenged by Lee in the UK employment tribunal, on the basis that this treatment was in violation of section 174 of the Trade Union and Labour Relations (Consolidation) Act 1992 (TULRCA). This statutory provision restricts the ability of trade unions to expel members if the reason for expulsion is membership of a political party. The UK courts found in favour of Lee. However, the European Court of Human Rights found that the union was entitled to expel Lee, and in so doing took the significant step of finding that a trade union as an organisation (or collective entity) could exercise a freedom protected under the ECHR, such as the negative right not to associate.

In this way, the Court attempted to give parity of treatment to the right of individuals not to join associations and the rights of associations not to have these individuals join. In so doing, the Court sought to treat trade unions in the same way as other sorts of associations.[65] This neutrality of treatment could be said to reveal the liberal underpinnings of its jurisprudence,[66] and such a formal application of the rule of law can, it would seem, sometimes assist workers' organisations.[67]

The conclusions of the Court were however stated to be subject to the proviso in Article 11(2) of the Convention that trade union autonomy can be restricted to the extent that this is prescribed by law and *'necessary in a democratic society'* for one of a number of aims. The Court was also prepared to recognise that *'a balance must be achieved which ensures the fair and proper treatment of minorities and avoids any abuse of a dominant position'*.[68]

What is now doubtful is whether the recent amendment of UK legislation, ostensibly designed to implement the decision of the European Court of Human

---

[63]   See *Conclusions of the Committee of Independent Experts XIV-1 and XV-1* in respect of Denmark. This is despite having previously determined that governments could not impose compulsory trade unionism, but that it was permissible for workers themselves to negotiate a 'closed shop' with their employers: See *Conclusions of the Committee of Independent Experts IV*, 47.

[64]   Application No. 11002/05; [2007] IRLR 361.

[65]   Ibid., para. 39.

[66]   V. MANTOUVALOU (2010), above n. 176.

[67]   E.P. THOMAS, *Whigs and Hunters: The Origins of the Black Act*, Pantheon, London 1976.

[68]   Application No. 11002/05; [2007] IRLR 361, para. 43.

Rights in *ASLEF*, does in fact do so. It is arguable that the amendments to section 174 of TULRCA implemented by the Employment Act 2008, far from giving trade unions latitude to exercise negative freedom of association, place additional burdens on trade unions which wish to expel certain individuals from membership on the grounds of their membership of a political party. Trade unions will be able to expel workers on the grounds of their membership of a political party only if this is in accordance with the rules or objectives of the union, if the objective is accessible to the individual in question, if certain procedural obligations are complied with first, *and* if representations made by the individual are considered fairly. These extensive and even draconian requirements are put in place, despite the worker's potential access to a common law remedy for expulsion in breach of trade union rules and the fact that the benefits of collective bargaining are *de facto* extended to any member of the workforce where a collective agreement is in place.[69]

More problematic was the jurisprudence of the European Court of Human Rights which at one time stated that the right to freedom of association in Article 11 did not extend to a right to consultation, participation in collective bargaining or the right to strike. In part, this would seem to be due to the parallel existence of the ESC which provided for such rights, but gave states the option whether or not to commit to compliance in respect of any one provision contained therein.[70] On this basis the Court took the view that '*[...] it cannot be supposed that such a right derives by implication from Article 11 [...] of the 1950 Convention, which incidentally would amount to admitting that the 1961 Charter took a retrograde step in this domain*'.[71] On their facts, early judgments on the European Court of Human Rights would seem to place emphasis on efficacy of collective bargaining, and as such are arguably defensible in terms of ILO jurisprudence. For example, in the *Swedish Engine Drivers' case*, the Swedish Government refused to enter into a collective agreement with the applicant union, preferring to agree terms with a larger, more representative organisation, which would automatically be extended to the applicant's members.[72] It was the general principle stated in these cases to the effect that there is no necessary connection between freedom of association and collective bargaining or industrial action which was to prove problematic.

---

[69] See K.D. EWING, 'Employment Act 2008: Implementing the ASLEF Decision – A Victory for the BNP?' (2009) 38 *ILJ* 50; and CEACR: Individual Direct Request concerning Freedom of Association and Protection of the Right to Organise Convention, 1948 (No. 87) United Kingdom: 2009.

[70] ESC, Art. 20.

[71] See *National Union of Belgian Police v Belgium* 1 EHRR 578 (1979), para. 38, in relation to claims made regarding a right to consultation, which is also provided for under Art. 6(1) of the ESC.

[72] 1 EHRR 617 (1979); applied *Schettini v Italy*, Application No. 29529/95, 9 December 2000, unreported.

The UK sought to rely in its submissions to the European Court of Human Rights in the *Wilson* case on the absence of any entitlement to collective bargaining under Article 11. This litigation concerned the ability of employers to offer incentives to workers to opt out of collective bargaining, although the workers remained free to accept other benefits of trade union membership. The UK argued that these workers were not deprived of freedom of association, since they had the opportunity to rely on trade unions to provide such services as representation in grievance and disciplinary hearings or access to social insurance schemes. The response of the Court was not quite what the UK Government had expected, for the judgment stated that '*by permitting employers to use financial incentives to induce employees to surrender important union rights, the [UK had] failed in its positive obligation to secure the enjoyment of rights under Article 11*'.[73] Nevertheless, while condemning UK legislation, the Court did reiterate its standard position that collective bargaining '*is not indispensable for the effective enjoyment of trade union freedom*' and that '*Contracting States enjoy a wide margin of appreciation as to how trade union freedom may be secured*'.[74]

In 2008 a significant victory was won by the trade union movement, when the Court made the decision to reverse its previous findings on this point and take a new tack.[75] The case of *Demir & Baykara v Turkey* concerned a trade union, Tüm Bel Sen, which was established in 1990 to represent civil servants. In 1993, this union concluded a collective agreement concerning pay and working conditions with the Gaziantep Municipal Council for a period of two years, but the agreement was not honoured. When the union sought to rely on the collective agreement in court proceedings, their claim was initially upheld by the District Court. However, the decision was eventually overturned by the Cour de Cassation. Moreover, during this time, the Constitution was amended (in 1995) and a Law introduced (in 2001),[76] which meant that while civil servants' unions could engage in collective bargaining under certain conditions, they were not entitled to enter into valid collective agreements directly with the authorities concerned. Monies originally paid out to civil servants by virtue of the District Court proceedings therefore had to be repaid. A complaint under Article 11 of the ECHR was brought by one of the union members, Mr Kemal Demir, who was asked to repay the sum originally granted to him by way of compensation and by Mrs Vicdan Baykara, the President of Tüm Bel Sen.

---

73 *Wilson, Palmer and others v UK*, Application Nos. 30668/96, 30671/96 & 30678/96, judgment of 02.07.02, para. 48. For background on the case, see, K.D. EWING, '*Dancing with the Daffodils?*' (2000) 50 Federation News 1 and T. NOVITZ, above n. 9.
74 *Wilson, Palmer and others v UK*, Application Nos. 30668/96, 30671/96 & 30678/96, judgment of 2 July 2002, para. 44.
75 See for detailed analysis of the implications of this landmark case, K.D. EWING and J. HENDY, 'The Dramatic Implications of *Demir and Baykara*' (2010) 39 *ILJ* 2.
76 Law no. 4688 on civil servants' trade unions, 25 June 2001.

The Turkish government responded to the complaint by arguing that:

> Turkey was not a party to Article 5 (the right to organise) or Article 6 (the right to bargain collectively) of the European Social Charter, which it ratified in 1989. An interpretation that rendered these provisions binding on an indirect basis was even more problematic where, as in the present case, the absence in the Convention of an express provision guaranteeing the right to enter into collective agreements was counterbalanced by consideration of other instruments to which the State concerned was not a party.[77]

This was not an argument accepted, either at first instance by the Chamber judgment or subsequently by the Grand Chamber, which delivered its judgment in 2008. Both judgments acknowledged that the Court had previously taken the view that Article 11 did not necessitate a right to enter into a collective agreement, or an entitlement in all circumstances to engage in collective bargaining. However, the Chamber judgment stated that:

> The Court observes that its case-law does not exclude the possibility that the right to enter into a collective agreement may represent, in the particular circumstances of a case, one of the principal means – even the foremost of such means – for trade unionists to protect their interests. It notes in this connection that the organic link between freedom of association and freedom to bargain collectively has been referred to by the Social Charter's Committee of Independent Experts, according to whom, when a Contracting Party does not ensure full freedom of association for workers, under Article 5 of the Social Charter, it cannot fully ensure respect for the right to bargain collectively under Article 6 either (see Conclusions XIV-1, p. 419 [Ireland], ibid. p. 179 [Denmark] and p. 530 [Malta]; Turkey has not yet agreed to apply Articles 5 and 6 of the Social Charter).[78]

It was considered significant in both hearings that Turkey had ratified ILO Convention No. 98 and the Grand Chamber further placed stress on general recognition that civil servants are entitled to collective bargaining, as is reflected in ILO Convention No. 151, which was also ratified by Turkey.[79] This would seem to reflect a more general trend towards citation of ILO Conventions and jurisprudence in the Court's judgments observed previously by VIRGINIA MANTOUVALOU.[80] The Grand Chamber was also cognisant of Article 28 of the EU Charter of Fundamental Rights 2000 which provides that '*workers and*

---

[77] Application no. 34503/97 *Demir and Baykara v Turkey*, Grand Chamber Judgment of 12.11.08.

[78] Application no. 34503/97 *Demir and Baykara v Turkey*, Chamber Judgment of 21.11.06, para. 35.

[79] Application no. 34503/97 *Demir and Baykara v Turkey*, Grand Chamber Judgment of 12.11.08, para. 147–8.

[80] V. MANTOUVALOU, 'Servitude and Forced Labour in the 21st Century: The Human Rights of Domestic Workers' (2006) 35 *ILJ* 395, 404–407 and (2010), above n. 5.

employers, or their respective organisations, have, in accordance with Community law and national laws and practices, the right to negotiate and conclude collective agreements at the appropriate levels'.[81] As a result, the Grand Chamber concluded that:

> In the light of these developments, the Court considers that its case-law to the effect that the right to bargain collectively and to enter into collective agreements does not constitute an inherent element of Article 11 [...] should be reconsidered, so as to take account of the perceptible evolution in such matters, in both international law and domestic legal systems. While it is in the interests of legal certainty, foreseeability and equality before the law that the Court should not depart, without good reason, from precedents established in previous cases, a failure by the Court to maintain a dynamic and evolutive approach would risk rendering it a bar to reform or improvement [...]

> Consequently, the Court considers that, having regard to the developments in labour law, both international and national, and to the practice of Contracting States in such matters, the right to bargain collectively with the employer has, in principle, become one of the essential elements of the *'right to form and to join trade unions for the protection of [one's] interests'* set forth in Article 11 of the Convention, it being understood that States remain free to organise their system so as, if appropriate, to grant special status to representative trade unions. Like other workers, civil servants, except in very specific cases, should enjoy such rights, but without prejudice to the effects of any 'lawful restrictions' that may have to be imposed on 'members of the administration of the State' within the meaning of Article 11 §2 – a category to which the applicants in the present case do not, however, belong.[82]

This is a decision which would seem to have significant repercussions for the UK, such that UK legislation and practice relating to collective bargaining could be regarded as coming within the scope of Article 11 and thereby the scrutiny of UK courts by virtue of the Human Rights Act 1998.

Potentially significant decisions have also been made regarding the connection between freedom of association and the right to strike, so that the latter also merits protection under Article 11. In the case of *Affaire Dilek et Autres v Turquie* (also known as the *Satilmis* case),[83] a Chamber of the Court concluded that the right to strike is so significant an aspect of the defence of workers' interests, that any interference with this right has to be assessed in term of whether it comes

---

[81] Application no. 34503/97 *Demir and Baykara v Turkey*, Grand Chamber Judgment of 12.11.08, para. 150. The practice of other European states and their willingness to allow collective bargaining by civil servants was also acknowledged at para. 151.

[82] Ibid., paras. 153–4.

[83] Applications Nos. 74611/01, 26876/02 et 27628/0, *Affaire Dilek et Autres v Turquie*, Judgment of 17.07.07 (available only in French).

within the defence provided in Article 11(2), namely whether that interference is *'prescribed by law'* and is *'necessary in a democratic society for the protection of the rights and freedoms of others or for the protection of public interest, national security, public health, or morals'*.

More recently, in the case of *Enerji Yapi-Yol Sen*,[84] a Chamber of the Court gave an even more firm indication that industrial action could arise as an entitlement under Article 11. This case concerned another civil servants' union, Enerji Yapı-Yol Sen, which like Tüm Bel Sen was founded in 1992, and was a member of the Federation of Public-Sector Trade Unions, which was planning a national one-day strike constituting peaceful action aimed at securing a collective agreement. On 13 April 1996 the Prime Minister's Public Service Staff Directorate published circular no. 1996/21, which, *inter alia*, prohibited all public sector employees from taking part in this action. Despite the circular, some of the trade union's board members took part in the strike and were subjected to sanctions as a result. The Court accepted that the right to strike was not absolute and could be subject to certain conditions and restrictions, but expressed concern that the sanctions imposed were such as to discourage trade union members and other persons from acting upon a legitimate wish to take part in such a day of strike action or other forms of action aimed at defending their affiliates' interests.[85] The Court concluded, according to the Registrar's summary, that *'the adoption and application of the circular did not answer a "pressing social need" and that there had been disproportionate interference with the applicant union's rights. There had therefore been a violation of Article 11.'*

Further case law decided by the Chamber of the European Court of Human Rights deals with the sanctions that may be placed on individual strikers. These cases are discussed at length by EWING and HENDY.[86] For example, in *Danilenkov v Russia*, discrimination against union members who had taken industrial action was found to be in breach of Article 11 of the ECHR, on the basis of Convention 98 as well as Convention 87.[87] It should also be noted that these cases indicate that public-sector strikes ought not to give rise to criminal conviction[88] or to any form of disproportionate disciplinary action.[89] Once again, these findings are wholly consistent with ILO jurisprudence.[90] There has been one anomalous case,

---

[84] Application No. 68959/01, *Enerji Yapi-Yol Sen v Turkey*, Judgment of 21.04.09 (available only in French).
[85] Ibid., para. 35.
[86] K.D. EWING and J. HENDY, above n. 75, 16–19.
[87] Application No. 67336/01, *Danilenkov v Russia*, 30.07.09.
[88] Application No. 23018/04, *Urcan v Turkey*, 17.07.08; and Application No. 22943/04, *Saime Özcan v Turkey*, 15.09.09.
[89] Application No. 30946/04, *Kaya and Seyhan v Turkey*, 15.09.09.
[90] *ILO Digest*, at paras. 658 *et seq.*

in which dismissal of a worker for participation in spontaneous strike action and picketing was upheld by the Court, *Trofimchuk v Ukraine*.[91] However, as has been noted by other commentators, this case makes no reference to ILO authority on this issue.[92]

These findings, although judgments delivered by only a Chamber (rather than the Grand Chamber) of the European Court of Human Rights, suggest that not only will national constraints on collective bargaining now be subject to scrutiny under Article 11, but that constraints placed on the right to strike should be likewise. However, it does not seem that UK courts have fully appreciated this development. In *Metrobus v Unite the Union*, John Hendy QC referred the Court of Appeal to the findings of the *Enerji Yapi-Yol Sen*. However, while their Lordships were willing to acknowledge the strength of the reasoning of the Grand Chamber of the European Court of Human Rights in *Demir and Baykara*, it was evident that they did not regard the judgment of the Chamber in *Enerji Yapi-Yol Sen* as being so compelling:

> The contrast between the full and explicit judgment of the Grand Chamber in *Demir and Baykara* on the one hand, and the more summary discussion of the point in *Enerji Yapi-Yol Sen* on the other hand is quite noticeable. It does not seem to me that it would be prudent to proceed on the basis that the less fully articulated judgment in the later case has developed the Court's case-law by the discrete further stage of recognising a right to take industrial action as an essential element in the rights afforded by article 11.[93]

Formally speaking, the Court of Appeal remains bound by this approach, but in a later judgment on two joined cases, *RMT and ASLEF*, it was noted that the European Court of Human Rights had now, in a number of cases, recognised a right to strike and that this could have a bearing on the issues before the Court. On this basis, Elias LJ preferred to adopt a neutral approach to UK legislation governing industrial action, such that statutory provisions would not be '*strictly construed against those seeking the benefit of the immunities*', but rather '*simply construed in the normal way, without presumptions one way or the other*'.[94]

---

91   Application No. 4241/03, *Trofimchuk v. Ukraine*, 28.10.10.
92   A. BUCKER, F. DORSSEMONT and W. WARNECK, 'The Search for a Balance: Analysis and Perspectives' in A. BUCKER and W. WARNECK (eds.), *Reconciling Fundamental Social Rights and Economic Freedoms after Viking, Laval and Rüffert*, Nomos, Baden-Baden 2011, p. 351.
93   *Metrobus Ltd v Unite the Union* [2009] IRLR 851, para. 35, per Lord Justice Lloyd. The other judges did not comment on this issue. For an excellent discussion of the implications of this case, see R. DUKES, 'The Right to Strike under UK law: Not Much More than a Slogan?' (2010) 39 *ILJ* 82 at 88–90.
94   *RMT v SERCO, ASLEF v London & Birmingham Railway Ltd* [2011] EWCA Civ 226 [2011] IRLR 399, discussed again by R. DUKES, 'The Right to Strike under UK Law: Something more than a slogan?' (2011) 40 *ILJ* 302, 304–5. See chapter 5.

6. THE EUROPEAN UNION

The more market-focused law of the European Union (EU) takes precedence over UK domestic law by virtue of the European Communities Act 1972.[95] EU law is, thereby, arguably even more compelling as a source of UK domestic law than the European Convention of Human Rights whose effect is mediated by the Human Rights Act 1998. This means that, while the EU has no specific competence to make legislation applicable to Member States relating to freedom of association, where UK labour law or that of another member state impinges on a vital aspect of EU law, such as freedom of movement of goods, services, persons and establishment between Member States, that legislation may be subject to challenge before national courts and, ultimately, the Court of Justice of the European Union (CJEU). The CJEU has, however, in its interpretation of EU law, sought to be guided in its general principles jurisprudence by the rights guaranteed under the ECHR, as well as the constitutional traditions of Member States.

The CJEU now also refers explicitly to the provisions set out in the EU Charter of Fundamental Rights 2000 (EUCFR), an instrument which also makes self-conscious reference to the ECHR.[96] Indeed, it is arguably now bound to do so due to the amendment secured by the Lisbon Treaty.[97] The EUCFR provides in Article 12(1) that: '*Everyone has the right to freedom of peaceful assembly and to freedom of association at all levels, in particular in political, trade union and civic matters, which implies the right of everyone to form and to join trade unions for the protection of his or her interests.*' This provision is distinct from the more specific protection of the right of collective bargaining and action set out in Article 28 of the EUCFR, which states that: '*Workers and employers, or their respective organisations, have, in accordance with Community law and national*

---

[95]   This is reiterated in the European Union Act 2011, s. 18 of which states that: Directly applicable or directly effective EU law (that is, the rights, powers, liabilities, obligations, restrictions, remedies and procedures referred to in section 2(1) of the European Communities Act 1972) falls to be recognised and available in law in the United Kingdom only by virtue of that Act or where it is required to be recognised and available in law by virtue of any other Act. The 2011 Act thereby maintains the status quo, while ensuring that certain decisions relating to the change of the UK's relationship with the EU (including further EU constitutional change) will require national referenda.

[96]   Case C–303/05 *European Parliament v Council* [2006] ECR I-5769, para.38. Note that the explanatory notes appended thereto make reference to the European Social Charter 1961 as well as the ECHR.

[97]   Consolidated Version of the Treaty on European Union (TEU), Article 6(1), which recognises the EUCFR, as adapted at Strasbourg in 2007, shall have 'the same legal value as the Treaties'. Also see P. SYRPIS, 'The Treaty of Lisbon: Much ado… but about what?', (2008) 37 *ILJ* 232; and V. BAZZOCCHI, 'The European Charter of Fundamental Rights and the Courts' and S. COPPOLA, 'Social Rights in the European Union: The Possible Added Value of a Binding Charter of Fundamental Rights' in G. DI FEDERICO (ed.), *The EU Charter of Fundamental Rights: From Declaration to Binding Instrument,* Springer, Dordrecht 2011.

laws and practices, the right to negotiate and conclude collective agreements at the appropriate levels and, in cases of conflicts of interest, to take collective action to defend their interests, including strike action.' Notably, by virtue of Article 51(2), the EUCFR (as amended in 2007) does not '*extend the field of application of Union law beyond the powers of the Union or establish any new power or task for the Union, or modify powers and tasks as defined in the Treaty*'.[98] Its provisions under Article 51(1) '*are addressed to the institutions, bodies, offices and agencies of the Union with due regard for the principle of subsidiarity and to the Member States only when they are implementing Union law. They shall therefore respect the rights, observe the principles and promote the application thereof in accordance with their respective powers and respecting the limits of the powers of the Union as conferred on it in the Treaties.*' It is very clear from this provision, and from the Protocol on the Application of the Charter in the UK and Poland, that the Charter does not create justiciable rights (whether in respect of Part IV solidarity rights or otherwise) '*except insofar as these are provided for under national law*'. The EUCFR constrains EU law and administrative action but not purely national legislative discretion. Moreover, both provisions are subject to the further proviso in Article 52(1) that: '*Any limitation on the exercise of the rights and freedoms recognised by this Charter must be provided for by law and respect the essence of those rights and freedoms. Subject to the principle of proportionality, limitations may be made only if they are necessary and genuinely meet objectives of general interest recognised by the Union or the need to protect the rights and freedoms of others.*'[99]

As is the case in respect of the UK Human Rights Act, so too Article 52(3) establishes that where the Charter contains rights which correspond to rights guaranteed by the ECHR, the meaning and scope of those rights shall be the same as those laid down by that Convention, and thus one would expect the case law of the European Court of Human Rights to be relevant. This would also seem to follow from the new commitment, post-Lisbon that the EU accede to the ECHR.[100] Indeed, this was long the practice of the CJEU (or European Court of Justice as it was previously known) prior to the adoption of the EUCFR.[101]

An example of the application of the case law of the European Court of Human Rights regarding negative freedom of association can be detected in the case of *Werhof*,[102] which concerned the extent to which a new employer should be

---

[98]   See also the Declaration attached to the TEU which confirms this statement.
[99]   See for past analysis of the equivalent limitations in the 2000 draft of the EUCFR, J. KENNER, *EU Employment Law: From Rome to Amsterdam,* Hart, Oxford 2003, pp. 528–543.
[100] TEU, Article 6(2).
[101] T. NOVITZ (2003) above n. 25, 250 et seq.
[102] Case C-499/04 *Werhof v Freeway Traffic Systems GmbH & Co KG* [2006] IRLR 400.

considered to be bound by a collective agreement after a transfer of an undertaking. Under EU law, it is standard for all of a worker's terms and conditions which apply before the sale of a business (a transfer of an undertaking) to apply afterwards.[103] However, while the CJEU accepted that terms set out in a collective agreement at the time of transfer could be incorporated into each individual worker's contract of employment, the judgment stated that the employer could not be considered to be bound by provisions contained in a subsequent collective agreement without the employer's consent; nor was the employer obliged to try to maintain relations with the relevant trade union. The justification given was the principle of negative 'freedom of association', namely the right of an employer not to have to associate or enter into an agreement with a union.[104] This is an approach which prioritises individual freedom of contract as opposed to collective bargaining within the EU labour market. It also acts as a limitation on the obligation of states to promote collective bargaining under Article 4 of ILO Convention No. 98. Curiously, it is also at variance with the more dynamic principle established previously under UK case law, whereby it was possible to incorporate in an individual contract of employment determination of key terms and conditions not just by a current, but by any subsequent collective agreement with a trade union. There has therefore been a subsequent reference of the matter to the CJEU by the UK Supreme Court to explain the extent of the principle stated in *Werhof* and further examine its ramifications.[105]

A second example of the application of ECHR jurisprudence on Article 11 is the treatment of the right to strike in the case of *Viking*.[106] This case concerned the extent to which trade unions could organise industrial action which affected an employer's freedom of establishment. The Finnish Seamen's Union (FSU) was contemplating action (supported by a circular asking for support from other unions issued by the International Transport Worker's Federation) to prevent sale of a vessel from Viking Shipping to its Estonian subsidiary, which would have allowed reflagging and thereby hire of a cheaper crew.

---

103 See Council Directive 2001/23/EC on the approximation of the laws of Member States relating to the safeguarding of employees' rights in the event of transfers of undertakings, businesses or parts of undertakings [2001] OJ L82/16.

104 Ibid., at para. 33.

105 Cf. *Alemo-Herron v Parkwood Leisure Ltd* [2010] IRLR 298 (CA) and the referral by the UK Supreme Court in [2011] UKSC 26.

106 Case C-438/05 *International Transport Workers' Federation (ITF) and Finnish Seamen's Union (FSU) v Viking Line*, judgment of 11 December 2007 [2008] IRLR 143; (hereafter *Viking*). The judgment delivered by the CJEU in this case was remarkably similar to its judgment in another case, Case C-341/05 *Laval un Partneri v Svenska Byggnadsarbetareförbundet*, judgment of 18 December 2007 [2008] IRLR 160; (hereafter *Laval*) referred from the Swedish courts.

The *Viking* case is notable as the first time that the CJEU recognised a right to strike. This recognition was accomplished primarily in reliance on Article 28 of the EUCFR, but also with reference to ILO Conventions and the ESC. However, the CJEU also contemplated that extensive limitations could be placed on exercise of a right to strike. This was a right which could only be relied upon where this was for 'the protection of workers' (narrowly construed)[107] and exercised in a proportionate fashion. The national court has to examine, on the one hand, whether, *under the national rules and collective agreement law applicable to that action, [the union] did not have other means at its disposal which were less restrictive of freedom of establishment in order to bring to a successful conclusion the collective negotiations [...] and, on the other, whether that trade union had exhausted those means before initiating such action*.[108] In defence of this proportionality test, the CJEU in *Viking* cited the view of the European Court of Human Rights that *collective action, like collective negotiations and collective agreements may, in the particular circumstances of a case, be one of the main ways in which trade unions protect the interests of their members*', but is not the only way.[109] The CJEU thereby drew the conclusion that the right to strike is only one of a variety of means by which workers and their organisations may promote and defend their interests.

A more extreme case is that of *Laval*, which concerned industrial action taken by Swedish unions in order to secure improved terms and conditions for workers posted from Latvia to Sweden to perform a building contract. In this scenario, the CJEU seemed to view it as entirely inappropriate for a union to take such action in respect of posted workers for this adversely affected the legitimate expectations of the service provider. It was extremely troubling that the employer '*may be forced, by way of collective action, into negotiations with the trade unions of unspecified duration at the place at which the services in question are to be provided*'.[110] On this basis, while accepting the existence of an entitlement potentially to take secondary action in the form of a boycott in pursuit of a right to strike, the CJEU only contemplated that this would be permissible in instances of 'social dumping', which one may take to understand as extreme inequity, as this was not considered to be applicable on the facts of the *Laval* case.[111] This

---

[107] See *Viking*, paras. 81–9; and *Laval*, at paras. 103–111, discussed in T. NOVITZ, 'A Human Rights Analysis of the *Viking* and *Laval* Judgments' in C. BARNARD (ed.), Vol. 10 *The Cambridge Yearbook of European Legal Studies*, Hart Publishing, Oxford 2007–8, pp. 556–8.

[108] *Viking*, para. 87. For discussion, see A.C.L. DAVIES, 'One Step Forward, Two Steps Back? The *Viking* and *Laval* Cases in the CJEU' (2008) 37 *ILJ* 126; and P. SYRPIS and T. NOVITZ, 'Economic and Social Rights in Conflict: Political and Judicial Approaches to their Reconciliation' (2008) 33 *European Law Review* 411.

[109] *Viking*, para. 86.

[110] *Laval*, para. 100.

[111] *Laval*, paras. 102–3.

attitude of the CJEU may now be called into question following *Demir and Baykara* and *Enerji Yapi-Yol Sen*,[112] but there is no assurance that this will be the case.

7.   CONCLUSION

It has been argued in this chapter that there are tensions between the individual and collective dimensions of freedom of association, which are reflected in international and European legal norms. These sources indicate that negative freedom of association should be respected in UK law, both as regards the entitlement of trade union members not to be members of a trade union, and also the entitlement of a trade union to expel what would be regarded under its rules as undesirable members. It is further apparent from the jurisprudence developed by supervisory bodies in the ILO and, more significantly from the more influential case law of the European Court of Human Rights that freedom of association is to be understood as connected to collective bargaining and industrial action. The result would seem to be that limitations which employers and the state place on trade union activities can be subjected to scrutiny before UK courts by virtue of the HRA, but the full potential for such scrutiny has yet to be realised. It remains to be seen how the development of legal principles concerning freedom of association will affect the approach taken by the CJEU to collective action, but there are indications that change is possible (if not probable), as shall be highlighted in Chapter 5.

---

[112]   See for the view of the ETUC in this regard, www.etuc.org/a/6174. See also the views of S. McKay from the European Industrial Relations Observatory (Online) at www.eurofound. europa.eu/eiro/2009/05/articles/eu0905029i.htm; and A. Bucker, F. Dorssemont, and W. Warneck above n. 92.

CHAPTER 3

COLLECTIVE BARGAINING

1. INTRODUCTION

One of the primary functions of trade unions is to bargain in the name of their members, to negotiate terms and conditions with the relevant employer.[1] In the context of the United Kingdom, this 'market'-related task[2] has tended to be lightly regulated. Collective bargaining itself is defined in law as negotiations relating to one or more of the following matters:

(a) terms and conditions of employment, or the physical conditions in which any workers are required to work;
(b) engagement or non-engagement, or termination or suspension of employment or the duties of employment, of one or more workers;
(c) allocation of work, or the duties of employment between workers or groups of workers;
(d) matters of discipline,
(e) a worker's membership or non-membership of a trade union;
(f) facilities for officials of trade unions; and
(g) machinery for negotiations or consultation, and other procedures relating to any of the above matters, including the recognition by employers or employers' associations of the right of a trade union to represent workers in such negotiation or consultation or in the carrying out of such procedures.[3]

In order for any negotiations between employers and trade unions to begin, a preliminary task must be fulfilled. The union must have been recognised by the employer. The process of obtaining recognition as representative of the workforce

---

[1]   This is part of the regulatory and representational functions of trade unions, see K.D. EWING, 'The Function of Trade Unions' (2005) 35 *ILJ* 1, 3 and 4.
[2]   See A. Fox's view of trade unions' role in counterbalancing power of the employer through collective bargaining. This was tagged 'market relations' as opposed to democratic relations which concern decision making. *Industrial Sociology and Industrial Relations*, Research paper 3, Royal Commission on Trade Unions and Employers' Associations 1966. Paras. 7 and 24.
[3]   TULRCA 1992, s. 178.

for the purpose of negotiation, the conduct of the bargaining process and its product, namely collective agreements, have traditionally been undertaken outside the legal arena except for a few safeguards. As was seen in chapter 1, this is primarily the result of the *laissez faire* approach in the industrial relations field. This was suited to both parties. Trade unions had the threat of industrial action as their ultimate weapon; while employers could utilise their economic power by imposing lock-outs or moving the location of a factory. However, the voluntary nature of the system came under pressure in various ways, notably a change in political ethos and the economic downturn of the 1970s. The combination of Conservative governments policies aimed at reducing the power of trade unions and the decline of sectors where trade unions were strongly anchored meant that legal support for trade unions' activities, in particular collective negotiations, became more pressing. Indeed, associated with declining trade union membership, the number of unions recognised was decreasing and the proportion of workforce covered by collective agreements was consequently diminishing. The figures stood at 64% in 1984 and 47% in 1990.[4] In 2004, 40% of all employees were covered by collective bargaining.[5] In 2010, just over 30% of UK employees said that their pay and conditions were affected by a collective agreement, down from 36.4% in 2000.[6]

When statutory intervention was introduced, the purpose was to tackle the preliminary condition for collective bargaining. The law essentially removed the pure discretionary nature of granting or withdrawing recognition. In essence, while employers can, at will, recognise a union for the purpose of collective bargaining or de-recognise it, a recalcitrant employer can be 'forced' by statute to recognise a union if it represents enough of the workforce affected. There were two early attempts at statutory recognition procedures. While they were both deemed unsuccessful, the reasons for their failure were in the mind of the drafters of the current statutory scheme.[7] In 1971, the Industrial Relations Act tried to give unions rights in relation to collective bargaining: in exchange for registration, the union could gain access to recognition as the sole bargaining agent for a given bargaining unit.[8] This would be done via specific institutions such as the Industrial Court, the Commission on Industrial Relations and the National Industrial Relations Court, created for the operation of the new

---

4   Findings from the Workplace Relations Surveys reported by G.S. MORRIS and S. DEAKIN, *Labour Law,* 5th ed., Hart, Oxford 2009, p. 755.

5   B. KERSEY, C. ALPIN, J. FORTH, A. BRYSON, H. BEWLEY, G. DIX and S. OXENBRIDGE, *Inside the Workplace – Finding from the 2004 Workplace Employment Relations Survey,* Routledge, 2006, p. 180.

6   J. ACHUR, *Trade Union Membership 2010,* Department for Business, Innovation and Skills (2011), <www.bis.gov.uk/assets/biscore/employment-matters/docs/t/11-p77-trade-union-membership-2010.pdf> accessed 22.10.2011.

7   T. NOVITZ and P. SKIDMORE, *Fairness at Work – A Critical Analysis of the Employment Relations Act 1999 and its Treatment of Collective Rights* Hart, Oxford 2001, p. 65.

8   Industrial Relations Act 1971, ss. 44–50.

legislation. The aim of the Conservative government was to try to control industrial relations by way of regulations, using primarily the US system. The non-cooperation of the unions with the registration system meant that the recognition procedure was essentially inoperative.[9] The 1974 Labour government enacted a new procedure in the 1975 Employment Protection Act[10] as part of the Social Contract it had entered into with the trade union movement.[11] The objective was to promote collective bargaining. This was done with the support of the unions and the creation of a new institution the Advisory, Conciliation and Arbitration Service (ACAS) whose role was to encourage collective bargaining.[12] ACAS was the body charged with recommending recognition provided that certain criteria were fulfilled. However, the brevity of the statutory scheme meant that ACAS had to be creative when assessing whether recognition should be granted.[13] This freedom of interpretation was challenged by the employers via judicial review.[14] Eventually, it was the combination of employers' opposition partly supported by a judiciary favourable to their requests of limiting ACAS' powers which were fatal to the system.[15] The procedure was subsequently repealed when the Conservatives came to power.[16]

As part of its Manifesto,[17] the Blair government had promised the re-introduction of a comparable procedure. Mindful of the previous drawbacks of statutory schemes, the government endeavoured to involve the social partners as much as possible in the drafting of the new statutory provisions. This was in order to avoid what were perceived as the failings of the 1970s procedure[18] and to fulfil the aim of promoting partnership.[19] While the TUC and CBI were clearly at loggerheads on a number of aspects, the final regulations reflect compromises and tend to favour employers rather than trade unions.[20] The statutory recognition procedure was adopted in the Employment Relations Act 1999 which inserted it into TULRCA 1992 through Schedule A1. The statutory schedule is detailed and complex but originally helped trade unions at least to

---

9   P. DAVIES and M. FREEDLAND, *Labour Legislation and Public Policy*, Clarendon Law Series, Oxford 1993, chapter 7 (principally from p. 301).

10   EPA 1975, ss. 11–16.

11   P. DAVIES and M. FREEDLAND, above n. 9, from p. 385.

12   T. NOVITZ and P. SKIDMORE, above n. 7, pp. 67–68.

13   A. BOGG, *The Democratic Aspect of Trade Union Recognition*, Hart, Oxford 2009, p. 66.

14   For examples of cases, see A. BOGG above from p. 68.

15   T. NOVITZ and P. SKIDMORE above n. 7, from p. 69.

16   Employment Act 1980.

17   *Fairness at Work* Cm 3968 1998, para. 4.11.

18   See for example, S. WOOD, S. MOORE, and P. WILLMAN, 'Third Time Lucky for Statutory Recognition Procedure in the UK' (2002) 33 *IRJ* 215.

19   T. NOVITZ and P. SKIDMORE above n. 7, p. 127.

20   See R. DUKES, 'The Statutory Recognition Procedure 1999: No Bias in Favour of Recognition' (2008) 37 *ILJ* 236.

stop the decline of recognition and collective bargaining.[21] Ten years on, considering the falling number of applications for statutory recognition, it has been argued that the impact of the procedure has been limited, primarily because the legal framework is too employer-oriented and presents too many obstacles for unions.[22] It should be pointed out, however, that the statutory machinery is viewed as the last resort. The idea behind the legislation is to encourage bargaining and assert that voluntary recognition should be the preferred option so as to promote partnership. Even when Schedule A1 is engaged, there are numerous steps where parties can return to negotiated solutions rather than applying the scenario provided for by law. Moreover, unlike the statutory procedure which operated under the 1975 Employment Protection Act, no award of terms and conditions can be imposed on the parties; any collective agreement remains entirely voluntary.

The purpose of this chapter is to examine how the three stages associated with collective bargaining are regulated. Considering the changes in the law, the greatest attention will be paid to the first phase of the process, namely recognition. While the outcome of the statutory recognition procedure is ultimately the imposition of a method of bargaining, the second phase of bargaining is very lightly regulated. The law guides the relevant parties in relation to the possible subject matters of bargaining and provides guarantees that trade unions receive the relevant information for negotiation. Finally, collective agreements, as the product of collective bargaining, are viewed as 'gentlemen's agreements' and therefore not legally binding. The conclusion will raise some questions about the future of collective bargaining and whether the law can have a positive impact.

2. THE PRE-CONDITION FOR COLLECTIVE BARGAINING – RECOGNITION OF TRADE UNIONS

As was seen in chapter 1, trade unions will seek recognition to enable them to perform their functions fully. The concept of recognition is defined by statute as *'the recognition of the union by an employer, or two or more associated employers, to any extent, for the purpose of collective bargaining'*.[23] Trade unions can be

---

[21]　See for example S. Oxenbridge, W. Brown, S. Deakin and C. Pratten, 'Initial Responses to the Statutory Recognition Provisions of the Employment Relations Act 1999' (2003) 41 *BJIR* 315.

[22]　G. Gall, 'The First Ten Years of the Third Statutory Union Recognition Procedure in Britain' (2010) 39 *ILJ* 444, p. 448. For a more complete assessment, see section 2.3 below.

[23]　TULRCA 1992, s. 178(3).

recognised in two ways: voluntarily by the employer or if the employer refuses to do so, the trade union can use the law and impose recognition with the aid of the statutory recognition procedure. The remainder of this section will consider the voluntary process of recognition and the mandatory scheme found in the statute. In conclusion, there will be qualitative and quantitative assessment of the result of the combination of voluntary and statutory mechanisms.

2.1. VOLUNTARY RECOGNITION

What constitutes 'recognition' in practice has been determined by case law. The most fundamental principle is that there must be evidence of an agreement between trade union and employer to negotiate on one or more of the subject matters specified in section 178(2), for example terms and conditions or matters of discipline, etc. However, this agreement can be express or implied. While the situation is simple with express agreements, case law has elaborated some guidelines regarding implied recognition. The courts have not easily conceded recognition by conduct because of the potential consequences for the employer. As stated in *National Union of Gold, Silver and Allied Trades v Albury Bros Ltd*: *'A recognition issue is a most important matter for industry; and therefore an employer is not to be held to have recognised a trade union unless the evidence is clear.'*[24] In that case, it was stated that there must be willingness to negotiate with a view to striking a bargain and that mere willingness to discuss is not sufficient.[25] An additional condition was the necessity of a course of conduct over a period of time.[26]

2.2. THE STATUTORY PROCEDURE FOR RECOGNITION

The current procedure was contentious because employers were not in favour of such legal intervention. The Labour government was however keen to involve the social partners in the gestation of the new law. Following talks between the TUC and CBI, they issued a joint statement on statutory trade union recognition and the government emphasised that the resulting schedule was a compromise between trade unions' demands and employers' resistance.[27] When the government reviewed the statutory procedure in 2003, a number of shortcomings were highlighted and some of these have now been addressed by the Employment

---

[24]   [1978] IRLR 504, para. 11.
[25]   Ibid. para. 19.
[26]   Ibid. para. 23.
[27]   *Statutory Trade Union Recognition Joint Statement by TUC and CBI* (December 1997) in R. Dukes, above n. 20, p. 246.

Relations Act 2004. However, the stamp of employers' opposition is still evident in the overall scheme.

The remaining part of this section considers the mechanics of the recognition process, although the intention is not to delve into the minutiae of the procedure.[28] The aim is to illustrate how trade unions have many hurdles to overcome and that a campaign for recognition is ultimately for a small reward if the employer is reluctant and refuses to negotiate.

2.2.1. Conditions for application

In order to apply for recognition via the statutory mechanism, trade unions must fulfil two important criteria. First, the union must have a certificate of independence.[29] Second, the employer must employ at least 21 workers.[30] This is a limiting factor in that a great number of undertakings are under no compulsion to recognise a union. EWING and HOCK estimated that as a result of this exclusion the procedure applies to less than 8% of British employers.[31] This has been the subject of criticism by the TUC which is interested in exploring whether a simplified modified form of statutory recognition could be applied in smaller workplaces. The ILO Committee of Experts in 2009 invited the UK Government to consider this possibility.[32] The response has been that, although there is evidence that the extent of collective bargaining is less significant in smaller undertakings, trade unions are not prevented from voluntarily engaging with employers in collective negotiations. Further, the government pointed to Partnership Funds initiatives which were financed by the government and which encouraged work of unions in smaller workplaces. In its submission to the ILO in 2010/11, the government clearly stated that it had no intention of reviewing the statutory recognition procedure.[33]

2.2.2. Application to the employer

The idea of the government in 1997 and the method encouraged by the statute is that voluntary recognition remains the preferred technique. Schedule A1 will

---

[28] For this, see J. BOWERS QC, M. DUGGAN and D. READE QC, *The Law of Industrial Action and Trade Union Recognition*, 2nd ed., Oxford University Press, Oxford 2011.

[29] TULRCA, Sch. A1, para. 6. See chapter 1 on how the certificate is granted.

[30] TULRCA, Sch. A1, para. 7.

[31] K.D. EWING and A. HOCK, *The Next Step: Trade Union Recognition in Small Enterprises* (2003, Popularis), p. 15.

[32] *Report of the Committee of Experts on the Application of Conventions and Recommendations – UK* (2009).

[33] *Committee of Experts on the Application of Conventions and Recommendations – Individual Observation concerning Right to Organise and Collective Bargaining Convention, 1949 (No. 98)* United Kingdom (ratification: 1950) Published: 2011.

only come into play if this first method has failed. This is reflected in the statutory scheme.

Practically, a trade union must give the employer a written request for recognition for a specified group of workers (called a bargaining unit). Two possible scenarios can be envisaged. Firstly, the employer accepts the bargaining unit and accepts to recognise the union within a specific time frame (10 days of the request) or accepts to negotiate on these issues within 20 working days. If this is done there is a recognition agreement and no need to take any further steps.[34] This agreement cannot be unilaterally terminated by the employer for three years.[35] Secondly, there is no response from the employer or no agreement within the specified time.[36] The union can apply to the Central Arbitration Committee (CAC)[37] to determine the bargaining unit and whether recognition can be granted. Before going onto these two critical points, the CAC must check the admissibility of the demand.

2.2.3. Conditions of admissibility of the request

The CAC can reject an application for recognition in four situations. Firstly, if a collective agreement is already in force with a union which is entitled to conduct collective bargaining on behalf of any workers falling within the proposed bargaining unit, the CAC can dismiss the request. This reflects the priority given to existing voluntary bargaining arrangements. However, it is not necessary for the pre-existing agreements to be with unions which are independent. This legal loophole could be used by some employers to avoid having to deal with some unions.[38] The TUC had reported such practice to be in breach of ILO Convention 98. It stated that '*the statutory procedure for recognition allows an employer to prevent an application for recognition to be made by an independent trade union by setting up an in-house company union and voluntarily extending to it recognition rights; the TUC referred to the case of POA and Securicor Custodial Services Ltd., where the union was denied the right to recognition – even though it had the support of a majority of members in the unit – as the employer had concluded a recognition agreement with a staff association*'.[39] Technically, a derecognition exercise of the non–independent union could be undertaken by

---

34   TULRCA, Sch. A1, para. 10.
35   TULRCA, Sch. A1, para. 56.
36   TULRCA, Sch. A1, paras. 11 and 12.
37   See chapter 1 on the functions of the CAC.
38   For a flagrant example of an abuse of para. 35 see *NUJ v (1) CAC, (2) Secretary of State and Industry, (1) Sport Division Mirror Group Newspaper, (2) British Association of Journalists* [2005] EWCA Civ 1309.
39   *Report of the Committee of Experts on the Application of Conventions and Recommendations – UK* (2009).

workers' application to end the arrangement.[40] However, the TUC has highlighted before the ILO that this is practically extremely difficult. In its 2011 report, the ILO recalls that *'it had also noted in its previous comments the TUC assertion that, where the incumbent trade union is non-independent, a request for de-recognition can only be made by an individual worker and not by an independent trade union; and that the independent trade union has no right of access to the workplace and no right to communicate with the workforce while de-recognition procedures are taking place, while the non-independent union has a statutory right to communicate with the workers during the de-recognition process'*.[41] The government had indicated that it is permissible for a non-incumbent trade union to assist the workers involved in making an application to derecognise the trade union. But the ILO Committee still requested the Government to provide observations thereon.

Secondly, a trade union that applies to the CAC for recognition must effectively demonstrate that it represents part of the workforce. The CAC must see evidence that 10% of the workforce in the bargaining unit are members of the union.[42] Further, the union must also establish that a majority of the workers in the bargaining unit would be likely to favour recognition.[43] This is more difficult to establish but can be demonstrated by a petition or if the majority of the workers in the bargaining unit are members of the trade union.

Thirdly, if more than one union applies for recognition, the CAC can reject the request.[44] However, if the various unions show that they will cooperate and bargain together on behalf of the workers in the bargaining unit, the applications may be admissible. In order to avoid inter unions conflicts and to maximise the effects of the legal support for recognition, the TUC provides help with application to the CAC and have also tried to centralise requests by asking unions preparing applications to notify the TUC in advance.[45] This has been the subject of concern in comments by the ILO Committee of Experts in 2009, which has suggested that there should be greater potential for more than one union to be recognised in respect of a bargaining unit.[46] The government responded that nothing prevents unions from making a joint application. This

---

[40] The de-recognition procedure of a union is envisaged in TULRCA 1992 (sch. A1, part IV). It mainly mirrors the recognition procedure and is not dealt with in details here but see J. BOWERS QC, M. DUGGAN, D. READE QC above n. 28 from p. 274.

[41] *Committee of Experts on the Application of Conventions and Recommendations* – above n. 33.

[42] This numerical information should be found in the application to the CAC.

[43] TULRCA, Sch. A1 para. 36.

[44] TULRCA, Sch. A1 para. 37.

[45] *TUC Disputes Principles and Procedures 2007.*

[46] *Report of the Committee of Experts on the Application of Conventions and Recommendations – UK* (2009).

enables minority unions to work with others. It also states that any union which does not reach the relevant threshold is still free to obtain voluntary recognition. This clearly ignores the fact that if a union is applying to the CAC, it means that voluntary recognition has been unsuccessful. However, the government concludes by stating that there is no plan to review the statutory recognition procedure.[47]

Fourthly, if a union had its application rejected by the CAC for a bargaining unit, it cannot make another application for three years in respect of the same group of workers.[48]

If these hurdles are passed, the first aspect on which the CAC is likely to have to make a decision is the bargaining unit.

2.2.4. The bargaining unit

If there is no agreement between the trade union and employer on the definition or extent of the bargaining unit, the CAC must determine whether the bargaining unit proposed by the union is appropriate.

Its first task is to try to get the parties to agree on the bargaining unit within a specific time of 20 days.[49] If this fails, the CAC will determine the bargaining unit. For this, the CAC must use a number of criteria given by Schedule A1 including the need for the unit to be compatible with 'effective management'.[50] This seems to be paramount over other factors, as the views of the employer and the union, the characteristics of the workers in the bargaining unit and the location of the workers must not conflict with that overall need.[51] This has rightly been analysed as favouring management.[52] Once the bargaining unit is determined, the next step for the CAC is to decide whether to grant recognition.

2.2.5. Deciding on recognition

The determining factor for the CAC is the conviction that recognition is wanted by the majority of the workforce in the bargaining unit. Two routes are available to demonstrate such support.

---

[47]   *Committee of Experts on the Application of Conventions and Recommendations* – 2011, above n. 33.
[48]   TULRCA, Sch. A1 para. 39.
[49]   TULRCA, Sch. A1, para. 18.
[50]   TULRCA, Sch. A1, para. 19B.
[51]   Ibid.
[52]   T. Novitz and P. Skidmore, above n. 7, p. 90.

2.2.5.1. Automatic recognition

If the majority of the workforce in the bargaining unit are members of the applicant trade union, the CAC can grant recognition.[53] However, this is not mandatory. Even with a majority of trade union members, the CAC can use the second method, which is to hold a ballot of the workforce in the bargaining unit. Statutes allow the CAC to depart from the automatic recognition route if any of three scenarios arise.[54] Firstly, the CAC is satisfied that holding a ballot would be in the interest of good industrial relations. Secondly, a significant number of union members have indicated that they do not wish the union to conduct collective bargaining on their behalf. It is questionable whether this would be a likely scenario as one of the principal reasons for joining a trade union is the defence of members' interests through collective bargaining. However, this provision was used by employers in such a twisted manner that it had to be amended by the Employment Relations Act 2004. It had emerged that employers would send evidence to the CAC that employees did not want the union to undertake collective bargaining on their behalf when subsequent evidence showed that this was done under pressure from the employer.[55] As a result paragraph 22(4) was amended to insert the provision that the evidence had to be 'credible' in the eyes of the CAC. Thirdly, there is 'membership evidence'[56] that casts doubt over members' willingness to have the union conducting collective bargaining on their behalf. Such evidence is defined by Schedule A1 and effectively relates to either the circumstances in which employees became members or the length of time that employees have been members of the union applying for recognition. This is a situation where, for example, a great number of workers have recently joined and this may have been due to pressure or offer of free membership for a given period.[57] Despite the possibility given to the CAC to organise a ballot in such circumstances, the CBI has argued that there should not be an automatic recognition and that a ballot should always be organised regardless of the membership of the bargaining unit.[58]

2.2.5.2. Ballot

If the CAC orders a ballot, a rigorous procedure must be followed. There are also stringent conditions attached to the result of the ballot. However, balloting requirements for recognition are not identical to the ballot procedure applied to

---

[53] TULRCA, Sch. A1 para. 22(1) and (2).
[54] TULRCA, Sch. A1 para. 22(3) and (4).
[55] See *R (on the application of Gatwick Express) v CAC* [2003] EWHC 2035 (Admin) and B. Simpson, 'Judicial control and the CAC' (2007) *ILJ* 287.
[56] In the words of Sch. A1: see para. 22(4)(c).
[57] See *AEEU v Huntleigh Healthcare Ltd* (TUR1/19/00).
[58] CBI, *Making Britain the Place to Work* (June 2010), p. 9.

strike action,[59] suggesting that the criteria chosen can be arbitrary. Some of the differences will be highlighted in the sections below.

The ballot procedure to follow is found in paragraph 25 of Schedule A1 and is detailed and complex. It is tainted by two factors. Firstly, there was a wish to make the process as neutral as possible, for example by involving independent personnel and by sharing the cost of the ballot between the employer and the union concerned.[60] Secondly, the intention was also to allow trade unions to communicate with workers, free of interference and undue pressure from employers. This aspect was underestimated by the government and the legislation had to be considerably strengthened when the procedure was reviewed in 2004.

The essence of the procedure is that the ballot must be conducted by a qualified independent person (QIP) appointed by the CAC. It must take place within a certain time period specified by the CAC. The ballot can be by post or at the workplace, or a combination of the two, depending on the kind of pressure that can be exerted by the employer or the union.[61] The balloting requirements for industrial action also involve independent scrutiny,[62] a time limit[63] but the vote must be done in secret so as to avoid the voter to be interfered with or constrained in exercising his right.[64]

Additionally, the union was given some protection against employers who would try to influence the results of the ballot by preventing the union to have access to the workforce and/or by putting pressure on employees. The first limb of the protection given to unions takes the form of duties imposed upon the employer during the ballot.[65] In the original 1999 Employment Relations Act, three duties were to be found in Schedule A1. Two were added by the Employment Relations Act 2004 as a result of lobbying from the unions following the experience of employers creating new tricks to put undue pressure on employees to vote against the recognition. The first duty is to co-operate with the union and the QIP. The second is to give union access to workers constituting the bargaining unit as it is reasonable to enable the union to inform the workers of the object of the ballot and seek their support and their opinion. This duty is considered as particularly fundamental as it is further dealt with by a Code of Practice on Access and Unfair Practices during Recognition and Derecognition

---

[59]   Full details of the balloting requirements for industrial action are discussed in chapter 5.
[60]   TULRCA, Sch. A1 para. 28.
[61]   TULRCA, Sch. A1 para. 25.
[62]   TULRCA, s. 226B.
[63]   TULRCA, s. 226 and 226A.
[64]   TULRCA 1992, s. 230.
[65]   TULRCA 1992, Sch. A1 para. 26.

Ballots.[66] There is emphasis on this aspect because employers are likely to put considerable pressure on employees and possibly prevent trade unions from contacting workers in the period prior to the ballot. It is therefore essential for the union to be able to have access to the workers to provide them with the relevant information. The Code of Practice encourages employer and union to agree on how access could take place, but ultimately if this fails, the CAC will have to adjudicate on the matters, with reference to the standards set out in the Code of Practice. These include making employer giving access to trade union officials or representatives in the bargaining unit; provide appropriate accommodation where unions can meet workers, if possible in private; provide a notice board for the union's use in a prominent location, etc. These measures should help, to a certain extent, to redress the imbalance between access that a union could have to workers to campaign in favour of recognition when employers have easy access to the workforce through meetings organised at the workplace during working time where anti-recognition campaigns could take place. However, the original provision was not enough as the Employment Relations Act 2004 had to qualify that duty further in response to employers' practices. A new paragraph 4(D) was inserted giving precise scenarios as to when an employer is deemed to have failed to fulfil his second duty. For example, this would be the case if a union requested a meeting with the workers without the employer or a representative and the employer refused.

The third duty requires employers to provide details of workers working in the bargaining unit to the CAC. The aim is to give the union the opportunity to contact all workers via the QIP. The fourth duty prevents employers from making offers which have the effect of inducing the workers not to attend meetings between the union and the workers. This additional provision was a direct response to evidence that employers had used direct or covert methods of intimidating workers during the ballot process.[67] In the same context, the fifth duty is to refrain from taking actions or threatening to take actions against an employee who attended or expressed an intention to attend meetings between the union and the workers.

The final aspect concerning the employer's duties is related to sanctions. The CAC can order the employer to remedy the failure in a specified time before the ballot; if this is not possible, it can order for the ballot to be rescheduled. If the employer does not comply with the orders and the ballot has not taken place, the CAC has the discretion to declare the union recognised without a ballot.[68]

---

[66] This is the 2005 version (<www.berr.gov.uk/files/file14418.pdf> accessed 20.10.2011) which was reviewed after the changes inserted by the Employment Relations Act 2004.

[67] See A. Bogg, 'Employment Relations Act 2004: Another False Dawn for Collectivism' (2005) 34 *ILJ* 72, 76.

[68] TULRCA 1992, Sch. A1 para. 27.

The second limb of the protection given to unions and the workers was fully introduced by the Employment Relations Act 2004. It creates a new concept of unfair practice. This was suggested by the TUC and ultimately agreed by the government despite original opposition to the idea.[69] Under paragraph 27A, both employers and unions must refrain from using such practices to influence the outcome of the ballot. Unfair practices are defined exhaustively by the statute and include the offer of money, the threat of or actual dismissal or the attempt to coerce a worker to disclose how s/he will vote.

If such a practice is found by the CAC, as for the breach of the duties, the CAC can make an order for the parties to take the necessary actions to mitigate the effect of the failure of the party.[70] The CAC can also order the ballot to take place again. If the unfair practice involves the use of violence or the dismissal of a union official, the CAC can grant recognition without the ballot.[71] The recognition can also be granted if the orders made by the CAC have been ignored.

The ILO Committee of Experts indicated in its report on the UK in 2009 that current protection from unfair labour practices is not enough. It made the following observations: *'In its previous comments, the Committee noted the Trades Union Congress's (TUC) indication that protection against anti-union discrimination (unfair practices) only applies in the framework of the organisation of a recognition ballot, whereas a lot of the misconduct by an employer may take place at a much earlier stage, where the union is trying to organise, recruit and build up some kind of structure. The TUC had expressed concern at the lack of protection in practice against unfair practices by employers taking place long before the balloting period, in order to discourage any organising campaign by a union (including threats of closure of the plant and individual job loss, actual dismissals, pay and promotion inducements, holding a company ballot in advance of an independently conducted ballot, denial of any access to a union including preventing leaflets being given to the employees, holding anti-union meetings at the workplace, one-on-one meetings, changes to the bargaining unit – either splitting it or combining it with others)'.*[72] Both in 2009 and 2011, the Committee noted that the TUC referred to various unfair practices and anti-union tactics in the framework of the statutory recognition scheme.[73] A study of the CAC decisions where unfair practices were raised confirms that some employers will

---

[69]   A. Bogg, above n. 67, 76–77.

[70]   TULRCA, Sch. A1 para. 27C.

[71]   TULRCA, Sch. A1 para. 27D.

[72]   *Report of the Committee of Experts on the Application of Conventions and Recommendations – UK* (2009).

[73]   *Committee of Experts on the Application of Conventions and Recommendations 2011*, above n. 33.

go to great length to avoid recognition, such as using consultants specialising in union avoidance.[74] However, it appears that the number of cases invoking the unfair practices provisions has been low[75] and that the CAC has not yet ruled in favour of a union alleging wrongdoing by the employer. BOGG argues convincingly that this may be explained by the formulation of the legislative provisions. They provide weak protection for trade unions as the protected period is only during the ballot while anti-union campaign could start before the union applies to the CAC. Further, the statutory language requires a high threshold of proof to demonstrate unfair practice[76] (for example that the use of the unfair practice changed or was likely to change the voting intention or the behaviour of the worker).[77] Finally, the small number of cases reported on unfair practices should not be regarded as evidence of the absence of such practices. Considering the statutory definition and the attitude of the CAC, trade unions may prefer to avoid using quasi-judicial institutions to resolve the matter and lobby other bodies such as the ILO.

In addition to the detailed procedure on the conduct of the ballot, the 1999 Employment Relations Act also complicated matters in relation to the result of the vote. It did not simply require a majority of votes in favour of recognition, it added a second limb to the formula: at least 40% of the workers constituting the bargaining unit must support recognition in the vote. This qualified majority has always been criticised vehemently by the trade union movement and academics.[78] It does not reflect other ballot requirements for trade unions where a simple majority is required (election of representatives or industrial action). It is also not in line with democratic principles. Such a formula does not apply to political parties when standing for elections. This was clearly a concession to the employers who feared that workers who were indifferent to the result of the vote would be counted against the employer. Considering the kind of difficulties that trade unions may encounter before the ballot even takes place, this is a significantly high threshold to meet.[79]

---

[74]   A. BOGG, 'The mouse that never roared: unfair practices and union recognition' (2009) 38 ILJ 390.

[75]   According to BOGG (ibid.), there were five cases since the 2004 insertion in TULRCA 1992 and the CAC annual reports since the article indicate that no case involving the unfair practice regulations has been brought before its panel.

[76]   A. BOGG, above n. 74, 392.

[77]   TULRCA, Sch. A1 para. 27B.

[78]   See TUC recommendations to abolish the threshold at the time of the review of the Employment Relations Act 1999 *Modern Rights for Modern Workplaces,* para. 82; see T. NOVITZ and P. SKIDMORE, above n. 7, p. 74.

[79]   See *R (on the Application of Ultrafame) v Central Arbitration Committee* [2005] EWCA Civ 560 where the union did not obtain recognition by 4 votes.

2.2.6.   Recognition and collective bargaining

The main consequence of recognition is the right to engage in collective bargaining. If this has been achieved under the statutory procedure, the next step relating to collective negotiations is also dealt with by statute, but still emphasising the need for the relevant parties to try and find agreement on how to conduct collective bargaining. Thus, the employer and the newly recognised union have 30 days to agree on a 'method' by which they will conduct collective bargaining.[80] If, subsequently, parties fail to carry out the agreement they can seek assistance of the CAC.[81]

If they cannot agree, the CAC has a duty to try and assist them agreeing on the method. If this is still unsuccessful, it is the CAC that specifies the method to conduct collective bargaining. The model used is found in The Trade Union Recognition (Method of Collective Bargaining) Order 2000,[82] although the CAC can depart from it. Such model lists the steps to be taken by both parties to start discussions on the items which will be the subject of collective bargaining. Consequently the method concerns procedural steps (composition of the group that will enter into negotiations, number of meetings, organisation of the agenda, etc). Further, the only items that need discussing are pay, hours and holidays. The scope of collective bargaining here is therefore notably more limited than under section 178(2) TULRCA 1992 (as described in the introduction of this chapter). Finally, such method does not require that a collective agreement is reached or that the parties negotiate in good faith. The imposition of collective bargaining relates to the obligation to meet and talk at certain intervals about certain topics. It is forcing to establish a pre-determined system, not the end result. However, the method imposed by the CAC is analysed as a contract that can be enforced.[83] For example, if one of the parties does not meet or provide the necessary information, the injured party can seek remedy that takes the form of specific performance. If the order made by the court is subsequently ignored this could lead to contempt of court and heavy fines for the offender. It is difficult to envisage a practical application of this sanction. Scrutiny of the CAC reports over the last ten years shows that there are instances where the CAC imposes the method to conduct bargaining (in a small minority of cases compared to the situation where agreement is reached between parties)[84] but that a complaint about a breach of the method has yet to be reported.

---

[80]   TULRCA, Sch. A1 para. 30.
[81]   TULRCA, Sch. A1 para. 32; see for example TUR1/206/(2002) *TGWU/GMB & Gala Casinos Ltd.*
[82]   SI 2000/1300.
[83]   TULRCA, Sch. A1 para. 31.
[84]   See for example CAC *Annual Report 2010–11*, p. 9.

2.3. EVALUATION: COLLECTIVE BARGAINING AND THE LAW

The statutory procedure has been in place for just over ten years. It clearly contributed to significant activity in industrial relations prior to the enactment of the Employment Relations Act 1999 and for a few years after the introduction of Schedule A1. Unions and employers came together to revisit or explore new ways of negotiating. In the legal arena, the CAC found a new dynamism and academic lawyers further analysed the role of the law in collective negotiations.

There are two important questions relating to quantity and quality. Firstly, has the introduction of the statutory recognition procedure had an impact on recognition numbers as a whole? As was seen in the introduction, the procedure came at a time when the union movement had suffered important blows because of the economy and a government which was anti-union. Secondly, the quality assessment questions whether the procedure is effective.

2.3.1. Quantitative evaluation

Numerous studies[85] reveal that at the outset voluntary recognition increased extensively. The shadow of the law had encouraged unions and employers to reach recognition agreements. They were signed in great numbers, especially from 1998 when it was clear that the government was going ahead with the statutory recognition procedure. However, this enthusiasm for the voluntary process slowed down as trade unions started campaigns seeking recognition from more recalcitrant and smaller organisations. It was therefore predictable that the number of voluntary agreements would decrease while the number of cases to be decided by the CAC might increase.

Trends in recognition deals

Period	Number of new deals
1996	110
July 1997 – February 1998	55
March – November 1998	34
December 1998 – October 1999	75
November 1999 – October 2000	159
November 2000 – October 2001	450

---

[85] For example, 'Focus on Recognition Survey' published yearly by the TUC and Labour Force Survey. Since 2005, the figures have not been available in such format.

Period	Number of new deals
November 2001 – October 2002	282
November 2002 – October 2003	137
November 2003 – October 2004	179
November 2004 – October 2005	61

Source: TUC /LCD

A snapshot review of the information in the CAC Annual Report gives an idea of the impact of the legislation and its problem areas. Originally the CAC thought it would receive about 150 applications per year.[86] However, the picture turned out to be slightly different. The cumulative receipt of recognition applications up to 31 March 2011 was 742.[87] The annual figures are:[88]

2000– 01	2001– 02	2002– 03	2003– 04	2004– 05	2005– 06	2006– 07	2007– 08	2008– 09	2009– 10	2010– 11	Total
57	118	80	106	83	58	64	64	42	42	28	742

Out of this total, the 2010–11 Annual Report showed some 441 cases were accepted for determination. This suggests a large number of rejected or withdrawn applications which could be explained by the criteria that trade unions have to fulfil before being able to apply. In some cases, the application is abandoned because voluntary agreement is reached.[89] The central issue of disagreement over definition of the bargaining unit is shown in that 151 of these cases had to be decided by the CAC whereas 213 cases were agreed directly by the parties. To date, it is reported that 104 unions were recognised without a ballot, 121 were recognised with a ballot and 75 were not recognised after a ballot. Out of 742 original applications trade unions were recognised in 225 instances.[90] Commentators' fears that automatic recognition could be a problem seem to be borne out, in that only in 104 applications recognition was granted without a ballot as opposed to 196 cases in which a ballot was needed.[91] Once the balloting hurdle has been overcome, however, it would seem that most parties then agree a method of collective bargaining without recourse to the CAC – in 199 cases, the parties agreed the method directly.[92] The CAC

---

86   G. GALL, above n. 22, 444.
87   CAC *Annual Report 2010–11.*
88   As collected from CAC annual reports.
89   See G. GALL above n. 22, 445.
90   CAC *Annual Report 2010–11,* p. 12.
91   Ibid.
92   Ibid.

attributes the decline in applications in part to trade unions taking more care when applying for recognition as the number of applications which were unsuccessful at the early stages has also fallen. Further, there seems to be a greater propensity to reach agreement on recognition.[93] Nevertheless, it could also be argued that unions have fought all the battles that they could win. The hurdles found in the procedure and the final outcome may eventually deter unions from engaging with the process.[94] GALL also shows that unions certainly withdraw applications because of uncertainty about meeting the criteria for recognition.[95]

2.3.2. Qualitative effect

It is undeniable that the introduction of the statutory procedure encouraged collective bargaining. There was 'widespread agreement among employers and union officials that the ERA has made a major contribution to achieving a change in both the atmosphere and conduct of employment relations'.[96] The TUC view is that the recognition legislation has generally been successful as far as it goes. 'One of the most important aspects of the statutory recognition scheme has been its success as a stimulus to voluntary agreements.'[97] The clear advantage is the growing number of employees whose terms and conditions are determined collectively.[98] It was also pointed out that the new law 'halted the rise in employer efforts to derecognise unions'.[99] However, there were numerous shortcomings in the legislation which rendered the task of obtaining recognition very difficult. This was addressed to a limited extent by the Employment Relations Act 2004, but many obstacles remain.

Firstly, there is an arbitrary exclusion of a significant part of the workforce from the scope of the recognition procedure as only employers with 21 employees or more can be compelled to recognise a union. Secondly, trade unions have significant thresholds to pass to be recognised: the 10% membership at the application stage and the controversial qualified majority showing support for recognition of the union. Thirdly, there have been considerable difficulties arising during ballot periods associated with intimidation and threats towards employees when unions apply for recognition. Cases before the CAC and

---

[93]   Ibid., p. 2.
[94]   C.F. WRIGHT, 'What role for trade unions in future workplace relations', (Acas Future of Workplace Relations Discussion paper series, September 2011), p. 4.
[95]   G. GALL, above n. 22, 444.
[96]   S. OXENBRIDGE, W. BROWN, S. DEAKIN and C. PRATTEN, above n. 21, 330.
[97]   TUC Modern Rights for Modern Workplaces, above n. 78, para. 37.
[98]   R. DUKES, above n. 20, 258.
[99]   C.F. WRIGHT, above n. 94, p. 3.

research showed that some employers engaged in surveillance of employees, misinformed the workforce about the union, threatened dismissals if employees voted in favour of union, etc.[100] Despite the positive changes brought by the 2004 Act to curtail these practices, there are still significant shortcomings in the lack of access to workers by unions before the CAC orders a ballot.[101]

Amendments to the legal provisions will not tackle the more fundamental issue that the procedure was not designed to promote collective bargaining, as the TUC would have liked.[102] As DUKES rightly identified, the purpose was to facilitate talks if the union could show support from the workers for representation.[103] As a consequence, the shadow of the law facilitated activity when it came to recognition, at least for the first few years and unions are clearly in a better position today than they would have been if the statutory recognition had not been in place. So far, it certainly has been the most successful statutory recognition procedure if the criterion is longevity on the statute book. However, the combination of statutory provisions biased towards employers,[104] a CAC that interprets too literally some of the crucial definitions when it comes to unfair practices[105] and employers ready to use the law and other methods to resist union recognition[106] has prevented the procedure from significantly changing the picture of collective bargaining. A stronger process that embraces collective negotiations and limits the hurdles for unions would be welcome, but the current political environment is not clement to such changes.

3. THE CONDUCT OF COLLECTIVE BARGAINING

While it was pointed out that the conduct of collective bargaining can be dictated by law when unions and employers are in the realm of the statutory recognition procedure, traditionally statute has very little to say about this process. The whole method of bargaining is left to the parties. There is primarily only one obligation for employers: the duty to disclose information for the purpose of collective bargaining. The relevant provision, now in TULRCA 1992, section 181, has been left untouched over the years. It will become clear that little recourse is made to the provision which is applied and interpreted by the CAC.

---

[100]   A. BOGG, above n. 74.
[101]   R. DUKES, above n. 20, 249.
[102]   TUC *Modern Rights for Modern Workplaces*, above n. 78 para. 46.
[103]   R. DUKES, above n. 20.
[104]   Ibid.
[105]   A. BOGG, above n. 74.
[106]   G. GALL, above n. 22.

3.1. THE DUTY TO DISCLOSE INFORMATION

Section 181 does not list the type of information that a trade union could expect to be disclosed by an employer. Instead it generally states that the information to be made available is the information without which the trade union could not conduct collective bargaining and information which is in conformity with good industrial relations practice. There is therefore a negative limb of the definition followed by the vague concept of *good industrial relations practice*. However, statutes expressly refer to a soft law source for additional assistance. ACAS produces a code of practice on the disclosure of information for collective bargaining purposes which elaborates on the two limbs of the definition.

The duty is further restricted by a prohibition on the disclosure of some information. The list in section 182 is exhaustive and covers a wide range of scenarios designed to protect the employer's interests and others. For example, the employer does not have to disclose information that would be against the interests of national security or information that relates specifically to an individual or which would cause substantial injury to his undertaking.

3.2. COMPLAINTS AND REMEDIES

Any complaint that the employer did not comply with the section 181 duty must be reported to the CAC.[107] At this stage, the CAC may suggest conciliation to the parties involved with the help of ACAS. If this is unsuccessful, and if the complaint is well-founded, the CAC will make a declaration to that effect and require the employer to disclose the relevant information within a certain time frame. If the employer fails to comply with the declaration, the trade union has at its disposal an effective weapon. It can make a further complaint to the CAC and if it is well-founded,[108] the union may make a claim requesting for terms and conditions to be included in the employees' contracts of employment. If the CAC find the complaint wholly or partly well-founded, it will make an award to that effect.[109] This sanction is therefore very effective but has been very rarely used. At first, although there were numerous complaints to the CAC for failure to disclose information in the 1970s and 1980s, the trend died down in the 90s and subsequently. In the last ten years, the CAC receives between 5 and 10 complaints a year, most of them being withdrawn because of resolution by further negotiations or being closed after informal meetings between parties CAC and/or ACAS. A study of the last ten years annual reports of the CAC shows that only one to three formal decisions are made per year and that roughly

---

107 TULRCA, s. 183.
108 TULRCA, s. 184.
109 TULRCA, s. 185.

50% are in favour of trade unions' requests.[110] In these cases, the unions usually request information on pay scales, promotion, turnover or simplified financial figures on the health of the company. There is only one case that reported the imposition of terms and conditions in contract of employment following the employer's refusal to provide information to the union after a CAC award.[111] The 1970s case highlighted the problem of what was claimed as appropriate as a term or condition when the union had requested information such as salary scale. The CAC would have preferred tangible terms and conditions to be claimed after a breach of the award. Nevertheless, the employer was ordered to insert salary scale and fixed increase so that they would take effect as part of the contract. No other reported case dealt with the issue of the ultimate sanction, presumably because employers have complied with the original award of the CAC to disclose information. The sanction may therefore have been an effective deterrent as any well advised employer would not take the risk to have terms and conditions imposed by the CAC.

4. THE PRODUCT OF COLLECTIVE BARGAINING – COLLECTIVE AGREEMENTS

The principal reason for collective bargaining is ultimately the improvement of terms and conditions, usually pay and typically on an annual basis. It is therefore expected that negotiations between the employer and the union would result in an agreement about the new terms and conditions which would subsequently be applicable to the relevant employees. While the formula and concept are simple, the legal application of such mechanisms is not as straightforward. First the notion of collective agreement needs to be defined before considering the impact it has on the contract of employment of the workers concerned.

4.1. PARTIES AND CONTENT

A collective agreement is defined by statute as '*any agreement or arrangement made by or on behalf of one or more trade unions and one or more employers or*

---

[110]   The CAC annual reports provide information on its annual case load and has a heading on disclosure of information for the purpose of collective bargaining. The section lists the number of complaints made per year and whether formal decisions were reached. The CAC decisions can be found at <www.cac.gov.uk/index.aspx?articleid=2256>, accessed 28.10.2011. For decisions upholding the unions' complaints, see TUR1/249/2003 (this decision is listed under the 'trade union recognition' jurisdiction because this was one of the complaints also intertwined); DI/8/(2006); DI /9/(2007) and DI /3/(2008).

[111]   See award No 79/451 *Holokrome – Association of Scientific Technical and Managerial Staff* available on the CAC website at <www.cac.gov.uk/CHttpHandler.ashx?id=2781&p=0> accessed 28.10.2011.

employers' associations.[112] The agreement must also relate to the topics that are listed for collective bargaining, for example terms and conditions of employment, allocation of work, etc.[113] There are therefore conditions relating to the identity of the parties signing up the collective agreement and the subject matter of the agreement.

Collective agreements tend to be the result of negotiations between a single employer and one trade union or a single employer and several trade unions representing different parts of the workforce. Central, sectoral or multi-employer bargaining is rare and company or undertaking level is the norm.

The content of the agreement is left to the parties, although statute indicates that one of the matters listed in section 178 should be covered to qualify for the designation of collective agreements. In practice, bargaining is primarily done over the issues of pay, holidays and working time.[114] The contents of collective agreements have recently come under scrutiny. Employers have questioned the validity of negotiated agreement clauses. For example, last in – first out (LIFO) clauses, which require the employer to make redundant those employees who have been employed for the shortest period of time first, and which are usually agreed as part of redundancy selection criteria, have been claimed to be discriminatory on grounds of age.[115]

In addition to what may be termed 'traditional collective agreement', the law permits the signing of agreements which are collective in nature but do not involve trade unions. Workforce agreements were a tool created by reaction to European law. A number of Directives[116] allow derogations from some of their own provisions if they are agreed through collective agreements. As collective agreements must be signed by trade unions, the legislator transposed the Directive by creating a mechanism where in the absence of trade unions, agreements can still be reached by other representatives of the workforce. Thus under the Fixed Term Employees Regulations,[117] collective or workforce agreements can be used to change the formula that limits the recourse to successive fixed-term contracts. Similarly, under the Working Time Regulations,[118] collective or workforce agreements can affect the maximum number of hours worked per week.

---

[112]   TULRCA, s. 178(1).

[113]   See introduction for the full list found in TULRCA, s. 178(2).

[114]   See B. Kersey, C. Alpin, J. Forth, A. Bryson, H. Bewley, G. Dix and S. Oxenbridge, above n. 5, p. 194.

[115]   *Rolls Royce Plc v Unite* [2009] IRLR 576.

[116]   For example, Council Directive 99/70/EC of 28 June 1999 concerning the framework agreement on fixed-term work concluded by ETUC, UNICE and CEEP [1999] OJ L175/43, clause 8(4).

[117]   SI 2002/2034, reg. 8(5).

[118]   SI 1998/1833, reg. 23.

The workforce agreements have been criticised for creating a parallel and potentially competitive channel to trade union representation and function.[119] There are always doubts about the independence of the representatives signing such an agreement and how they are manipulated by management. Nevertheless, the existence of such alternative collective voice could be beneficial where trade unions are less present or have not been able to secure recognition. Despite not being recognised, they could still potentially influence the outcome of the agreement and use this tool to recruit and convince workers to join the union. The existence and proliferation of such agreements is less clear.

4.2. STATUS AND IMPACT ON CONTRACTS OF EMPLOYMENT

The reaching of an agreement between the relevant parties does not lead to immediate enforceability in the sphere of collective relations. Statute presumes that collective agreements are not binding, unless the agreement is in writing and includes a clause expressly stating that the parties intend the agreement to be a legally enforceable contract.[120] The statutory presumption applied what had been found in case law.[121] A collective agreement is therefore often referred to as a *gentlemen's agreement*, denoting the moral obligation to abide by it. The statutory position was also a reflection of the parties' intentions and of the legal analysis of such conventions. At first, trade unions and employers were reluctant to make the instruments binding. On the one hand, trade unions had experienced the antipathy of the judiciary and did not want the courts to deal with the breach of the agreement by fear of losing out and making the process too legalistic.[122] On the other hand, the employers also preferred to be outside the court's reach as the only weapon available to the unions in case of breach was recourse to industrial action which could be contained. Legally, a collective agreement does not fulfil the conditions required to define a contract. The latter must be signed between parties which will be bound directly by the agreement. The unions represent workers and therefore act as 'agents' when signing the collective agreement. For example, the union will not be the recipient of the new working arrangements or the new pay. Individuals who work for the employer will benefit from the agreement. This process is not permitted under English contract law. There is a further anomaly in relation to collective agreement when compared to contract law. When the agreement is signed, it is applicable to the

---

[119]   See C. KILPATRICK, 'Has New Labour Reconfigured Employment Legislation' (2003) 32 *ILJ* 135, 160.
[120]   TULRCA, s. 179(1).
[121]   *Ford Motor Co Ltd v AUEFW* (1969) 2 All ER 481.
[122]   P. DAVIES and M. FREEDLAND, above n. 9, p. 271.

whole workforce and not only to the members of the union within that bargaining unit. There is therefore an *erga omnes* effect that does not tally with normal contractual principles.

English law did not create a new category of contractual arrangement for collective agreements or analyse it in a different way. Case law and then legislation simply created a presumption that such an agreement was not intended to have legal effect. The difficulty then laid in the legal construct of how such agreements can benefit the workers. It is case law which created the mechanisms whereby the collective agreement can be applied to workers. In essence, collective agreements are 'incorporated' into individual contracts of employment. Such incorporation can be express or implied. In the first scenario, parties expressly indicate in the collective agreements which provisions will be incorporated in the individuals' contracts. Implied incorporation can occur by different means, such as, for example, custom and practice.[123] The disputes arise when there is uncertainty on whether incorporation has taken place, but also as to the extent of the incorporation.

The relevant clause must be appropriate for incorporation. Clearly, illegal terms would not be considered appropriate; nor would terms that are specifically stated to be binding in honour only. Negotiated clauses relating to pay, working hours, holidays would naturally be suitable for incorporation. Enhanced redundancy payments for example have been deemed apt for incorporation.[124] The judiciary had tried to explain that collective agreement clauses that would benefit the employee directly could be incorporated whereas provisions which concern the 'administration' of the collective relations could not. For example, early cases suggested that procedural terms could not be incorporated. This was how certain commentators understood the case of *Alexander v Standard Telephone and Cables Ltd (No. 2)*,[125] which concerned the application of a LIFO redundancy selection procedure. Such redundancy arrangement is favoured by trade unions, as the use of objective criteria (length of service) stops the employer stigmatising certain employees as being unproductive. In *Alexander*, the court refused to treat the selection procedure as being incorporated into the contract of employment, leading to speculation that procedural terms *per se* were not appropriate for incorporation. A more useful precedent for workers appeared to be set in *Anderson v Pringle of Scotland*,[126] which also concerned a LIFO policy agreed with the union. The employer had decided to breach this agreement and use a selective

---

[123]   *Henry v London General Transport Services Ltd* [2002] IRLR 473.
[124]   *Keeley v Fosroc International Ltd* [2006] IRLR 961, applied in *Harlow v Artemis International Corporation Ltd* [2008] IRLR 629.
[125]   *Alexander v Standard Telephone and Cables Ltd (No. 2)* [1991] IRLR 286.
[126]   *Anderson v Pringle of Scotland* [1998] IRLR 64.

scheme, under which Anderson was made redundant. The Scottish Court of Session found that the terms of the collective agreement relating to redundancy had been incorporated into Anderson's employment contract and he was reinstated accordingly. This was perhaps a sign that the courts were beginning to recognise how crucial procedural standards are to the welfare of individual employees in the employment relationship.

The finding of the Court of Appeal in *Malone and others v British Airways plc*[127] is however less promising in terms of what aspects of a collective agreement are treated as potentially capable of incorporation into the individual employment contract. The employees were arguing that a clause of the collective agreement which specified the staffing level per flight (the crew complement) was part of their contract of employment and could therefore not be altered unilaterally by BA without being in breach of contract. The High Court and the Court of Appeal considered that the clause was not 'apt' for incorporation because it was not directed to individuals and there was no 'intention' of the parties to make this clause binding. The first finding is curious because the number of crew on flights is closely linked to pay, safety and productivity, in which each individual employee clearly has an interest. The second limb is more problematic, as essentially the judiciary found that, because the consequences for BA would have been unpalatable if the parties had intended for this clause to be enforceable by individual employees, this could not have been intended. As RUSSELL rightly points out, the test of 'aptness' seemed to have been replaced by a test of 'appropriateness' which firmly favours the employer and could undermine collective bargaining if hard fought provisions are left ineffective.[128]

Finally, revocation of incorporation cannot, according to contractual principles, be unilateral. The employer cannot do this alone.[129] However, it has been established that employers can vary the incorporation of terms, with the consent of the recognised trade union, as long as the union has ostensible authority to enter into negotiations of this kind.[130]

In relation to workforce agreements, it is not clear what their legal status is. The relevant regulations simply acknowledge their existence and function. Section 179 does not mention them in relation to enforceability. For the reasons highlighted above in relation to collective agreements, they would seem not to

---

[127] *Malone and others v British Airways plc* [2010] EWCA Civ 1225. For comments, see R. RUSSELL, '*Malone and others v British Airways plc*: protection of managerial prerogative?' (2011) 40 *ILJ* 207.

[128] R. RUSSELL, ibid. 208 and 213.

[129] *Robertson v British Gas Corporation* [1983] ICR 351.

[130] *Burke v Royal Liverpool University Hospital NHS Trust* [1997] ICR 730; *Harris v Richard Lawson Autologistics Ltd* [2002] IRLR 476.

constitute contracts, but they permit derogation from statutory protection and must therefore have some force. The question remains as to the remedy available if such agreement is breached.

5. CONCLUSION

The legal framework on collective bargaining underwent major changes under the Labour administration as a statutory recognition procedure was re-introduced. It clearly had some impact on trade unions and industrial relations. However, the original enthusiasm has died down. Collective bargaining is still in decline.[131] Recent Labour governments facilitated recognition to an extent, but failed to promote collective bargaining as a fundamental instrument for the regulation of the employment relationship. There is no intention to remedy this situation at present under a Coalition government that does not seem amenable to collective representation by trade unions.[132] The question therefore is whether the trend can be reversed for collective bargaining, where the law, imperfect as it was, failed. There is potentially some hope with the development of information and consultation mechanisms. Trade unions may be able to regain a more prominent place as representatives and to gain some negotiation rights via the backdoor, as will be discussed in chapter 6.

---

[131] J. ACHUR, above n. 6.
[132] See the Employment Review process and the Red Tape Challenge (<www.bis.gov.uk/policies/employment-matters/employment-law-review> accessed 20.12.2011) discussed in chapter 1. The government does not mention collective actors in its review and vision of employment law.

CHAPTER 4

TRADE UNIONS AND THEIR MEMBERS: THE REGULATION OF INTERNAL AFFAIRS

1. INTRODUCTION

This chapter turns to the relationship between the trade union as an organisation and its members. There was a time where this relationship was nearly as important as the relationship between the employee and employer because a contract of employment could be dependent on union membership. The closed shop was an *'arrangement whereby employers and trade union could agree that union membership was a prerequisite to employment'*.[1] While this was permissible, being refused entry or being expelled from a union could mean the end of the employment relationship and serious difficulties in finding work in the same trade or profession. The closed shop was however made impossible by statute in the 1980s[2] and as membership of trade unions continues to decline,[3] the nexus between a trade union and its members does not appear as fundamental. However, this chapter intends to show that the organisation of trade unions and the relationship with its affiliates are still the subject of controversy. The intervention of the law, either via the judiciary or statute, has encroached upon the independence of trade unions over the years. In particular, members have been given extensive powers to challenge the governance or decisions of their trade union. An individualistic approach to the relationship

---

[1]   C.F. Wright, 'What role for trade unions in future workplace relations', (ACAS Future of Workplace Relations Discussion paper series, September 2011), p. 3. See chapter 2 for international standards approach to the closed shop.

[2]   By systematic statutory attacks, first by the limitation of the operation of the closed shop and then by making it discriminatory practice to either request union membership for job applicants or by making it automatically unfair to dismiss for non-membership of a union – see Employment Act 1982, Employment Act 1988 and Employment Act 1990. Help was also found in the European Court of Human Rights judgment of *Young, James and Webster v UK* [1981] IRLR 408 which held that art. 11 of the European Convention on Human Rights allows freedom not to join a union as well as freedom to join a union. See chapter 2.

[3]   J. Achur, *Trade Union Membership 2010*, Department of Business, Innovation and Skills, 2011, <www.bis.govuk/assets/biscore/employment-matters/docs/t/11-p77-trade-union-membership-2010.pdf> accessed 14.11.2011.

between a member and that union to which they belong has developed. The judiciary and policy makers do not seem comfortable with the collective dimension of trade union activities.

Rules governing the organisation and administration of trade unions are originally and generally found in the 'rule book'. This effectively amounts to the constitution of the union, containing provisions on the object of the union, elections of its officers and executive, membership (including discipline and expulsion), political funds, finance, etc.[4] The rule books allowed unions to have transparent systems of governance and procedural safeguards for members. However, this chapter will show that trade union rules have been subjected to interference by the courts (at first) and by parliament (subsequently). The rationale for such interventions was generally the defence of the individual. The judiciary used various contractual and public law mechanisms to interpret and review internal rules and procedures enacted by trade unions democratically. Legislation had only regulated very lightly trade union governance before the Conservative era of the 1980s and 1990s.[5] During that period, so-called 'democratisation' of trade unions was concretised by empowering members to resist leadership that the government of the day regarded as a few left wing extremists.

A series of Green Papers[6] expressly stated the government agenda in relation to union governance. In the first document considering trade unions, it was made clear that '*much public concern had been voiced about the need for trade unions to become more democratic and responsive to the wishes of their members*'.[7] The government subsequently summed up its position in relation to the state of the law: '*it is necessary to consider whether the rights of individual members of trade unions are adequately protected and whether those who exercise powers in the name of the membership are properly accountable to the members*'.[8] This was translated into practice in different ways.

---

[4] Trade unions have a statutory duty to supply copies of their rules to any person who requests it (TULRCA, s. 27). A number of national union rules book are available to consult on the internet, for example UNITE at <www.unitetheunion.org/pdf/rule%20book%20sept10.pdf> accessed 14.11.2011; GMB, <www.gmb.org.uk/pdf/RulebookfollowingCongress2011fnl.pdf> accessed 14.11.2011; or one of the higher education unions UCU <www.ucu.org.uk/media/pdf/d/h/ucurules_2011–12.pdf> accessed 14.11.2011.

[5] The Trade Union Act 1871 required trade union to have rules on object and trustees; the 1913 Act regulated political funds; the Industrial Relations Act 1971 Act tried to regulate internal affairs but was repealed in 1974. See P. ELIAS and K.D. EWING, *Trade Union Democracy – Members' Rights and the Law*, Mansell Publishing Limited, London 1987, chapters 1 and 5.

[6] *Democracy in Trade Unions*, Cmnd 8778, 1983 and *Trade Unions and their Members*, Cm 95, 1987.

[7] *Democracy in Trade Unions*, Cmnd 8778, 1983, para. 1.

[8] Ibid. para. 3.

Firstly a whole host of measures were enacted, applying the ideology and views expressed in the Green papers: the Employment Acts 1980, 1982, 1988, 1989 and 1990; the Trade Unions Act 1984 and the Trade Union Reform and Employment Rights Act 1993. Concrete example of reforms included introduction of ballots for the election of the union leaders and new rules for the financial organisation of the union, emphasising the rights of individuals against the collective interests. Trade union members became more protected against discipline and exclusions. The abolition of the closed shop removed pressures to join trade unions and to act in solidarity with other workers.

A specific agency was also created during that period to help union members take legal actions against their union for breach of the union rules or of the statutory obligations. The Commissioner for the Rights of Trade Union Members (CRTUM) could provide advice to members on the merit of their case and even had a budget to financially assist members who had a grievance they wished to take to court. The additional support given to members was justified by the government at the time because *'individuals may otherwise be deterred from bringing cases to the courts because of their complexity, the financial costs involved or for any other reason'*.[9] The new system ran the risk that 'rebel' union members would disrupt the running of the organisation. This could have negative consequences in terms of public image for the unions, but there was also financial cost involved if unions were sued. However, very few cases were taken by CRTUM.[10] The Labour Government used this lack of activity as a reason to abolish the institution.[11] This was however a cost-saving exercise[12] rather than an ideological re-balancing of powers as the government still indicated that it had *'no wish to protect poorly run trade unions'*.[13] Overall, the remaining details and complexities of the legislation of the Conservative era were mainly left untouched by the Labour government. Two reasons could be advanced: firstly, the discourse of 'democracy' and 'accountability' were a more popular formula,[14] and secondly *'trade union autonomy could potentially enhance collective bargaining power, conjuring up the negative images associated with British industrial relations of the 1970s'*.[15]

---

9   *Trade Unions and their Members*, Cm 95, 1987, para. 6.5.
10 See for example D. MORRIS, 'The Commissioner for the Rights of Trade Union Members – a framework for the future' (1993) 22 *ILJ* 307.
11 ERelA 1999, s. 28.
12 T. NOVITZ and P. SKIDMORE, *Fairness at Work – A Critical Analysis of the Employment Relations Act 1999 and its Treatment of Collective Rights*, Hart, 2001, p. 57.
13 *Fairness at Work*, Presented to Parliament by the President of the Board of Trade by Command of her Majesty, May 1998. Cm 3968, para. 4.31.
14 T. NOVITZ and P. SKIDMORE, above n. 12, p. 47.
15 Ibid., p. 54.

In addition to the specific measures targeting union internal affairs, other 1980s and 1990s legislative reforms had a significant impact on trade union organisation. For example, as the scope of the ability to call strikes diminished, recruitment problems started to present themselves. As a result, the number of amalgamation and mergers of trade unions increased, raising new problems of internal governance and dilemmas relating to collective action.[16]

The outcome of such intervention has also been exposed as contravening international obligations, both by the International Labour Organization[17] and the European Committee of Social Rights[18] on the basis that trade unions should be free of state intervention when organising their own affairs. This was most recently and strongly demonstrated by the European Court of Human Rights (ECtHR) in the *ASLEF* case[19] where the Court indicated that the autonomy of trade unions is crucial to freedom of association.[20]

Adopting a relative chronology, this chapter will consider first how the judiciary, drawing on the common law, have intervened in trade unions' internal affairs. Secondly, the involvement of statute will be examined in relation to four aspects of trade unions' organisations: the ability to discipline members, the elections of officials, financial management and the use of political funds. In conclusion, the resulting state of the law, which combines statutory rules and case law, is assessed against international standards such as ILO Conventions, the European Social Charter and the European Convention of Human Rights. Such evaluation demonstrates the need for future reforms.

2. UNIONS' RULES AND THE COMMON LAW

Unions establish their way of functioning by enacting rules applicable to all members. They are found in the rule book which serves as a constitution for the union and as a contract that binds the members and the union. Rule books do not always have the same content but usually start with the object and aim of the union which is to promote and defend the interests of its members. With more or

---

[16] P. WILLMAN, 'Structuring Unions: The Administrative Rationality of Collective Action' in J. KELLY and P. WILLMAN, *Union Organization and Activity*, Routledge, London and New York 2004.

[17] Committee of Experts on Application of Conventions and Recommendations. Individual Observation Concerning Freedom of Association and Protection of the Right to Organise Convention (No. 87) (2007).

[18] European Social Charter, European Committee of Social Rights, *Conclusions XIX-3* (2010) (United Kingdom).

[19] *ASLEF v UK* [2007] IRLR 361 and see M. FORD and J. HENDY QC, *Briefing Note ASLEF v UK*, Institute of Employment Rights, London 2007.

[20] Ibid. *ASLEF* para. 38.

less details, the rules usually refer to membership (criteria to be admitted, procedures if members have to be disciplined), but also to governance (how officials and executive committees come to office) and finances. While the content of the documents are now largely influenced by statutory requirements, trade unions' constitutions included similar headings prior to the intervention of the law.[21] If there were disputes between members and the trade unions, for example, in relation to disciplinary measures, union rules would usually have internal procedures to deal with such conflict. However, questions arose as to whether members could take the difference of opinion to courts. Judges had first to determine the status of the rule book to decide whether they could intervene. Were the rules equivalent to a private contract between members and the union or were they equivalent to bylaws, considering the nature and functions of trade unions, which as influential social actors could potentially allow access to or deprive members of employment? Regardless of the label given to the rules, the judiciary seldom shied away from enforcing or interpreting the rules, often in favour of the individual. The techniques were to construe the book like a contract or to use principles of natural justice. While these issues are not so contemporary following the heavy regulations of trade union affairs in the 1980s–90s, the principles remain and current cases still refer to rule books as will be seen in this section.

2.1. STATUS OF THE RULE BOOK AND CONTRACT OF MEMBERSHIP

When asked to adjudicate on the breach of the rules or their interpretation, the courts had to decide how to analyse the rule book and its legal status in relation to the union and its members. Originally, section 4 of the Trade Unions Act 1871 prevented trade union members from enforcing the rule book, thus leaving courts and Parliament out of the unions' internal affairs. However, despite this bar, the House of Lords still considered that union members could sue their unions if they were in breach of union rules and be awarded damages.[22] This is now academic as, since the Industrial Relations Act 1971, trade unions are quasi-corporate bodies against which legal actions can be taken.[23] Case law however struggled to be consistent in its analysis of the rule book. It was either regarded as a code of practice or as a bylaw, or assimilated to and interpreted as a contract. Lord Denning was a keen defender of the first approach: *'the rules are in reality more than a contract. They are a legislative code laid down by the council of the*

---

21 Although the detail of the procedures and content vary from union to union, see P. ELIAS and
    K.D. EWING above n. 5, pp. 279–283.

22 *Bonsor v Musicians' Unions* [1956] AC 104.

23 Now in TULRCA, s. 10(1).

union to be obeyed by the members. This code should be subject to control by the courts just as much as a code laid down by Parliament itself.[24] The second approach eventually prevailed. The House of Lords clearly stated that: '*trade union rule books are not drafted by parliamentary draftsmen. Courts of law must resist the temptation to construe them as if they were*'.[25] This has been since reiterated clearly: '*the right of a member to complain of a breach of the rules is a contractual right*'.[26] As a result, courts can imply terms through custom and practice in order to complement union rules.[27] Accordingly, despite the uncertainty hovering above the status of the rule book, the courts still found sufficient justification to intervene in union affairs.

2.2. BREACH AND INTERPRETATION OF THE RULES

Courts interceded where the union rules had been breached or needed interpretation. Union rules usually provided for internal bodies to deal with disputes.[28] However, courts had no difficulties giving themselves jurisdiction to hear a complaint in order to have the final say.[29] In those cases, the courts would effectively interpret the rule and substitute their finding to what had been found internally. The cases relate primarily to disciplinary offences and particularly where members were expelled. For example, when a member was expelled for not paying his subscription fees according to the rule that stated that a member could not be in arrears of more than six weeks, the court annulled the union's decision on the basis that the wrong 'body' had expelled the member. In *Bonsor v Musicians' Union*,[30] the rule book stated that the branch committee had the power to expel the member and not the branch secretary as had occurred in this instance. The court would also grant injunction before any disciplinary action was taken because no reasonable tribunal would come to a conclusion that a member could be expelled in the given circumstances. In *Esterman v NALGO*,[31] the court held that a member who refused to follow orders not to assist returning officers in local election, to put pressure on local government during pay negotiations, could not be disciplined as it was unclear whether the rules allowed such orders and therefore no reasonable tribunal would reach a decision of expulsion. When the closed shop was effective and the withdrawal of the union

---

[24]   *Breen v AEU* [1971] 2 QB 175 at 190.
[25]   *Heatons Transport (St Helens) Ltd v TGWU* [1972] ICR 308 at 393 per Lord Wilberforce.
[26]   *Wise and another v Union of Shop, Distributive and Allied Workers* [1996] IRLR 609, para. 34.
[27]   See *Heatons Transport (St Helens) Ltd v TGWU* [1972] ICR 308 where the court implied a general authority of shop stewards to act in the interest of their members.
[28]   See for example GMB Rule book 2011 version, above n. 4, rule 60.
[29]   *Lee v Showmen's Guild of Great Britain* [1952] 1 All ER 1175.
[30]   [1956] AC 104.
[31]   [1974] ICR 625.

card would mean loss of livelihood, the courts were particularly keen to scrutinise the unions' rules and how they had been considered by internal panels.

The possibility to have recourse to the judiciary despite the existence of internal mechanisms to deal with a dispute was superseded by section 63 of TULRCA 1992. Trade unions members have the right not to be denied access to the courts, even if union rules state that internal conciliation or determination of a matter is final.

2.3. PRINCIPLES OF NATURAL JUSTICE

The courts intervened via a second route in internal union affairs. The principles of natural justice were found to apply to internal disciplinary proceedings when taking decisions against members. This was established in *Lee v Showmen's Guild of Great Britain*.[32] The principles of reaching decisions without bias and following a fair hearing were formulated as requiring notice of the charge to the person concerned, the opportunity to be heard and a fair hearing by an unbiased judge. The first component means that charges cannot be amended. In *Eccleston v NUJ*,[33] the deputy general secretary of the National Union of Journalists had publicly expressed views on the running of the union that were contrary to what had been advocated by the General Secretary. He was asked to attend a disciplinary hearing for misconduct. At the hearing, new evidence, charges and possible outcomes were presented to him, which led to a vote of no confidence. In turn, this disqualified him from being shortlisted for re-election. The High Court considered that there was a breach of natural justice which rendered his prohibition to stand as a candidate unlawful. The third element of the formula prevents a person from being a prosecutor and judge when deciding whether a member should be expelled especially when the 'judge' has been directly involved in the case and is therefore biased. In *Roebuck v NUM (Yorkshire Area) No2*,[34] the president of the miners' union, Arthur Scargill, had sued a local newspaper for libel and had won. During the court proceedings, two members gave evidence which was either contradictory to what had been originally said to the union's solicitor, or had been the result of showing internal correspondence to the newspaper's solicitors. The president had considered those actions as detrimental to the union and had instigated disciplinary proceedings which led to the suspension from office of one of the members and

---

[32] [1952] 1 All ER 1175.
[33] [1999] IRLR 166.
[34] [1978] ICR 678.

the ban from standing as candidate for the other. The procedure was started by the president and the disciplinary hearing was chaired by the same person. The High Court decided that the president's bias meant that the disciplinary decisions could not stand.

Most of the cases and findings discussed above pre-date the Conservative onslaught on the internal affairs of the trade unions but remain valid, especially considering the remedies available to union members.

2.4. REMEDIES

Where union rules have been improperly applied or ignored, a member of the union has two possible routes for enforcement: either the traditional civil court or, since 1999, the Certification Officer (CO).[35] The latter may be more popular as it does not involve legal costs, judicial delays or formality. From a trade unions' perspective, their relationship with the courts had historically been difficult and the recourse to an independent body could also be welcome.[36] However, the grounds for complaints are exhaustively limited by statute and concern disciplinary matters, appointment or election or removal from office, ballots (other than on industrial action) and constitution or proceedings of relevant decision-making meetings.[37] The array of remedies available through the CO is more limited than the courts' panoply. While the High Court can issue declaration, award injunctions and damages, the CO is restricted to declarations and orders to take the necessary steps to remedy the breach or abstain from certain acts to avoid repetition of the breach.[38] The time-limit for application is also tighter as a claimant would have six months[39] to make an application to the CO as opposed to six years for the High Court. While the number of cases relating to breach of union rules has died down in the civil courts, the number of applications and decisions by the CO vary over the years. The annual reports of the COs[40] show that the number of decisions may go from 18 at its lowest in 2003/4 to 79 at its highest in 2006/7 as seen in the table below:

---

[35] TULRCA, ss. 108A-108C as inserted by ERelA, 1999.
[36] T. NOVITZ and P. SKIDMORE, above n. 12, p. 58.
[37] TULRCA, s. 108A.
[38] TULRCA, s. 108B.
[39] TULRCA, s. 108A(6) and (7).
[40] See *Certification Officer Annual Reports* all available on-line since 1999 at <www.certoffice. org/Publications/Annual-Reports.aspx> accessed 14.11.2011.

CO– number of decisions for breach of union rules[41]

Annual reports	1999/2000	2000/1	2001/2	2002/3	2003/4	2004/5	2005/6	2006/7	2007/8	2008/9	2009/10	2010/11
Decisions	0	48	57	28	18	27	35	79	29	23	28	39

Decisions of the CO can be appealed to the EAT on a point of law.[42]

3. TRADE UNION GOVERNANCE AND STATUTES

Trade unions' constitutions today are heavily influenced by statute and cannot be drafted as freely as was possible in the past. While legislation regulating unions' conduct and activities existed prior to the Thatcher era,[43] most of the current body of law originates from the 1980s and 90s. This section aims to illustrate the extent of interference in four activities of the unions: the ability to discipline and expel members, the appointment of union officials, the financial management and the support of political activities.

3.1. DISCIPLINARY ACTIONS

As in other organisational settings, trade unions should be able to discipline their members if they breach the rules applicable to the union. Such discipline could start with withdrawing some benefits and could go as far as expulsion if the misconduct is serious enough. However it has been pointed out that the common law has given some safeguards to members in this field, notably by applying natural justice principles to disciplinary actions. Additionally, statutes have limited the possibility to take such actions in two ways. Firstly by defining extensively what would be unjustifiable discipline and secondly by listing exhaustively the reasons for which members can be expelled.

3.1.1. Unjustifiable discipline

TULRCA 1992 does not list when a union is entitled to discipline, but instead prescribes the kinds of conduct which cannot give rise to sanctions by unions. Section 64(1) states that *'an individual who is or has been a member of a trade*

---

41 Some of the decisions concerned the same application but several breaches are alleged. Further, annual reports do not always state how many applications are received but always indicate the number of decisions for the period concerned.
42 TULRCA, s. 108C.
43 For example in the field of political funds in the Trade Union Act 1913, see section below.

union has a right not to be unjustifiably disciplined by the union'. Falling within the ethos of Conservative policies to empower members against their unions, the provision is classified as a right. The term discipline is further defined by statute as a number of actions that would cover financial sanctions, withdrawal of union services or advice to other unions to refrain from accepting the offending member, expulsion (treated separately below), or being subject to any other detriment.[44] The latter has been interpreted widely by the EAT, meaning that a variety of actions can be caught by statute and therefore scrutinised by the courts. For example, naming a member as a strike breaker in a circular distributed to the whole membership because she had crossed the picket line during an industrial action was considered as subjecting her to a detriment as the naming was clearly aimed at embarrassing her.[45] The meaning of 'unjustifiably disciplined' is subsequently explained, as section 65 exhaustively lists ten types of conduct that cannot be reasons for disciplining members. Without inventorying them all, examples of conduct that cannot be subject to disciplinary measures include asserting that the union has broken its own rule or any other rule of law, or working with employees who are not members of the union. However, the most significant limit is the prohibition to discipline members who do not partake in or support industrial action. The government of the time considered that individuals should be free to choose whether to go to work or strike, as a matter of principle.[46] It even used human rights language to justify its policy: *'the right of the individual to choose to go to work despite a call to take industrial action is an essential freedom'*.[47] Essentially, union members are given carte blanche to ignore the collective side and solidarity aspect of trade unionism. As a consequence, more individual rights were given to members of an organisation but, in parallel, the organisation was deprived of an essential democratic function, namely that the members of the group should abide by decisions taken by the majority. Combined with the imposition of strict balloting rules for organising lawful industrial actions, the attack on trade unions' autonomy meant that their main industrial 'weapon' was being disarmed on all fronts. The limitation imposed on trade unions to discipline members when refusing to take part in industrial action has been criticised particularly by the European Social Charter Committee of Experts (now the European Committee of Social Rights or 'ECSR') as contravening Article 5 on the right to organise. In its latest conclusion on section 65, the Committee considers the provision as limiting too restrictively the grounds upon which a union can discipline its members and therefore interfering unjustifiably with union autonomy.[48] This

---

[44]   TULRCA, s. 64(2)(a)-(f).
[45]   *NALGO v Killorn and Simm* [1990] IRLR 464.
[46]   *Trade Unions and their Members*, Cm 95, 1987 para. 2.22.
[47]   Ibid. para. 2.10.
[48]   See European Committee of Social Rights – *Conclusions XIX-3* (2010) (United Kingdom), 11.

view is echoed by the ILO Committee of Experts.[49] Nationally, the Court of Appeal has however interpreted narrowly what constitutes *'failure to support strike or other industrial action'*. In *Knowles v Fire Brigade Union*,[50] members were expelled because they agreed to take on additional duties as fire-fighters when the union policy was clear that there was opposition to such practice. The employers had tried to re-introduce retained duties for full-time fire-fighters (for example, being on standby outside their normal working hours) but this had not been agreed by the union. The expelled employees argued that they were disciplined for failure to support industrial action. The Court of Appeal disagreed because the trade union pressure was not to enter into additional contracts. The employees were therefore not breaking their contract of employment.

If a member considers that he has been unjustifiably disciplined, he can bring an action before an employment tribunal within three months.[51] Where the claim is well-founded and the situation was not remedied (i.e. a member was found to be unjustifiably expelled but not re-admitted subsequently by the union), a further claim can be brought requiring financial compensation.[52] The amount of the compensation will be what is just and equitable in the circumstances but a substantial minimum can be claimed (£7,600 at the time of writing) while the maximum is capped at the highest compensation available for unfair dismissal.[53] The courts did compensate members when expelled for not taking part in industrial action but originally were not necessarily prepared to go beyond the statutory minimum unless there were grounds to do so.[54] Injury to feelings however have been included and the Court of Appeal has recently even gone as far as to re-assess the amount awarded by the EAT.[55] As a consequence wrongly disciplining a trade union member seems to equate to discrimination in terms of remedies while compensating injury to feelings is not available to employees unfairly dismissed.[56] The burden on trade unions appears therefore heavier than for employers when a contractual relationship has ended.

3.1.2. Expelling and excluding members

The ultimate sanction in disciplinary matters is the expulsion of the members. Unions cannot exclude (i.e. refuse entry to membership) or expel members

---

[49] See M. FORD and J. HENDY, *o.c.*, above n.19, p. 12 listing the number of ILO Individual observations where ss. 64–67 were mentioned.
[50] [1996] IRLR 617.
[51] TULRCA, s. 66.
[52] TULRCA, s. 67.
[53] TULRCA, s. 67(8).
[54] *Bradley and others v NALGO* [1991] IRLR 159.
[55] *Massey v UNIFI* [2007] IRLR 907.
[56] *Dunnachie v Kingston upon Hull CC* [2004] IRLR 733.

unless it is for one of the four reasons catalogued by statute. Section 174 effectively lists three categories which are linked to qualifying membership criteria and are not controversial.[57] In other words, a member can be expelled if s/he does not fulfil one of the requirements listed by the union's rules in relation to his / her profession,[58] or if the union only operates in some geographical areas where the member is not working, or finally if the union deals with one or several employers which do not employ the member. The fourth heading has lead to difficulties because of its subjective nature. A union member can be excluded because of his or her conduct. Originally, section 174 further stated that conduct did not include being a member of another union, or working for a specific employer or being a member of a political party.[59] As a consequence, trade unions could not exclude a member for belonging to the Conservative party for example. However, the meaning of conduct was put to the test relatively recently by a series of cases involving unions expelling members who were also affiliates of extreme right wing political parties, notably the British National Party (BNP). In *Lee v ASLEF*[60], the member had taken an action against the union for expelling him on the ground that he had been a candidate for the BNP. This was found to be contravening statute. As a result of this case however, the Employment Relations Act 2004[61] amended section 174 to the effect that conduct did not cover membership of a political party, but could include activities for the political party.[62] This was not entirely satisfactory as members of the BNP could still not be excluded. Unhappy with such outcome, ASLEF took the matter to the European Court of Human Rights on the basis that section 174 was in breach of Article 11 of the European Convention of Human Rights. The ECtHR delivered an exceptional judgment that Article 11 cannot be interpreted as imposing an obligation to admit any person in an association that espouses certain values and ideals.[63] Unions should have some control over their membership:

> 'Article 11 cannot be interpreted as imposing an obligation on associations or organisations to admit whosoever wishes to join. Where associations are formed by people, who, espousing particular values or ideals, intend to pursue common goals, it would run counter to the very effectiveness of the freedom at stake if they had no control over their membership'.[64]

---

[57]   TULRCA, s. 174(2)(a),(b),(c).
[58]   TULRCA, s. 174(3).
[59]   TULRCA, s. 174(4)(a)(iii) before amendments inserted by ERelA 2004.
[60]   [2004] All ER (D) 209.
[61]   Via ss. 33–34.
[62]   Now s. 174 (4A) and (4B).
[63]   See chapter 2: the ECtHR used the negative freedom available to employees not to join a trade union as a counterpart to the freedom of unions to choose who can belong to their association.
[64]   *ASLEF v UK* [2007] IRLR 361, para. 39.

As a result section 174 was amended again by the Employment Act 2008.[65] The new formulation that adds paragraphs 4(C) to 4(H) is complex and unnecessarily cumbersome. It effectively allows exclusion of members on the basis of membership of a political party but under certain stringent conditions. The political party in question must be contrary to the rules or objectives of the trade union. The objective of the union must be easily ascertainable.[66] Procedural guarantees are included in that the decision to expel must follow union rules and not be taken unfairly (namely the member has to be notified and be given a chance to make representation). Finally, loss of union membership must not cause the individual to lose his/her livelihood.[67] It is not clear that these were absolutely necessary, as principles of natural justice and union rules book must be followed. Further, the latter guarantee regarding livelihood seems to have limited practical application today as it resonates with past days of the closed shop and it is difficult to envisage how this condition could be fulfilled.[68]

The remedies for exclusion or expulsion mirror the ones found for unjustifiable discipline.[69] There are minor differences as a member has six months to bring his claim under section 174 (whereas it is three under section 66) and the individual does not have to mitigate his loss (whereas section 66 requires the member to do so). As there could be overlap between actions taken under unjustifiable discipline and expulsion, statutes indicate that if a complaint is made under section 64, the other provision (section 174) cannot be invoked.[70]

3.2. ELECTIONS

Union rules were shown to have mechanisms in place to appoint or elect decision makers. Case law illustrates how the common law has intervened in this field by preventing officials from taking their posts if the rules are not respected.[71] However, direct election of trade unions' decision makers was one of the Conservative government mantra as part of the campaign to make unions more democratic and accountable. It was asserted that even when election rules were included in union rule book, they could be obscure[72] or if providing for indirect

---

[65]   S. 19.
[66]   Subs. 4(D) and (E).
[67]   Subs. 4(F), (G) and (H).
[68]   For a full analysis of the legislative changes, see K.D. Ewing, 'Employment Act 2008. Implementing the *ASLEF* decision – A victory for the BNP?' (2009) 38 *ILJ* 50.
[69]   TULRCA, ss. 175–176.
[70]   TULRCA, s. 66(4).
[71]   See *Leigh v NUR* [1970] Ch 326.
[72]   *Democracy in Trade Unions*, Cmnd. 8778, 1983 para. 7.

elections, the degree of support for the candidates could not be determined.[73] Further, low participation in elections increased the '*risk of placing powers in the hand of unrepresentative minorities*'.[74] The various employment legislation enacted during the 1980s and 1990s aimed to allow members to have a voice when choosing their leaders and to have the mandate renewed on a regular basis. This ideology has been criticised as encouraging a model of democracy that favours direct and individualistic participation as opposed to collective debates, perhaps with a view to silencing activists or inhibiting more creative forums for joint decision-making, for example by imposing postal ballot.[75]

A whole chapter of TULRCA 1992 is devoted to the elections of union officials. The President of the union, as well as the general secretary and members of the executive must be directly elected by the membership and cannot hold a post for more than five years without being re-elected.[76] The election process is subject to detailed procedures.[77] The more important requirements to be satisfied are the need to appoint an independent scrutineer, who oversees the election process and reports on it.[78] All members must be allowed to vote[79] and they should not be unreasonably excluded from standing as candidates.[80] In the recent case of *Unison v Bakhsh and another* which went before the Employment Appeal Tribunal,[81] Mr Bakhsh had argued breach of the union rules and of section 47 because he had not been allowed to stand for election. The exclusion was based on its suspension during disciplinary investigation. The CO and the EAT both upheld the complaint as the rule did not preclude a suspended member from standing for office. Such action was also in breach of section 47 as the exclusion was unreasonable. The voting system imposed by statute is postal[82], although originally the ballot could be secret at the workplace.[83] If the requirements are not fulfilled, an 'interested party', who is defined as a member

---

[73]   Ibid. para. 39.

[74]   Ibid. para. 1.

[75]   S. FREDMAN, 'The New Rights: Labour Law in the Thatcher Years' (1992) *OJLS* 24, 29–30; T. NOVITZ and P. SKIDMORE, above n. 12, p. 51.

[76]   TULRCA, s. 46.

[77]   One example is the detailed provision concerning the opportunity for candidate to give an address. See TULRCA, s. 48.

[78]   TULRCA, ss. 49 and 52. There were fears of malpractice if the process was not overseen by independent actors, see *Trade Unions and their Members*, Cm 95, 1987, para. 5.15 and 5.17.

[79]   TULRCA, s. 50.

[80]   TULRCA 1992, s. 47. See *Paul v NALGO* [1987] IRLR 43, where NALGO had a procedure which was deemed as precluding ordinary members of knowing that they could stand for the post of junior vice president.

[81]   UKEAT/0375/08/RN and D/1–6/10 for the CO decision (available on the CO website).

[82]   TULRCA, s. 51.

[83]   This was amended by the Employment Act 1988.

or a candidate,[84] may make a complaint to the CO[85] or the court,[86] (but cannot do both) within a year of the election. After making an inquiry and hearing the evidence, the CO may make a declaration that the union has failed to comply with the obligations and make an enforcement order stating the steps to be taken to remedy such failure (for example, to *'secure the holding of an election in accordance with the order'*[87]). Such order can be enforced as if it was an order of the court and would therefore constitute a contempt of court if ignored. The number of decisions made by the CO is not very high and varies between 3 and 18 every year.

CO – number of decisions and enforcement orders for breach of statutory rules on elections[88]

Annual reports	1999/2000	2000/1	2001/2	2002/3	2003/4	2004/5	2005/6	2006/7	2007/8	2008/9	2009/10	2010/11
Decisions	18	11	8	7	4	4	6	9	1	4	14	3
Enforcement orders	1	0	2	1	0	0	0	0	0	0	3	1

The Certification Officer's ruling can be appealed before the EAT.[89] The court has the same power as the CO, except that it can grant interlocutory relief.[90] These exercises are costly and perhaps not necessary for all the posts currently covered.

3.3. FINANCIAL AFFAIRS

This is an additional aspect where the Conservative government was keen to regulate, giving members the possibility to question the management of the unions' funds, but also submitting the organisation to weighty duties in terms of reporting and transparency. Regardless of the content of the rule book, the trade unions are obliged to keep accounting records;[91] to send an annual report to the

---

[84]   TULRCA, s. 54.
[85]   TULRCA, s. 55.
[86]   TULRCA, s. 56.
[87]   TULRCA, s. 55(5A).
[88]   Some of the decisions concerned the same application but several breaches are alleged. Further, annual reports do not always state how many applications are received but always indicate the number of decisions for the period concerned.
[89]   TULRCA, s. 56A.
[90]   TULRCA, s. 56(7).
[91]   TULRCA, s. 28.

CO;[92] to appoint an auditor[93] who audits the annual report and has various powers, such as right of access to records or attendance at general meetings;[94] and to send a statement to members containing the auditor's report and other predetermined information within eight weeks of sending the annual report to the CO.[95] The CO may also conduct investigations in the financial affairs of the union.[96] He (or she) can do so when alleged irregularities are raised by members, but the CO can have recourse to other sources such as media reports.[97] An investigator can be appointed[98] but most issues are resolved informally through correspondence or meetings with the interested parties.[99] If any of the above requirements are not fulfilled the union and its individual members could ultimately face criminal sanctions.[100] Members of the union also have a right to access the accounting records and can complain to the CO or the court (but not both) if such right is denied.[101] Only one to three applications per year are made to the CO under this heading according to the annual reports since 1999. The infrequent abuse of powers by trade unions would be a legitimate reason for such low number. It could therefore be advanced that the provisions on financial affairs constitute unwarranted interference in trade unions activities.

3.4. POLITICAL ACTIVITIES AND POLITICAL FUNDS

The final area to consider is the link between trade unions and political parties. The Labour Party was born from the trade union movement and has therefore always enjoyed a special relationship with the labour organisations.[102] Trade unions had found that they could not increase workers' rights and benefits only

---

[92] TULRCA, s. 32. Over 99% of trade unions are now compliant according to the CO (Annual Report 2010/11, para. 3.13).

[93] TULRCA, s. 33.

[94] TULRCA, s. 37.

[95] TULRCA, s. 32A.

[96] TULRCA, s. 37A-37E. Documents can be required from the union. See for example, Certification annual report 2003/4, para. 3.23.

[97] See for example, CO Annual Report 2010/11 para. 3.20.

[98] See for example, CO Annual Report 2008/9 para. 3.21.

[99] See for example, CO Annual Report 2010/11 para. 3.21.

[100] TULRCA, ss. 45 and 45A. Two prosecutions were reported in the CO's annual reports between 1999 and 2011. They were both for failure to submit annual reports and the unions were fined £1,500 each (see annual report 2002/3 para. 3.14 and annual report 2000/1 para. 3.13). Trade unions can also alert the CO that an irregularity has been reported to the police. This would stop the investigation of the CO on that specific matter – see for example annual report 2007/8 para. 3.21.

[101] TULRCA, ss. 30 and 31. The powers of the CO were enlarged in this context by the ERelA 1999.

[102] See for example the social contract between Labour government and trade unions in 1974 where policies on labour law were agreed. For discussion, see M. FREEDLAND and P. DAVIES, *Labour Legislation and Public Policy* Oxford University Press, 1993, chapter 8.

by collective bargaining but that they also needed to lobby lawmakers and be elected as representatives of workers' interests.[103] As such trade unions used their funds to support political activities. The alliance between the Labour Party and trade unions attracted the attention of the legislator and was the subject of early regulation. In 1913, the Trade Union Act established the first limits on how trade unions could contribute to political activities by imposing the creation of a specific political fund.[104] The Conservatives also wanted to address the funding of political parties, once again ostensibly in the name of the individual members that might not want necessarily to be associated with a political objective, but effectively to curtail unions' potential input into the broader democratic process.[105] This was done by amending statutory provisions on two fronts: on the one hand, by regulating further the administration of this unions' activity and on the other, by granting additional rights and powers to individual members in order to limit the union's freedom.

Firstly, statute imposed the isolation of the part of the unions' finance used for political reasons. In fact, the statutory language effectively presumes that the use of trade unions' funds for political purpose is not acceptable unless certain conditions are fulfilled. Section 71 TULRCA 1992 states that '*The funds of a trade union shall not be applied in furtherance of the political objects [...] unless [...]*'. There are effectively three requirements. Firstly, there should be a ballot approving the existence of a political fund by a 'political resolution'.[106] Secondly, even if such political fund exists, members can be exempted from contributing to it. Thirdly, the activities for which the political fund is spent are exhaustively listed by statute. As far as the first condition of balloting members is concerned, this has to be done according to the rules applicable in other contexts, such as union officials' elections.[107] However, it is not enough that rules relating to political funds are enumerated in details in the statute. They have to be incorporated in the union rules and approved by the CO,[108] every time a ballot takes place and the rules are amended. If the majority of the members participating in the ballot vote in favour of a political fund, the political resolution will not remain in place indefinitely. It has a limited life of ten years.[109] Any breach of the rules can be reported to the CO or the court. They can take the necessary steps to remedy the breach by declarations and enforcement

---

[103] For a general discussion, see K.D. EWING, *Trade Unions, the Labour Party and the Law: a Study of the Trade Union Act 1913*, Edinburgh University Press, 1982.

[104] This was as a reaction to *ASRS v Osborne* [1910] AC 87 which made the funding of political activities *ultra vires* for trade unions.

[105] *Democracy in Trade Unions*, Cmnd 8778, 1983, chapter 4.

[106] TULRCA, s. 73.

[107] Appointment of independent scrutineer (s. 75), method of voting (s. 77), etc.

[108] TULRCA, s. 74.

[109] TULRCA, s. 73(3).

orders.[110] A decision of the CO can be appealed before the EAT on a point of law. Even if the political fund is in place, members have the power to withdraw the part of the subscription that would go towards political activities. Legislative provisions require trade unions to inform members that they can be exempted from the payment of such subscription.[111] TULRCA even spells out the relevant notice of objection in section 84. Finally, unions are limited to spend money on six activities which fit in the political objects defined by statute. Essentially, the expenditures covered relate to donations to political parties, organisations of conferences or meetings for or on behalf of the party, maintenance of holder of political offices or productions of materials encouraging members to vote or not to vote for a political party.[112] The CO is also the guardian of the political fund when it comes to its use, but parties could also go to court as with other remedies concerning unions' governance.[113]

In March 2011, 28 unions were reported to have a political fund.[114] The number has been in slow decline since 1999 when the figure was 38. This is primarily the result of amalgamations and mergers of unions. Most unions have renewed their political fund over the last ten years, usually by a substantial majority even if the turn out tends to be less than 50%.[115] £17 million was spent on political activities in 2010/11,[116] a figure that corresponds to the average spent over the last 12 years.[117] Very few complaints about political funds are brought to the CO. There were no more than 2 a year over the last 10 years and they rarely reached the point where the union was found to be in breach of the rules. FORD and HENDY argue that the complex rules that exist in relation to the political fund could be classed as unduly interfering with the autonomy of trade unions, and are therefore contrary to Article 11 ECHR (as was the case with ASLEF and exclusions). This is an interesting hypothesis that may need testing before the ECtHR.[118]

---

110   TULRCA, ss. 80 and 81.
111   TULRCA, s. 82(1)(b).
112   TULRCA, s. 72(1).
113   TULRCA, s. 71 and 72(A).
114   CO Annual Report 2010/11, para. 7.11.
115   See for example CO Annual Report 2004/5 para. 7.13 where 14 unions held a review ballot. There are also instances where a union created a political fund for the first time (National Association of Teachers – see CO Annual Report 2008/9 para. 7.9). There was only one case reported over the last 12 years where the resolution to have a political fund was rejected (by UNIFI – see para. 7.11 CO Annual Report 2000/1) and one case where the political fund lapsed following the trade union failure to hold a review ballot (CO Annual Report 2007/8 para. 7.13).
116   CO Annual Report 2010/11, para. 7.16.
117   The annual reports since 1999/2000 show that the amounts vary from £12.5 to £20.5 millions.
118   M. FORD and J. HENDY QC, above n. 19, p. 13.

4. CONCLUSION: TRADE UNION INTERNAL AFFAIRS AND THE LAW

The law regulating trade union internal affairs changed substantially and incrementally from the 1980s. While the common law struggled with the status to be given to the union and started encroaching on union freedom, statute imposed detailed rules to be respected on many fronts of union organisation. Most union rules have been superseded by statute. Trade unions must therefore ensure that they act in conformity with their own rules and that the latter are not in breach of relevant legislative provisions. This has increased costs and administrative burdens for unions, while seriously limiting their ability to discipline members who do not abide by union rules. While there was perhaps too much latitude and scope for mismanagement in the past and a case for increasing transparency and protection of individual members, the pendulum has swung too far the other way. This is notably demonstrated by the continued criticisms of the legal system by significant international bodies which protect fundamental social rights. Under the European Convention on Human Rights, the UK legislation was found to be in breach of Article 11.[119] This was a major achievement for the trade union movement as it was the first time that the court referred to trade union autonomy as part of freedom of association.[120] This has potentially wider implications for the national legislation if further put to the test before the European Court. TULRCA 1992 is still considered in breach of Article 5 of the European Social Charter which protects the right to organise.[121] The European Committee of Social Rights still considers that section 65 on discipline constitutes unjustified incursions into the autonomy of trade unions.[122] Further, before it was amended, section 174 was also analysed as putting excessive restrictions on trade unions' rights to determine their membership conditions. The latest changes introduced by the Employment Act 2008 may go towards answering some of the concerns previously raised by the Committee but the provisions remain cumbersome. Finally, the ILO Committee of Experts on Application of Conventions and Recommendations came to similar conclusions in relation to section 174 (before amendments)[123] and its incompatibility with

---

[119]   *ASLEF v UK* [2007] IRLR 361.

[120]   Ibid. para. 38 and M. FORD and J. HENDY QC, above n. 19, p. 6.

[121]   'With a view to ensuring or promoting the freedom of workers and employers to form local, national or international organisations for the protection of their economic and social interests and to join those organisations, the Parties undertake that national law shall not be such as to impair, nor shall it be so applied, as to impair this freedom [...]'.

[122]   The European Committee of Social Rights, *Conclusions XIX (2010)*.

[123]   See Committee of Experts on Application of Conventions and Recommendations. Individual Observation Concerning Freedom of Association and protection of the Right to Organise Convention (no87). (2007) available at <www.ilo.org/ilolex/english/newcountryframeE.htm> accessed 14.11.2011; see also chapter 2 and K.D. EWING, *Britain and the ILO*, Institute of Employment Rights, London 1994 and T. NOVITZ, 'Freedom of Association and 'Fairness at

Article 3 of Convention No 87 on Freedom of Association and Protection of the Rights to Organise 1948 which refers to trade unions' *'[...] right to draw up their constitutions and rules, to elect their representatives in full freedom, to organise their administration and activities and to formulate their programmes'*.[124] Considering the criticisms of the legislation and the legacy of the Conservative era, the Labour government remained surprisingly lifeless when it came to review the law. Since 1997, most of the changes have been prompted by decisions of the European Court of Human Rights. As seen, the current result is still not satisfactory. Prospects of change remain very slim under the current Coalition (Conservative-Liberal Democrat) Government. However, reforms are clearly needed because the system still reflects an out-dated reaction to a closed shop (which has now been abolished) and strong unions (which no longer exist in the same way that they did during the 1970s). It may be that further changes will be provoked by litigation before the European Court of Human Rights, as policy makers and courts are inactive. What is naturally always a disappointment is the fragmentary approach to reform forced by supranational rulings rather than a more comprehensive revision of the law.

Work': an Assessment of the Impact and Relevance of ILO Convention 87 on its Fiftieth Anniversary' (1998) 27 *ILJ* 169.

[124] The right of workers' and employers' organisations to draw up their constitution and rules without interference from public authorities.

CHAPTER 5

INDUSTRIAL CONFLICT

1. FORMS OF INDUSTRIAL CONFLICT AND THEIR MOTIVATIONS

Industrial conflict occurs where workers and their organisations, usually trade unions, disagree fundamentally with employers. Their disagreements may concern such matters as terms and conditions, closure of plants and redundancies, pension changes or even other issues, such as the ethics of particular employers' actions. Workers and their organisations may respond to the failure to resolve these disagreements by commencing industrial action, which can take a variety of forms.

The most common form of industrial action is the complete withdrawal of labour in a 'strike'.[1] Also used is action 'short of a strike', such as an overtime ban or a call out ban.[2] Action short of a strike can also include a 'work to rule' (following an employer's instructions to the letter so that performance of the contract takes a greater period of time),[3] or simply a 'go slow' (performing the tasks required more slowly).[4] Normally, action is authorised or endorsed by a trade union, because, as shall be discussed in this chapter, without such authorisation or endorsement, the worker who takes such action is exposed to dismissal.[5] Secondary or, as it is more commonly known, sympathetic action in support of another worker's dispute with a different employer, is illegal in the UK and therefore relatively rare. A trade union which authorises or endorses such action would be liable under the common law of tort to compensate an employer, and the employer would be able to seek an injunction to prevent such action

---

[1] As discussed in T. NOVITZ, 'Collective Action in the UK' in E. ALES and T. NOVITZ (eds.), *Collective Action and Fundamental Freedoms in Europe: Striking the Balance* Intersentia, Antwerp 2010, p. 173.

[2] Questions on the ballot paper, which have to be asked of workers if a trade union is to claim immunity from liability in tort, must differentiate between a 'strike' or 'industrial action short of a strike'. See Trade Union and Labour Relations (Consolidation) Act 1992 (TULRCA), s. 229(2) and (2A).

[3] See, for example, *Secretary of State v ASLEF* (No. 2) [1972] 2 QB 455.

[4] See, for example, *General Engineering Services Ltd v Kingston and St Andrew Corp* [1988] 3 All ER 867.

[5] TULRCA, ss. 237, 238 and 238A.

from taking place, as ordinary persons would be affected adversely by the action.[6] This makes sympathetic action unlikely to be authorised or endorsed by a trade union, exposing any worker who takes such action vulnerable to dismissal.

Notably, employers can also take industrial action, in the form of a full or partial lock-out which prevents workers from performing work at the workplace and thereby being paid to do so. However, exercise of a lock out is not specifically regulated by statute.[7] Instead, it may be understood to be governed by contractual principles, such that if workers are willing to work, the employer's conduct may entitle an employee to seek compensation for lost wages and potentially dismissal, but only where there has been a repudiatory breach.[8]

Clearly, the continuation of employment and avoidance of redundancies is a major issue in a time of recession. In 2009, when the credit crunch led to retrenchment in the private sector, there emerged a spate of industrial action. For example, when a wind turbine manufacturer decided to shut down, causing severe job losses, workers went on strike and (together with protestors in the green movement) occupied the employer's premises.[9] The maintenance of local jobs has also been a live issue, as was reflected in sympathetic action taken in support of workers protesting against the contracting out of work to posted workers at the Lindsey Oil Refinery.[10]

The public sector is more highly unionised than the private sector, so one would normally expect more industrial action in the latter. However, in the wake of the financial crisis in the month of June 2009, many more working days were lost due to labour disputes in the private sector (38,000) than in the public sector (9,000).[11] There has been a shift again, as the UK Conservative and Liberal-Democrat Coalition Government has sought to cut public spending, leading to

---

6   TULRCA, s. 224.

7   The sole exception is the Employment Rights Act 1996, s. 136(2) which prevents an employee claiming for dismissal by reason of redundancy where the employee could otherwise claim constructive dismissal by reason of a lock-out.

8   S. DEAKIN and G.S. MORRIS, *Labour Law*, 5th ed, Hart Publishing, Oxford 2009, p. 981.

9   P. LEWIS, Vestas workers fight on after eviction attempt fails, *The Guardian* 29.07.09.

10   A. GILLIAN and A. SPARROW, Strikes spread across Britain as oil refinery protest escalates *The Guardian* 30.01.09; A. SEAGER, I understand fears over jobs, says Brown on refinery strike, *The Guardian*, 31.01.09; R. BOOTH, Mediators called in as wildcat strikes spread across UK, *The Guardian*, 31.01.09; and P. WINTOUR, M. WAINWRIGHT and A. STRATTON, Refinery strike is over – but jobs fight goes on, *The Guardian*, 05.02.09. As regards subsequent action taken in June 2009, see G. WEARDEN, Deal ends Lindsey oil refinery dispute, *The Guardian*, 26.06.09; P. STIFF, Lindsey dispute settled as workers reinstated, *The Times*, 26.06.09.

11   See 'Labour Disputes statistics 1931 – 2011', available from Office for National Statistics at: <www.ons.gov.uk/ons/publications/re-reference-tables.html?newquery=*&newoffset=50&pageSize=25&content-type=Reference+table&edition=tcm%3A77–222441> accessed 31.10.11.

the loss of 111,000 public sector jobs in the second quarter of 2011 (while in the same period private sector employment rose by 41,000).[12] The vast majority of labour disputes in 2010–11 have therefore taken place in the public sector and are related to redundancies and changes to terms and conditions, including pensions. For example, between April – June 2011, there were 46 work stoppages in the public sector, resulting in 268,000 working days lost; whereas, in the private sector, there were only 19 work stoppages resulting in 29,000 days lost.[13] It is certainly no easier in the public sector to take industrial action, as shall become apparent when outlining the additional constraints which potentially arise in respect of such workers; this seems to be more a reflection of concern over public spending policies and their impact on workers.

This chapter examines the ways in which UK law seeks to regulate very different forms of industrial conflict, being responsive to the manner of collective action taken by workers and unions, as well as the motivations for such action.

2. AN INTRODUCTION TO UK REGULATION OF INDUSTRIAL CONFLICT

2.1. THE EDIFICE OF COMMON LAW AND STATUTE

In the UK, a common law country, it is not surprising that legal regulation of industrial conflict is built on UK courts' construction of the obligations arising from a contract of employment and the law of tort. The 'contract of employment' is understood to be breached by the worker who participates in industrial action. This is so, even in respect of what could be called a 'defensive' strike, itself a response to a repudiatory breach of contract by the employer.[14] Moreover, action short of a strike, such as an over-time ban, while not in strict breach of the express terms of the contract of employment, may still be regarded as in breach of implied terms of mutual trust and confidence and a duty of fidelity.[15] The

---

12   'Public Sector Employment – Q2 2011' Office for National Statistics, available at: <www.ons. gov.uk/ons/rel/pse/public-sector-employment/q2–2011/stb-public-sector-employment--q2–2011.html>, accessed 31.10.11.

13   'Labour Disputes statistics 1931 – 2011', above n. 11.

14   *Wilkins v Cantrelll and Cochrane (GB) Ltd* [1978] IRLR 483; *Solihull Metropolitan Borough v NUT* [1885] IRLR 211. This is despite the arguments of P. Elias, 'The Strike and Breach of Contract: A Reassessment' in K.D. Ewing, C. Geary and B. Hepple (eds.), *Human Rights and Labour Law: Essays for Paul O'Higgins*, Mansell, London 1994. See S. deakin and G.S. Morris n. 8 above, pp. 970–973. It would seem to be only where there is no contract of employment in existence, or notice of termination has been given by the employer, that breach will not be found. See, for example, *Boxfoldia v NGA* [1988] ICR 752 and *Burgess v Stevedoring Services* [2002] IRLR 810.

15   *Secretary of State v ASLEF* (No. 2) [1972] 2 QB 455; and in respect of a refusal to work overtime, see *Express & Star v Bunday* [1987] IRLR 423.

---

result is that, under common law, unless the employer is willing to accept a return to work after a strike has taken place, which has occurred for example (at least initially) in the Lindsey Oil Refinery dispute discussed above, it is unlikely that an employee will be able to do so. The employer has entirely free discretion to dismiss. This rather harsh result for employees is modified by statute, namely the Trade Union and Labour Relations (Consolidation) Act 1992 (TULRCA) in conjunction with protection from unfair dismissal provided by the Employment Rights Act 1996 (ERA). However, there is no statutory blanket protection from dismissal, even for those participating in strikes deemed lawful under this legislation. This construction of industrial action as a breach of contract also has implication for the payment of wages over the duration of a strike,[16] and it seems that employers can suspend or remove discretionary (non-contractual) benefits in retaliation for such action.[17]

In addition, the courts have accepted that where industrial action constitutes a breach of the contract of employment, to call a strike can be regarded *inter alia* as an inducement of breach of contract, giving rise to civil liability in tort.[18] Even when there is no breach of the contract of employment, liability may arise in tort for the way in which collective action has led indirectly to breach of a contract of supply of goods or services.[19] On this basis, and in reliance on other economic torts, such as interference with trade or business by unlawful means, civil liability can be imposed on an organiser of industrial action, whether the organiser is an individual or a union. In past years, the range of economic torts applicable to industrial action has been expanded and elaborated upon by the judiciary, more often by allowing an employer to gain an injunction to prevent action from taking place, rather than providing compensation after the fact.[20]

Once again, statute limits the effect of common law in the sphere of industrial disputes. There is no express provision made for a 'right to strike' in TULRCA, but the statute does provide for trade unions to claim statutory limitations on liability for having taken industrial action[21] and even statutory immunity from

---

[16] See discussion of *Cooper & Ors v The Isle of Wight College* [2008] IRLR 124 below at n. 57.

[17] 'BA strikers to forfeit cheap travel perks', BBC news, 24.03.10 available at: <http://news.bbc.co.uk/1/hi/8584720.stm> accessed 31.10.11. See also K.D. EWING, *Fighting Back: Resisting 'union busting' and 'strike breaking' in the BA dispute*, Institute of Employment Rights, London 2011 at 9.8.

[18] *Taff Vale Railway v Amalgamated Society of Railway Servants* [1901] AC 426.

[19] *DC Thomson & Co v Deakin* [1952] Ch 646; and *Torquay Hotel Ltd v Cousins* [1969] 2 Ch 106.

[20] For a useful outline of developments relating to economic torts, see S. DEAKIN and G.S. MORRIS, n. 8 above, pp. 899–914; G.S. MORRIS and T. ARCHER, *Collective Labour Law*, Hart, Oxford 2000, pp. 395–408; N. HUMPHRIES, *Trade Union Law*, Blackstones, London 1999, Chapter 6; C. BARROW, *Industrial Relations*, Cavendish, London 1997, pp. 283–302; and H. CARTY, 'Intentional Violation of Economic Interests: The Limits of Common Law Liability' (1988) 104 *Law Quarterly Review (LQR)* 250.

[21] TULRCA, s. 22 et seq.

liability in tort subject to certain stringent conditions relating to the aims of the industrial action taken and the procedures followed before such action takes place.[22] The relevant statutory provisions do not require, as in other jurisdictions, that a distinction be drawn between disputes of interest (for example, over the level of pay to be included in a new collective agreement) and disputes of right (for example, the legitimate interpretation of a collective agreement). However, they are restrictive nonetheless, and the scope of statutory immunity was eroded considerably from 1979 onwards, when Margaret Thatcher's Conservative Government first took power, such that employers have sought to rely increasingly on legal measures, such as injunctions, so as to prevent strikes from taking place.[23] There seems to have been little substantial change to the *status quo* under Labour Governments from 1997 onwards or under the Coalition Conservative-Liberal Democrat Government from 2010. This is despite the adoption of further pieces of industrial relations legislation (two Employment Relations Acts in 1999 and 2004). What may however have some impact is the development of domestic case law regarding injunctive relief which is slightly more lenient towards trade unions.[24] While trade unions have expressed considerable dissatisfaction with the state of the law and have proposed their own 'Trade Union Freedom Bill' as an alternative basis for labour legislation,[25] they remain unsuccessful.

2.2. THE POTENTIAL RELEVANCE OF INTERNATIONAL HUMAN RIGHTS LAW

The right to strike is explicitly recognised under international instruments ratified by the UK, such as Article 8 of the International Covenant of Economic, Social and Cultural Rights 1966 and Article 6(4) of the European Social Charter 1961. The supervisory bodies responsible for monitoring application of these obligations have criticised domestic UK law. For example, the UN Committee on Economic, Social and Cultural Rights held in 1997 and reiterated in 2002, in its regular reviews of the UK:

> that failure to incorporate the right to strike into domestic law constitutes a breach of Article 8 of the Covenant [...]. The Committee recommends that the right to strike be

---

22 TULRCA, s. 219 and s. 244.

23 See S. Fredman, 'The New Rights: Labour Law and Ideology in the Thatcher Years' (1992) 12 *OJLS* 24; B. Simpson, 'From *Thomson v Deakin* in 1952 to *P v NASUWT* in 2003' in K.D. Ewing (ed.), *The Right to Strike: From the Trade Disputes Act 1906 to a Trade Union Freedom Bill 2006*, Institute of Employment Rights, London 2006; and P. Davies and M. Freedland, *Labour Legislation and Public Policy*, Clarendon Press, Oxford 1993.

24 *RMT v SERCO* and *ASLEF v London & Birmingham Railway Ltd* [2011] IRLR 399 discussed below at n. 129.

25 J. Hendy and G. Gall, 'British Trade Union Rights Today and the Trade Union Freedom Bill' in K.D. Ewing, above n. 23.

established in legislation, and that strike action does not entail any more the loss of employment, and it expresses the view that the current notion of freedom to strike, which simply recognises the illegality of being submitted to an involuntary servitude, is insufficient to satisfy the requirements of Article 8 of the Covenant [...].[26]

However, the UK operates under a 'dualist' rather than a 'monist' system of law, such that actual legislation needs to be adopted to give international treaty obligations effect in domestic law. For this reason the UN Committee on Economic, Social and Cultural Rights has also asked that further legislative action be taken to ensure that the Covenant be incorporated in the domestic legal order,[27] but no UK Government has taken action to do so. References to a right to strike in point 13 of the Community Charter on the Fundamental Social Rights of Workers 1989 (CCFSRW) and Article 28 of the EU Charter of Fundamental Rights 2000 likewise have no binding legal status in the UK legal system, except insofar as they affect EU law.[28]

As a member of the ILO, the UK has been called upon to defend its practices relating to the right to strike before the ILO Governing Body Committee on Freedom of Association (ILO CFA) (which hears complaints relating to violations of freedom of association) and the ILO Committee of Experts on the Application of Conventions and Recommendations (CEACR) (which considers annual reports regarding compliance with ILO Conventions and Recommendations). These supervisory bodies have indicated that various aspects of UK law are in breach of ILO Conventions Nos. 87 and 98, which relate to the right to organise and to engage in collective bargaining, as well as constitutional guarantees of freedom of association applicable to all ILO members by virtue of their membership of the organisation. For example, in 2009 and again in 2011, the ILO CEACR found that lack of any legal protection for sympathy action in the UK is highly problematic, that there should be more effective measures to enable reinstatement of workers which employers wish to dismiss following collective action, and that the notice requirements imposed in respect of industrial action should be simplified.[29] Moreover, the ILO CFA has

---

[26]   Concluding Observations of the UN Committee on Economic, Social and Cultural Rights 1997 (UK), para. 11 and 2002 (UK), para. 16.

[27]   Concluding Observations of the UN Committee on Economic, Social and Cultural Rights 2002 (UK), para. 11; and 2009 (UK), para. 13.

[28]   Note that the Protocol on the Application of the Charter of Fundamental Rights of the European Union to Poland and to the United Kingdom, appended to the Lisbon Treaty, states, *inter alia*, that 'for the avoidance of doubt, nothing in Title IV – Solidarity of the Charter creates justiciable rights applicable to Poland and the United Kingdom except in so far as Poland and the United Kingdom has provided for such rights in its national law'.

[29]   Report of the ILO CEACR 2009 and 2011, (in relation to the UK and Convention No. 87). For similar views expressed by the European Social Rights in relation to compliance with Art. 6(4) of the European Social Charter, see Conclusions XIX-3 (2010) at pp. 14–15.

found that restrictions placed on the right to strike in the prisons service are problematic insofar as these are not accompanied by adequate, impartial and speedy conciliation and arbitration proceedings, the outcomes of which are fully and properly implemented.[30]

Nevertheless, while this last finding of the ILO CFA was cited in a judgment of the English High Court delivered by Mr Justice Wyn Williams, *The Ministry of Justice v POA*, it was not considered to be determinative. Instead, the court respected the UK Government's assertion of an entitlement under domestic legislation to depart from the findings of the Pay Review Body on the basis of 'affordability'.[31] Even propositions presented by John Hendy QC in reliance on Article 11 of the ECHR were rejected.[32] As this judgment illustrates, international legal sources have relatively little influence on determinations in UK courts.

The only recent development which might affect the outcome of that case is the subsequent judgment of a Chamber of the European Court of Human Rights in *Enerji Yapi-Yol Sen v Turkey*.[33] In the *POA* case, the UK government's submissions made reference to past case law of the European Court of Human Rights which suggested that a right to strike is not a necessary aspect of freedom of association under Article 11 of the ECHR.[34] However, the judgment in *Enerji Yapi-Yol Sen*, in a manner comparable to *Demir & Baykara v Turkey*,[35] makes a clear connection between freedom of association and industrial action, such that the latter cannot be restricted other than in narrowly defined circumstances which must be provided for by law, have a legitimate aim and be necessary in a democratic society.[36] In this way, the barriers otherwise arising by virtue of the UK's dualist legal system, could be overcome. As was explained in Chapter 2, should UK legislation be itself in violation of Article 11, it will not be regarded as invalid; the UK courts have a power to issue a 'declaration of incompatibility', thereby placing political pressure on the UK Parliament to engage in legislative

---

30 Case No. 2383 (UK), 336th Report of the ILO Committee on Freedom of Association (2005) paras. 773 and 777, cited in *The Ministry of Justice v POA* [2008] IRLR 380 at para. 42.

31 *The Ministry of Justice v POA* [2008] IRLR 380 at para. 42.

32 Ibid., at paras. 58–61.

33 Application No. 68959/01, *Enerji Yapi-Yol Sen v Turkey*, judgment of 21 April 2009, discussed above in Chapter 2.

34 Application No. 5589/72 *Schmidt and Dahlstrom v Sweden*, para. 36 and *UNISON v UK* [2002] IRLR 497, para. 497. See E. Szyszczak, 'The United Kingdom' in R. Blanpain and A.M. Swiatkowski (eds.), *The Laval and Viking Cases: Freedom of Services and Establishment v Industrial Conflict in the European Union* (2009) 69 *Bulletin of Comparative Labour Relations* 168, 175.

35 Application No. 34503/97 *Demir and Baykara v Turkey*, judgment of 12 November 2008, discussed in chapter 2 above.

36 See this volume, above chapter 2, for more extensive discussion of this case law on freedom of association, collective bargaining and the right to strike.

reform.[37] In the meantime, UK courts are now bound to interpret legislation (insofar as this will not distort the meaning of the statute),[38] and arguably apply common law principles[39] in accordance with Strasbourg jurisprudence on this point.[40] This may, at least, have some impact on the extent to which judges are willing to issue injunctions, moving to a more 'neutral' approach, rather than one wholly sympathetic to the perspective of employers.[41]

3. THE LEGAL DEFINITION OF A STRIKE

It should be reiterated that UK law on industrial action is peculiar in its failure to provide a right to strike. British courts have refused to contemplate such a development at common law and the legislature has been reluctant to ensure its introduction via statute. Instead, UK legislation provides only for narrowly circumscribed protections from dismissal for striking workers and restricted immunity for trade unions from liability in tort.

This state of affairs was defended by the Donovan Commission Report back in 1968 on the following basis:

> The right to strike is, basically, a right to withdraw labour in combination without being subject to the legal consequences which would, in the past, have followed. This situation is now well recognised and we do not think it can be improved by granting the right in express terms.[42]

This argument does not, however, withstand closer scrutiny. As A.C.L. DAVIES has noted common law is apt to develop further and statutory immunities have not altogether kept pace with the innovations of the courts. This is particularly true in terms of the public sector. Moreover, as DAVIES also observes *'the concept of an "immunity" does not have the same rhetorical force as the term "right" and may even have negative connotations'*.[43] Immunities are more vulnerable to challenge.[44]

---

[37]   Human Rights Act 1996 (HRA), s. 4.
[38]   HRA, s. 3.
[39]   HRA, s. 6; see also K.D. EWING, 'Human Rights and Labour Law' (1998) 27 *ILJ* 275.
[40]   HRA, s. 2. See G.S. MORRIS and T. ARCHER, above n. 20, chapter 1.
[41]   *RMT v Serco Docklands; ASLEF v London Midland* [2011] IRLR 399 discussed further below at n. 129.
[42]   *Royal Commission Report on Trade Union and Employers' Associations 1965–1968 (Donovan Royal Commission Report)* Cmnd 3623 (1968) para. 935.
[43]   A.C.L. DAVIES, *Perspectives on Labour Law*, 2nd ed., Cambridge University Press, Cambridge 2009, p. 229.
[44]   See for detailed discussion of these challenges, see T. NOVITZ and P. SKIDMORE, *Fairness at Work: A Critical Analysis of the Employment Relations Act 1999 and its Treatment of Collective Rights*, Hart, Oxford 2001, chapter 5.

Not only are judges prone to adopt a narrow construction of statutory immunities,[45] but as HAYEK and others at the Institute of Economic Affairs demonstrated in the 1980s, the language of 'immunities' makes trade unions sound like an indefensibly privileged group.[46] The Institute of Employment Rights, on the opposite side of the political spectrum, acknowledges the force of the language of rights,[47] but has yet to be successful in persuading recent governments to introduce such an entitlement through legislation.

While there is no right to strike under UK legislation, a definition of a strike is nevertheless provided by statute. The term is understood to mean 'any concerted stoppage of work',[48] and:

(a)   the cessation of work by a body of employed persons acting in combination, or

(b)   a concerted refusal, or a refusal under a common understanding, of any number of employed persons to continue to work for an employer in consequence of a dispute,

done as a means of compelling their employer or any employed person or body of employed persons, or to aid other employees in compelling their employer or any employed person or body of employed persons, to accept or not to accept terms or conditions of or affecting employment.[49]

Statute thereby acknowledges the crucial role that strikes play in enhancing workers' bargaining position in negotiations with their employer. This is, however, a definition which does not contemplate collective action taken for any reason other than workers' self-interest and complements statutory constraints placed elsewhere on secondary action and political strikes, discussed below.

---

[45]   See *Express Newspapers v MacShane* [1979] IRLR 210.

[46]   F.A. HAYEK, *1980s Unemployment and the Unions: Essays on the Impotent Price Structure of Britain and Monopoly in the Labour Market*, 2nd ed., Institute of Economic Affairs, London: 1984; A. SHENFFIELD, *What Right to Strike? With Commentaries by Cyril Grunfeld and Sir Leonard Neal*, Institute of Economic Affairs London 1986. See also for a contemporary discussion of this rhetoric, K. SYRETT, '"Immunity", "Privilege" and "Right": British Trade Unions and the Language of Labour Law Reform"' (1998) 25 *JLS* (*Journal of Law and Society*) 388 especially at 390–3.

[47]   K.D. EWING and C. JONES, 'From the Trade Disputes Act to the Trade Union Freedom Bill' in K.D. EWING, above n. 23, p. 5.

[48]   TULRCA, s. 246.

[49]   Employment Rights Act 1996, s. 235(5).

4. THE CONSEQUENCES OF INDUSTRIAL ACTION FOR PARTICIPANTS

Collective action will almost invariably be regarded as a breach of the contract of employment. This breach entitles an employer to elect a variety of responses, which can be taken cumulatively. For example, an employer may deduct wages and also dismiss the employee who takes industrial action, subject to limited protections available to the employee under UK statute.

4.1. PROPORTIONATE WITHDRAWAL OF PAY (AND DISPROPORTIONATE REMOVAL OF BENEFITS)

It has been established at common law that an employer is entitled to withdraw pay from any worker participating in collective action. In the event of a strike which entails the complete withdrawal of labour for a period of time, this is relatively straightforward to calculate, in that no payment needs to be made for the period that the employee is absent from work.[50] It has been less clear whether this calculation should take account of annual holiday entitlements and how it should be calculated when employees pursue action short of a strike, such as a go-slow or a work-to-rule. Moreover, the legal basis on which an employer is entitled to do this is not settled.

In *Sim v Rotherham Metropolitan Borough Council*[51] the employer – the education authority – deducted a percentage of the salary of teachers who were taking part in industrial action and refused to cover the teaching of absent colleagues. Their breach of the implied contractual duty of trust and co-operation caused damage to the employer, the cost of which became deductible from their wages under the doctrine of equitable set-off.[52]

By way of contrast, in *Wiluszynski v London Borough of Tower Hamlets*,[53] the Court of Appeal found that an employer may withhold all of an employee's salary where industrial action results in only partial performance of the contract by the employee. In that case, the employees had refused to answer queries from Borough constituents, but were able to deal with the queries swiftly when the action had ended. The employer was held to have acted lawfully in completely withholding pay for the entire period of the industrial action.[54] Subsequently,

---

[50] *Ticehurst v British Telecom* [1992] ICR 383.
[51] *Sim v Rotherham Metropolitan Borough Council* [1987] Ch 216.
[52] See for analysis of the case law, T. Novitz and C. Villiers, 'The 2006 Higher Education Pay Dispute: The Reality of Partnership Rhetoric?' (2007) 27 *Legal Studies* 486, 499–501.
[53] *Wiluszynski v London Borough of Tower Hamlets* [1989] IRLR 259.
[54] Ibid., 262.

the decision in *Wiluszynski* has been criticised on the basis that the reasoning sits uncomfortably with the law of restitution.[55] This rule also allows employers to impose a disproportionate penalty on industrial action in violation of the European Social Charter 1961 and International Labour Organization (ILO) Convention No. 87.[56]

In *Cooper & Ors v The Isle of Wight College*,[57] Blake J acknowledged the lack of an 'unambiguous authority' on the question in point.[58] He decided that the calculation of a proportionate deduction from pay had to be calculated on the basis, not of what overall losses were suffered by the employer by reason of partial non-performance, but what an employee could properly claim in respect of the one day's lost pay had the employer not been entitled to withhold remuneration. If an employee were wrongly not paid one day's wages, the most he could recover would be one day's pay, namely 1/260 of salary. This then was what, in this instance, the employer could lawfully withhold by virtue of industrial action.

Nevertheless, in the recent BA dispute of 2009–10, the particularities of air crew roster systems led, in some circumstances to docking of up to two weeks' pay for one day's industrial action, as well as removal of travel allowances indefinitely.[59] These were restored under a settlement agreement in May 2011, suggesting that industrial realities are sometimes more likely to determine the repercussions of a strike for workers than legal constraints on employer sanctions.[60]

4.2. DISMISSAL

Another option available to an employer under common law is dismissal, on the basis that there has been a fundamental breach of the contract of employment.[61] This power is affected by statute in two ways.

Firstly, where 'official industrial action' is taken, there is protection from 'selective dismissal'. This means that an employer must either dismiss all or none of the striking workers and cannot seek to penalise only perceived

---

[55] G. MEAD, 'Restitution within Contract?' (1991) 11 *Legal Studies* 172, 179.

[56] See European Committee of Social Rights, *Conclusions* XV-I, 254–7; and *Freedom of Association: Digest of Decisions and Principles of the Freedom of Association Committee of the Governing Body of the ILO*, 4th edn, ILO, Geneva 1996, paras. 595 and 570–574.

[57] *Cooper & Ors v The Isle of Wight College* [2008] IRLR 124.

[58] Ibid. at para. 5.

[59] H. WALLOP, BA Strike: strike for one day – lose up to two weeks' pay, *The Telegraph* 27.03.10.

[60] For terms of the settlement, see <http://uniteba.com/LATESTNEWSUPDATES.html.> accessed 31.10.2011 and K.D. EWING, above n. 17, chapter 9.

[61] See above ns 14–15.

'troublemakers'.[62] Employers may re-engage some but not all striking employees, but only after a three month period has expired.

It was a Conservative Government which introduced the requirement that industrial action be 'official' via the Employment Act 1990. This was a clever strategy for it has the effect of placing trade unions in a very awkward position.[63] Industrial action will be 'official' where none of those taking part in industrial action are members of the union or where the trade union authorises or endorses action taken by a group of workers which include its members. British unions then face a difficult choice where the 'rank and file' are enthusiastic participants in and instigators of industrial action. A union will expose its members to selective dismissal if it does not authorise and endorse the action taken,[64] but by providing authorisation or endorsement, the union exposes itself to potential civil liability in tort (and a union without assets is of little use to its members).[65] This is a difficulty which has arisen particularly in the context of secondary action. For example, when the Liverpool dockers refused to cross a picket line, the Transport and General Workers' Union (TGWU) could not endorse their actions so as to protect them from dismissal, without exposing the union to substantial liability.[66]

In 1999, a Labour Government introduced further legislative protection from dismissal, which was further consolidated in 2004.[67] This is available only to employees taking 'protected' industrial action, which is 'official' *and* which will not give rise to liability in tort. Such a requirement places an even greater burden on trade unions to ensure that the action taken will be immune from liability in tort, not only by reason of its aims and objectives, but also by satisfying ballot and notice requirements.[68] In other words, the Labour Government was not minded to remove the dilemma which the requirement of 'official action' imposed on trade unions, but to further reinforce it. This legislative provision shields the employees from dismissal for a limited 'protected period', which was initially eight weeks, but has now been extended to twelve weeks, after amendment by the Employment Relations Act 2004. An employee can also claim

---

62   TULRCA, ss. 237–238.
63   Employment Act 1990 s. 9. See also *Unofficial Action and the Law* Cm 821 (1989).
64   Moreover, this provision was introduced in conjunction with the requirement that trade unions be regarded as legally responsible for organisation of industrial disputes not only by full-time officials but also shop stewards, unless the trade union unequivocally repudiated the action by notifying all its 'relevant' members in writing. See Employment Act 1990, s. 6; and now TULRCA 1992 s. 21. See B. Simpson, 'The Employment Act 1990 in Context' (1991) 54 *MLR* 418, 427–9.
65   TULRCA, s. 20.
66   <www.labournet.net/docks2/9702/bmrecord.htm> accessed 31.10.11.
67   TULRCA, s. 238A.
68   For comment, see T. Novitz and P. Skidmore above n. 44, pp. 41–2.

protection after that period where the employer (and not the union) has acted unreasonably. Other changes were made in 2004 which can be linked to concerns arising from the *Friction Dynamics* case, where an employer had sought to deprive employees of protection from dismissal by implementing a lock-out which went beyond the protected period for dismissal.[69] The Labour Government's legislative response was to extend the protected period by a day for every day that the employee is locked out,[70] and to impose new procedural duties on employers to seek a resolution to the dispute.[71] However, it should still be noted that, even where a claim for unfair dismissal for industrial action is established, the likelihood of reinstatement or re-engagement by the same employer is minimal.[72]

In commenting on the twelve week period of protection under UK labour legislation, the ILO Committee of Experts has observed that:

> The Committee recalls the importance it attaches to the maintenance of the employment relationship as a normal consequence of the recognition of the right to strike [...] it considers that restricting the right to maintain the employment relationship to industrial action of twelve weeks or less places an arbitrary limit on the effective protection of the right to strike in a manner contrary to the Convention [...] The Committee therefore once requests the Government to review the [TULRCA] [...] with a view to strengthening the protection available to workers [...].[73]

Unsurprisingly, the European Committee of Social Rights responsible for supervision of implementation of the European Social Charter has come to the same conclusion, namely that the twelve week period is merely 'arbitrary' and therefore an indefensible restriction on the right to strike.[74]

The current Coalition government has not altered this system since coming to power in 2010, but is carrying on an extensive Employment Law Review, the

---

[69] *Davis v Friction Dynamics*, Employment Tribunal (Liverpool), no. 6500432, unreported. See discussion of the case by Ms Hewitt, HC Hansard, 14.1.4, vol. 416, col. 826; and Lord Sainsbury HL Hansard, 29.4.4, col. 905.

[70] Employment Relations Act (ERelA) 2004, s. 26 amending s. 238A TULRCA 1992.

[71] ERelA 2004, s. 28, amending s. 238A and inserting s. 238B TULRCA 1992.

[72] Ministry of Justice Tribunals Services, *Employment Tribunal and EAT Statistics 2009–10* (2010) reported that unfair dismissal cases were only successful in 10% of all instances, and that reinstatement or re-engagement was ordered only in 6 cases involving unfair dismissal, representing less than 1% of all unfair dismissal cases that went to a hearing. This has been the subject of concern in Report of the ILO CEACR 2011, (in relation to the UK and Convention No. 87).

[73] Report of the ILO CEACR 2011 (in relation to the UK and Convention No. 87).

[74] See Conclusions XIX-3 (2010) at 14–15.

outcomes of which are (at the time of writing) largely unclear.[75] It does however seem unlikely that there will be any legislative response to criticism of this aspect of domestic legislation emanating from the ILO and Council of Europe.

5. CONSEQUENCES OF COLLECTIVE ACTION FOR ORGANISERS

Within the British common law tradition, long established 'economic' or 'industrial' torts allow trade unions and workers to be held liable as organisers to third parties affected by the collective action, despite the lack of any contractual nexus between them. These include the torts of direct and indirect inducement of breach of contract, unlawful interference with performance of a contract, inducement of breach of statutory duty, intimidation and conspiracy.[76]

A strike organiser may be liable for inducing breach of contract either directly and indirectly. Direct inducement of a breach of contract is said to take place '*if A intentionally induces B to breach a contract between B and C to the damage of C*'.[77] C then has a cause of action against A. For example, where a union induces the breach of a contract of employment between a worker and an employer, then an employer can claim against the union.[78] Indirect inducement will occur where A does not directly induce the breach of contract between B and C, but uses unlawful means to achieve this end. For example, '*where A persuades B's employees to take industrial action in breach of their contracts of employment and by these unlawful means produces the result that B is unable to fulfil a commercial contract with C*'.[79] C may then claim against A.[80]

The tort of *inducement* of breach of contract came to be supplemented by the tort of *interference* with contract, business or trade. This 'genus' or 'supertort' tort seemed to remove the requirement of actual breach of the contract, so that mere interference will suffice, where this causes economic loss. However, the expansion of this tort seems to have been halted by the intervention of the House

---

[75]   See <www.bis.gov.uk/policies/employment-matters/employment-law-review> last checked 19.1.12.
[76]   See LORD WEDDERBURN, *The Worker and the Law*, 3rd ed., Pelican, London 1986, chapter 7; and also H. CARTY, above n. 20.
[77]   S. DEAKIN and G.S. MORRIS, *Labour Law*, 4th ed., Hart Publishing, Oxford 2005, p. 976. See also S. DEAKIN and G.S. MORRIS, above n. 8, pp. 900 et seq. for the impact on this tort of *OBG v Allan* [2007] IRLR 608, discussed below at n. 82.
[78]   *South Wales Miners' Federation v Glamorgan Coal Co Ltd* [1905] AC 239.
[79]   S. DEAKIN and G.S. MORRIS, 2005, above n. 77, p. 979. See also S. DEAKIN and G.S. MORRIS, 2009, above n. 8, p. 905 et seq.
[80]   See *J.T. Stratford and Son Ltd v Lindley* [1965] AC 269.

of Lords, which has circumscribed its application.[81] *'Bare interference with a contract which does not amount to a breach [...] will not suffice for the purposes of this tort.'*[82]

The tort of intimidation can be linked to that of unlawful means and again has a direct and indirect form. It is committed where unlawful threats are made directly to the plaintiff or where unlawful threats are made to a third party with the intention of causing the plaintiff loss. Furthermore, industrial action can also be regarded as a 'conspiracy' in the law of tort. While section 3 of the Conspiracy and Protection of Property Act 1875 abolished the application of criminal conspiracy to collective action, the tort of conspiracy remained untouched. However, the House of Lords finally established, in *Crofter Hand Woven Harris Tweed Co v Veitch*,[83] that if the industrial action is aimed at legitimate subjects of collective bargaining, namely a lawful trade dispute, as itemised below, there can be no actionable conspiracy in tort.

Most notable is the tort of breach of statutory duty, which would seem to place particular constraints on public service employees. There is only one case on point today, which did not itself concern the liability of the union, but indicated that organisation of strike action could be regarded as inducing the local authority to breach its statutory duty to provide full-time education to school students.[84] Liability for breach of statutory duty is now set out in various statutes, including those regarding supply of telecommunications,[85] gas,[86] electricity,[87] water.[88] It also applies to prison officers.[89]

An employer's entitlement to bring an action on the basis of the economic torts has, however, been limited by statute in two significant respects.

---

[81]   *OBG Ltd v Allan* [2008] 1 AC 1 and *Total Network SL v HMRC* [2008] 1 AC 1174 discussed in S. DEAKIN and J. RANDALL, 'Rethinking the Economic Torts' (2009) 72 *MLR* 519.

[82]   S. DEAKIN and G.S. MORRIS above n. 8, pp. 901–2.

[83]   *Crofter Hand Woven Harris Tweed Co v Veitch* [1942] AC 435.

[84]   *Meade v Haringey* [1979] ICR 494. Note that the scope of this tort was restricted in *Associated British Ports v Transport and General Workers' Union* [1989] IRLR 399, where there was a statutory scheme which required 'work for such periods as are reasonable in the circumstances of the case'. The claim was made that the union, by organising industrial action, was inducing a breach of a non-actionable statutory duty. The House of Lords rejected this claim on the basis that the clause imposed a contractual obligation (as opposed to a statutory) obligation to work.

[85]   Telecommunications Act 1984, s. 18; now Communications Act 2003, s. 104(3).

[86]   Gas Act 1986, s. 30.

[87]   Electricity Act 1989, s. 27.

[88]   Water Industry Act 1991, s. 22. See S. DEAKIN and G.S. MORRIS, above n. 8, at p. 904.

[89]   See Criminal Justice and Public Order Act 1994, since amended by Criminal Justice and Immigration Act 2008.

The first is by a statutory cap on damages. Section 22 of TULRCA sets out a scale of maximum awards of damages which may be awarded against a trade union which is liable in tort. The exceptions not covered by the statutory provision are:

(a) proceedings for personal injury as a result of negligence, nuisance or breach of duty;
(b) proceedings for breach of duty in connection with the ownership, occupation, possession, control or use of property; and
(c) product liability in the context of consumer protection.

The maximum award for a union of more than 100,000 members is £250,000; for a union of 25,000 or more but less than 100,000 members it is £125,000; for a union of 5,000 or more but less than 25,000 members it is £50,000; and for a union of less than 5,000 members it is £10,000. Notably this provision only applies to a 'trade union' within the meaning of sections 1 and 2 of TULRCA, that is, an organisation which meets the criteria necessary to be kept on the Certification Officer's list of trade unions.[90]

The second is the statutory immunity provided for industrial action which makes provision for definition of a 'lawful trade dispute'.[91] This requires that the collective action pursue one of a number of narrowly defined objectives,[92] and that detailed procedural notice and balloting requirements are met.[93] Despite the amendments to these provisions by New Labour governments in 1999 and 2004,[94] it remains difficult to be certain that any given industrial action meets all of the detailed statutory requirements and has acquired immunity from liability in tort.[95] This has significant implications for the availability of injunctive relief to employers who have only to establish a *prima facie* case that the conduct of the union lies outside the scope of the statutory immunity and that the balance of convenience falls in the employer's favour.[96]

---

[90] See this volume above chapter 1.
[91] TULRCA 1992, s. 219 and 244. See K.D. EWING, above n. 23, which traces the history of this statutory immunity and its restrictive interpretation by British courts.
[92] TULRCA 1992, s. 244(1).
[93] See, in particular, reforms made by the Employment Acts of 1980, 1984, 1988, and 1990, which were incorporated into TULRCA 1992. See P. DAVIES and M. FREEDLAND, n. 23 above, Chapter 9. Note also the amendments made to TULRCA by the Trade Union Reform and Employment Rights Act (TURERA) 1993, discussed in S. McKAY, *The Law on Industrial Action under the Conservatives*, Institute of Employment Rights, London 1996.
[94] See for example the current wording of TULRCA, s. 232B, following amendment by the Employment Relations Act 2004.
[95] For an example of this uncertainty in practice, see T. NOVITZ and C. VILLIERS, above n. 52.
[96] For the application of *American Cyanamid Ltd v Ethicon Ltd* [1975] AC 396, see this chapter further below.

5.1. THE LEGITIMATE AIMS OF INDUSTRIAL ACTION

The Trade Disputes Act 1906, albeit in modified form, provides the foundation of British labour legislation governing the lawful aims of industrial action, now set out in sections 219 – 245 of TULRCA.[97] These statutory provisions establish that, in order for a person to claim immunity for liability from the economic torts, that person must demonstrate that the act in question was done '*in contemplation or furtherance of a trade dispute*'.[98]

A '*trade dispute*' is said in section 244 to be a '*dispute between workers and their employer*'. This wording can be linked to the clear legislative statement that secondary action in support of another dispute is not permissible under British legislation.[99] This rule has various implications. Firstly, there is no immunity for industrial action relating to demarcations disputes, that is, disputes between trade unions as to who should represent a group of workers.[100] Secondly, a canny domestic employer can artificially divide its workforce by creating ostensibly separate 'buffer companies' and thereby avoid combined industrial action. In *Dimbleby & Sons Ltd v NUJ*,[101] the House of Lords refused to pierce an artificial corporate veil, with the result that workers could no longer take action in solidarity with one another, even though they had previously been employed within a single enterprise. A further illustration was the recent dispute between the NUJ and Johnston Press. The NUJ had attempted to call industrial action to fight the closure of a pension scheme and prevent a wage freeze, but Johnston Press successfully argued that 600 journalists were not employees of the publishing group but of the smaller subsidiary businesses running each individual newspaper. As a result, an injunction was granted in the High Court to prevent the strike taking place.[102] The NUJ were informed that they could not call co-ordinated action of this kind, even though decisions regarding all workers' pensions and pay were, as a matter of fact, taken at a higher level by Johnston Press. In other words, there is an onus on unions to bargain at the level of the enterprise, when in reality the employer is not deciding on terms and conditions at that level. Finally, this prevents coordinated action across national borders where workers might otherwise wish to take action in support of each other where they work in the same or related industries, or where they work for interconnected companies (which have the same multinational parent

---

[97]   Lord Wedderburn, 'Labour Law 2008: Forty Years On' (2007) 36 *ILJ* 397, 422.

[98]   Meeting the requirements of TULRCA, s. 219.

[99]   TULRCA, s. 224.

[100]   See T. Novitz and P. Skidmore, above n. 44, pp. 139–40.

[101]   *Dimbleby & Sons Ltd v NUJ* [1984] IRLR 161.

[102]   *Johnston Press v National Union of Journalists*, May 2010, High Court, unrep. See <www.personneltoday.com/articles/2010/05/19/55623/johnston-press-secures-high-court-injunction-against.html> accessed 31.10.11.

company).[103] In this way, UK legislation on secondary action deters British workers from engaging in such an endeavour to secure international or European-level collective agreements.[104] It is on this basis, amongst others, that the ILO CEACR has been critical of UK legislation relating to collective action:

> The Committee emphasizes that the globalization of the economy and the delocalization of work centres may have a severe impact on the right of workers' organizations to organize their activities in a manner as to defend effectively their members' interests should lawful industrial action be too restrictively defined. The Committee therefore recalls that workers should be able to participate in sympathy strikes, provided the initial strike they are supporting is lawful, and to take industrial action in relation to social and economic matters which affect them [...]'[105]

The term 'trade dispute' also does not cover a dispute aimed at ensuring terms and conditions are extended to future employees or in respect of an unidentified future employer.[106] This means that in the situation where there is a 'transfer of an undertaking' such as 'contracting out of services' from the public to the private sector (that is, 'privatisation'), workers are only entitled to take action to defend their present terms and conditions enforceable against their present employer; they cannot oppose any plan which proposes to offer lower terms and conditions to future workers of the new employer. This has been described by the European Committee of Social Rights, responsible for supervision of the European Social Charter, to constitute a breach of the right to take collective action set out in Article 6 of that instrument. On this basis the Committee has found that '*the scope for workers to defend their interests through lawful collective action*' is '*excessively circumscribed in the United Kingdom*'.[107]

Notably, in this scenario of a transfer in the public sector, workers are also unable to oppose the policy of privatisation itself. This would amount to a political strike.[108] Political strikes aimed at challenging Government policy are likewise not covered by statutory immunity.

---

[103]   See K.W. WEDDERBURN, 'Multi-national Enterprise and National Labour Law' (1972) 1 *ILJ* 12; and W. WARNECK, 'Transnational Collective Action – Already a Reality?' in F. DORSSEMONT, T. JASPERS and A. VON HOEK (eds.), *Cross-Border Collective Actions in Europe: A Legal Challenge*, Intersentia, Antwerpen-Oxford 2007.

[104]   K.D. EWING, 'British Labour Law and Private International Law' in F. DORSSEMONT et al, above n. 103.

[105]   See most recently Report of the ILO CEACR 2011, (in relation to the UK and ILO Convention No. 87).

[106]   *University College London Hospital NHS Trust v Unison* [1999] IRLR 31; found not to be in violation of Article 11 of the European Convention on Human Rights by the European Court of Human Rights in *Unison v UK* [2002] IRLR 497.

[107]   See Conclusions XIX-3 (2010) at 14.

[108]   See *Mercury Communications Ltd v Scott-Garner* [1983] IRLR 494, discussed further below.

This state of affairs follows from the requirement, under section 244(1) of TULRCA, that a trade dispute relates 'wholly or mainly' to one or more matters listed therein. They are:

(a) terms and conditions of employment, or the physical conditions in which any workers are required to work;

(b) engagement or non-engagement, or termination or suspension of employment or the duties of employment between workers or groups of workers;

(c) allocation of work or the duties of employment between workers or groups of workers;

(d) matters of discipline;

(e) a worker's membership or non-membership of a union;

(f) facilities for officials of trade unions; and

(g) machinery for negotiation or consultation, and other procedures, relating to any of the above matters, including the recognition by employers or employers' associations of the right of a trade union to represent workers in such negotiation or consultation or in the carrying out of such procedures.

There is no requirement under UK law to consider whether the action taken is in any way proportionate to the aims pursued.

In the UK, prior to 1982, industrial action which related to broader issues was lawful if a connection could be found with the matters listed as the appropriate subject of a 'trade dispute'. It did not matter whether a strike had more than one object in mind, or that the predominant object was political, as long as the actual demand resisted by the employer had some relationship to a matter on that list.[109] Concerned by the scope this gave to unions to organise lawful industrial action, the Conservative Thatcher Government introduced the 'wholly or mainly' requirement.[110] From this date, the 'predominant motive' test has been used to exclude industrial action from statutory protection. For example, in the case of *Mercury Communications v Scott-Garner*,[111] the Post Office Engineers Union (POEU) had called on members to oppose to privatisation in the telecommunications industry and to refuse to connect Mercury, a private company, to the British Telecommunications (BT) network. Mercury sought an injunction on the grounds that this was unlawful industrial action. The Court of Appeal found that the main aim of the strike was not to oppose the particular job losses that would follow from privatisation, but to express general opposition

---

[109] See the judgments of Lord Diplock in *NWL v Woods* [1979] IRLR 478 and *Duport Steels Ltd v Sirs* [1980] IRLR 116.

[110] Discussed in P. DAVIES and M. FREEDLAND, *Labour Law: Text and Materials*, 2nd ed., Weidenfeld and Nicolson, London 1984, pp. 802–5.

[111] *Mercury Communications v Scott-Garner* [1983] IRLR 494.

to this government policy. They considered that had job security been the union's chief concern, the union could have sought to have the matter dealt with under a Job Security Agreement. The union had therefore failed to satisfy the 'wholly or mainly' test and could not establish the existence of a lawful 'trade dispute'.[112] Nevertheless, it should be observed that this test can be and has been applied more leniently in certain instances, reflecting the broader interests of workers. For example, a dispute over whether teachers were obliged to teach a disruptive pupil was held, in these terms, to constitute a 'trade dispute'.[113]

A dispute between workers and Ministers of the Crown can only constitute a lawful trade dispute where it relates to matters which have been referred for consideration by a joint body on which the Minister is represented by virtue of any enactment or which cannot be settled without the Minister exercising a power conferred on the Minister by or under any enactment. The application of this provision seems to be confined to the situation where an employer (usually in the public sector) has to rely on the government to authorise the grant of the workers' demands,[114] and industrial action is not otherwise rendered inappropriate by legislation governing that sector of employment.[115]

In addition, two judgments of the European Court of Justice have added an additional substantive limitation on the legitimate substance of a trade dispute, despite their preparedness to recognise a right to strike.[116] It would now seem that where action is taken which is aimed at or has the effect of impeding free movement of goods, services, establishment or workers between EU Member States, this will be the subject of particular scrutiny.[117] UK unions will, it seems, be unable to take industrial action lawfully in support of improved terms and conditions for workers posted from one EU Member State to another, unless some form of 'social dumping' can be established,[118] which may be taken to mean the worst kind of discrimination by employers, leading to a detrimental effect on terms and conditions of local workers. In other cases involving free movement principles, it seems that UK unions will need to establish that the

---

[112]   P. DAVIES and M. FREEDLAND, above n. 110, p. 621.

[113]   *P v National Association of Schoolmasters/Union of Women Teachers* [2003] IRLR 307.

[114]   See *Sherrard v AUEW* [1973] IRLR 188 per Lord Denning MR.

[115]   Such as the prison service, see above n. 30.

[116]   Case C-438/05 *International Transport Workers' Federation (ITF) and Finnish Seamen's Union (FSU) v Viking Line* [2007] ECR I-10779 (hereafter *Viking*); Case C-341/05 *Laval un Partneri v Svenska Byggnadsarbetareförbundet* [2007] ECR I-11767 (hereafter *Laval*). See A.C.L. DAVIES, 'One Step Forward and Two Steps Back? The *Viking* and *Laval* Cases in the ECJ' (2008) 37 *ILJ* 126; and P. SYRPIS and T. NOVITZ, 'Economic and Social Rights in Conflict: Political and Judicial Approaches to their Reconciliation' (2008) 33 *European Law Review (ELRev)* 411.

[117]   See Chapter 2, above, for its discussion of the impact of these two cases.

[118]   *Laval*, paras. 102–3.

measures taken in the form of collective action can be tied to 'the protection of workers' (narrowly construed)[119] and exercised in a proportionate fashion. UK employers have asserted that the normal statutory immunity and statutory limitations on liability on tort[120] will not apply to civil liability which arises through breach of EU law when trade union action is considered to be 'disproportionate'.[121] The sheer uncertainty surrounding the question of how courts should assess what is proportionate would itself seem to have a 'chilling effect' on the willingness of trade unions to call or support industrial action which has an intra-EU trade element.[122] This legal development, when taken together with the ways in which injunctions can be granted by UK courts in respect of industrial action, to be discussed further below, has led to additional criticism of the UK by the ILO Committee of Experts on this basis.[123]

Immunity for picketing is also granted by statute, but is regulated separately under section 220 of TULRCA, which makes provision for persons '*in contemplation or furtherance of a trade dispute*' to attend at their own place of work, or if recently dismissed, what was previously their place of work '*for the purpose only of peacefully obtaining or communicating information, or peacefully persuading any person to work or abstain from working*'. This entitlement extends to an official of a trade union who is allowed to attend '*at or near the place of work of a member of the union whom he is accompanying and whom he represents*'. There is no statutory definition of what is meant by 'near' but the Court of Appeal has attempted to expand the term generously, since the purpose of the legislation is to give a right to picket.[124] Nevertheless, the courts have tended to limit its exercise with reference to the Code of Practice on Picketing introduced in 1980 and revised in 1992, which recommends that the number of pickets be restricted to six.[125] In the case of *Gate Gourmet London Ltd v TGWU*,[126] the High Court admitted that there was a right to picket by virtue of Article 11 of the European Convention on Human Rights, but took the view that the threatening behaviour of picketers was unacceptable and, as trade union officials were aware of the conduct of picketers, the union was to be regarded as vicariously liable for their actions. An interlocutory injunction was issued to limit the number of

---

[119] See *Viking*, paras. 81–9; and *Laval*, at paras 103–111, discussed in T. NOVITZ, 'A Human Rights Analysis of the *Viking* and *Laval* Judgments' in C. BARNARD (ed.), *The Cambridge Yearbook of European Legal Studies,* Vol. 10, Hart Publishing, Oxford 2007–8, pp. 556–8.
[120] TULRCA, s. 22.
[121] K. APPS, 'Damages Claims Against Trade Unions after Viking and Laval' (2009) 34 *ELRev* 141.
[122] See T. NOVITZ, 'UK Country Report' in *Viking- Laval – Rüffert: Consequences and Policy Perspectives,* ETUI, Brussels 2010.
[123] See Report of the CEACR 2010 and 2011.
[124] *Rayware Ltd v TGWU* [1989] IRLR 127.
[125] SI 1992/476.
[126] [2005] IRLR 881.

pickets on one site to six and restrictions were imposed to keep them within a particular area, so that they could not approach those going to work. Injunctions were issued to named defendants who were placing pressure on others and to unnamed defendants in respect of such conduct as assault, threats, harassment and intimidation.

5.2. PROCEDURAL REQUIREMENTS: BALLOTING AND NOTICE PROVISIONS

For a trade union to claim statutory immunity from liability in tort, certain other procedural criteria must be satisfied: namely, the trade union must satisfy balloting and notice requirements set out in TULRCA.[127] The overly onerous nature of these requirements has been highlighted by the European Committee of Social Rights which considers that *'the requirement to give notice to an employer of a ballot on industrial action, in addition to the strike notice that must be issued before taking industrial action, is excessive'*.[128] What has, in fact, proved particularly onerous for UK unions is the ability of employers to seek injunctive relief, on the basis of failure to comply with rather convoluted and sometimes vague statutory balloting and notice requirements. A turning point in UK labour law may be a recent statement made by members of the Court of Appeal that they will not apply statutory criteria to undermine entirely worker (and union) access to industrial action.[129]

Industrial action must have the support of a ballot, that is, a majority of those voting in the ballot have answered 'yes' to a question concerning the type of industrial action 'to which the act of inducement relates'.[130] However, this in itself is not sufficient to escape civil liability. The way in which the ballot itself is organised has to satisfy a detailed set of criteria.

The trade union in question must, not less than seven days before the ballot, provide the employer with written notification of the intention to hold a ballot and its date, providing a sample voting paper and specifying also the categories of employee to which employees belong and a list of their workplaces, the total number of employees involved and the number in each category. An explanation must also be given of how these calculations were reached. In the alternative, where the employer makes union deductions direct from wages, information

---

[127] TULRCA, s. 219(4).
[128] See Conclusions XIX-3 (2010) at 14.
[129] *RMT v Serco Docklands; ASLEF v London Midland* [2011] IRLR 399 discussed further below at n. 170.
[130] TULRCA, s. 226(1) and (2).

may be provided merely 'as will enable the employer readily to deduce' the relevant information.[131] There is no need to provide the names of relevant employees, as there was prior to 1999,[132] but it is evident that unions cannot merely refer to 'all members of the union employed in all categories at all workplaces'.[133]

An independent scrutineer must be appointed to report on the secret ballot,[134] which must take place by post.[135] The balloting paper must follow a particular form, which distinguishes between strikes and action short of a strike, and includes a warning relating to the potential for dismissal.[136] Moreover, every person who is entitled to vote must be allowed to do so without constraint by the union and without cost.[137] All persons entitled to vote are to be informed, as soon as is reasonably practicable, of

(a)   votes cast in the ballot;
(b)   individuals answering 'yes' to each question;
(c)   individuals answering 'no' to each question; and
(d)   spoiled voting papers.[138]

The same information is also to be supplied to the employer 'as soon as is reasonably practicable'.[139] The scrutineer must also report on the legitimacy of the ballot, and that report can be requested by any one entitled to vote or by the employer.[140]

To these stringent requirements, a Labour Government has offered some relief, such that certain 'small accidental failures' that do not affect the result of the ballot can be disregarded, where these concern omission of certain members entitled to vote or failure to provide an opportunity for postal voting, including the special circumstances of merchant seamen.[141] However, this latitude is very narrowly circumscribed.

---

131   TULRCA, s. 226A.
132   *Blackpool and Fylde College v NATFHE* [1994] IRLR 227.
133   *National Union of Rail, Maritime and Transport Workers v London Underground* [2001] IRLR 228.
134   TULRCA, s. 226A(2F). Except in cases where the number of members entitled to vote is 50 or less. See TULRCA, s. 226C.
135   TULRCA, s. 226B – s.234A.
136   TULRCA, s. 229.
137   TULRCA, s. 230.
138   TULRCA, s. 231.
139   TULRCA, s. 231A.
140   TULRCA, s. 231B.
141   TULRCA, s. 232B.

The ballot will only be effective for four weeks or up to eight weeks if that longer period is agreed between the union and the members' employer.[142] Moreover, even when the support of a ballot is established, statutory provision is made for how the industrial action is to be called by the trade union.[143]

Particular information must be provided to the employer prior to the start of any industrial action (which must be received by the employer at least seven days before the action is due to begin, but after notification provided to the employer of the result of the ballot).[144] This information is phrased in a similar way to that concerning notice of a ballot, but more detail must be given as regards, for example, whether the action will be continuous or discontinuous.

Guidance as to the appropriate application of these statutory provisions is given by the Code of Practice on Industrial Action Ballots and Notice to Employers 2005. Commenting on the Code, BOB SIMPSON has observed that:

> It may be lawful for trade unions to organise industrial action within the 'golden formula' of contemplation or furtherance of a trade dispute only if they give employers of the workers concerned the information necessary for them to first, influence members' votes in the ballot which unions must hold and second, to take action necessary to reduce the effect of any industrial action which does occur, thereby reducing both the impact of the action and the unions' bargaining power. Unions have the right to organise industrial action only when they have taken extensive steps to minimise its impact. The more intelligible prose of the Code, now in its fifth version, makes this more apparent than the ever-increasing inaccessibility of the legislation.[145]

6. THE RELEVANCE OF INJUNCTIVE RELIEF

Where trade unions organise industrial action which does not come within the scope of the substantive or procedural preconditions for statutory immunity, there is scope for employers,[146] trade union members,[147] and members of the public[148] to seek injunctive relief which would stop such action from taking place. This is likely to be interlocutory, that is, prior to the action commencing, and is therefore unlikely to involve a full hearing of all the issues. Instead, all

---

[142] TULRCA, s. 234.
[143] TULRCA, s. 233.
[144] TULRCA, s. 234A.
[145] B. SIMPSON, 'Strike Ballots and the Law: Round Six' (2005) 34 *ILJ* 331.
[146] TULRCA, s. 221.
[147] For a recent summary, see S. DEAKIN and G.S. MORRIS, *Labour Law*, n. 8 above, pp. 1001–1003.
[148] TULRCA, s. 235A.

that is required is that the party seeking the injunction has made out a *prima facie* case and should be granted the request on the basis of a 'balance of convenience' test, otherwise known as the *American Cyanamid* test.[149] This is despite the express statutory provision made in TULRCA for *'restrictions on grant of injunctions and interdicts'* in respect of industrial action, such that all efforts should be given to those affected to be heard and that the courts should *'in exercising its discretion whether or not to grant the injunction, have regard to the likelihood of that party's succeeding at the trial of the action in establishing any matter which would afford a defence to the action under section 219 (protection from certain tort liabilities) or section 220 (peaceful picketing)'.*[150] Instead, given that it is the employer who is likely to suffer economic loss by virtue of a strike, UK courts have tended to be very generous to employers in their grants of interim injunctive relief, a state of affairs that has been criticised by the ILO CEACR and the Council of Europe's Social Rights Committee.[151]

Breach of an interim injunction or, indeed any injunction, can lead to a finding of 'contempt of court' which has consequences under criminal law. A trade union which defies an injunction faces significant fines (as do their officials) and there may even be ordered 'sequestration' (confiscation) of a union's assets.[152] It was not therefore surprising that a Trade Union Freedoms Bill proposed by the TUC advocated reform of this aspect of UK labour law.[153]

There has however arguably been some sign that the attitude of UK courts to grant of an injunction is shifting, potentially for the benefit of UK workers and trade unions. The cases in question relate to the balloting requirements and consequential notice to workers and employers outlined above. Curiously, it seems that where notice to workers is concerned, employers are keener to seek compliance with the letter of the law than the workers affected. It may be assumed that the actions of employers in these circumstances are not wholly altruistic or concerned with the democratic aims of the legislation. In these cases, and even in those cases which concern notice given to employers to enable them to make preparations for eventual industrial action, change seems to be afoot. In the last two years, it appeared that ever more strenuous requirements were being imposed by the courts on unions which sought to organise industrial action. Two recent decisions of the Court of Appeal suggest that this trend has been at least partially corrected, with a steer towards a more modest *de minimis* rule and a more neutral stance to regulation of industrial conflict.

---

[149]   *American Cyanamid Ltd v Ethicon Ltd* [1975] AC 396, 407.
[150]   TULRCA, s. 221.
[151]   See J. HENDY and G. GALL, above n. 25, p. 276.
[152]   TULRCA, ss. 15–16. See also S. DEAKIN and G.S. MORRIS, above n. 8, pp. 949–50.
[153]   See J. HENDY and G. GALL, above n. 25, pp. 262–3.

The recent sequence of cases regarding injunctive relief began with *Metrobus v Unite the Union*,[154] where the Court of Appeal accepted that informing the employer of the result of the ballot for industrial action 48 hours after it was known to the employer constituted unreasonable delay, in breach of the relevant statutory provisions which required notice as soon as was reasonably practicable. This was arguably a more stringent requirement than that which followed from the text of the statute, but the injunction issued at first instance on this basis was nevertheless upheld. Moreover, minor technical inaccuracies in the provision of notice regarding employees (whose union dues were not automatically paid or 'checked-off' by the employer), which were in breach of the Code of Practice, but not the letter of the statute, were also fatal to the legality of industrial action. Not only was the injunction granted at first instance upheld, but a more general statement was made to the effect that UK legislative balloting and notice requirements were consistent with Article 11 of the European Convention on Human Rights, which UK courts are bound to respect by virtue of the UK Human Rights Act 1998. The case is notorious now for the statement made by Lord Justice Maurice Kay that: *'In this country, the right to strike has never been much more than a slogan or a legal metaphor.'*[155]

The response to the precedent seemingly set by *Metrobus* was a spate of cases in which injunctions were issued to prevent industrial action. In *BA v Unite*, the High Court ruled that a strike by Unite members at British Airways (BA) was unlawful even though 92.49% of those voting had voted in favour of strike action, because the ballot included members who had opted to take voluntary redundancy.[156] This was despite the fact that the union had no way of knowing or checking for itself which of its members were in that position and that the inclusion of those members in the ballot could not have affected its result. The judge presiding, Cox J, considered herself bound by the Court of Appeal's finding that UK legislation complied with Article 11 of the ECHR, but commented regarding ILO obligations that: *'Sooner or later, the extent to which the current statutory regime is in compliance with international obligations and with relevant international jurisprudence will fall to be carefully reconsidered'.*[157]

In *EDF v RMT*,[158] the union had made mistakes as to the location where members worked, using job descriptions which were not identical to those used

---

[154] *Metrobus Ltd v Unite the Union* [2009] IRLR 851. See also for detailed discussion, R. DUKES, 'The Right to Strike: Not Much More Than A Slogan?' (2010) 39 *ILJ* 82.

[155] *Metrobus Ltd v Unite the Union* [2009] IRLR 851, para. 118.

[156] *British Airways v Unite* [2009] EWHC 3541, at para. 82. See K.D. EWING above n. 17, chapter 6.

[157] Ibid. at para. 27.

[158] *EDF Energy Powerlink Ltd v National Union of Rail Maritime and Transport Workers* [2010] IRLR 114.

by the employer. In order to meet the statutory requirement of what was *'reasonably necessary'*,[159] Blake J ruled that a union had a duty to do its *'reasonable best'*[160] to address the essential criteria laid out in the legislation. The fear seems to have been that, otherwise, trade unions would be tempted *'to record minimal information in their record-keeping of members in order to diminish the content of the duty to supply categories to the employer'*.[161] The Court did not accept union claims that the employer had deliberately changed the job titles of its employees in the run up to the ballot notice period and blocked access to information about job categorisations. In frustration, the RMT sought leave to appeal, which having been refused culminated in an application to the European Court of Human Rights to the effect that UK legislation (and its application by UK courts) is in breach of Article 11 of the ECHR. That case has yet to be heard at the time of writing.[162]

Then in May 2010, British Airways initiated new injunctive action against the union, Unite, in respect of a ballot previously assumed to have been lawful (and under which industrial action had already been taken). The reason given was that Unite the Union had not adequately informed its own members of eleven spoilt ballot papers. This was despite Unite's efforts at communication, namely placing records of the result of the ballot (including the spoilt ballot papers) on workplace noticeboards and on their website; as well as informing members by text message and e-mail of the outcome (again including the number of spoilt ballot papers). At first instance McCombe J granted an injunction on the basis of the precedent set by *Metrobus*.[163] The only question was whether a *prima facie* argument existed to the effect that the union had not fully complied with the statutory provision and, *'once one reaches that conclusion, it is in my judgment inevitable that the balance of convenience comes down in favour of the airline'*.[164] This finding was, however, ultimately overturned by the Court of Appeal by a 2/1 majority. It is notable that the employer was arguing that there had been a breach of notice requirements intended for the benefit of workers, but only to serve their own interests.[165] In this context, the judgment of Smith LJ also offered the prospect of a significant change to the courts' understanding of the application of notification provisions. Her view was that *'the policy of this part of the Act is not to create a series of traps or hurdles for the Union to negotiate. It is to ensure*

---

[159]   TULRCA, s. 226A.
[160]   [2010] IRLR 114 at para. 18(6).
[161]   Ibid., para. 18(7).
[162]   <www.rmt.org.uk/Templates/Internal.asp?NodeID=136131> accessed 31.10.11. For the precise terms of the application, see <www.rmt.org.uk/files/136487/FileName/SMAN-TS012510060810080.pdf> accessed 31.10.11.
[163]   *British Airways v Unite* [2010] EWHC 1354. See K.D. EWING, above n. 17, chapter 6.
[164]   Ibid., para. 50.
[165]   *British Airways v Unite* [2010] EWCA 669, para. 20.

fair dealing between employer and Union and to ensure a fair, open and democratic ballot.[166] This was the first case which suggested a shift away from the ready availability of injunctive relief to employers.

Since then, the Court of Appeal has had the opportunity to consider two further cases, which do not so much establish a right to strike as might follow from ILO or Council of Europe requirements, but at least suggest a more 'neutral' approach in the balance of employer and employer interests.

In *Milford Haven Port Authority v Unite the Union*,[167] the Court of Appeal again considered the extent of notice requirements in the context of injunctive relief. In that instance, despite an apparent softening of requirements, such that a single notice could be given by the union in respect of both continuous industrial action short of a strike and discontinuous strike action, the injunction was ultimately upheld since the union had given notice that both species of action would start on the same day, which could not logically be the case. As the union would ultimately elect to take one or the other, this had to be specified to the employer under the terms of the statute and the Code of Practice, *'the authority was unclear as to what action the unions members intended to take and would take between these times and dates and so was unclear "as to how best to try to cover for the industrial action which is going to take place"*.'[168] This was considered to be unacceptable.

> 'The notice should have set out the intended position accurately. It should not need to be a matter of inference or assumption as to which part of the action will bite at which time; neither is it difficult to achieve. It simply requires the union to pay proper attention to the very important notice that it is giving of its intended action, which will allow it to avoid what would otherwise be unanswerable liability at the very least for the tort of inducing breach of contract.'[169]

This perhaps suggested that where the notice was for the employer's as opposed to the worker's benefit, a higher standard of scrutiny would be applied by members of the Court of Appeal.

The most recent authority on the question of sufficient notice, which provides a degree of respite for trade unions alongside some limited recognition of the right to strike, comes from the judgment of the Court of Appeal of two joined cases,

---

[166] Ibid., para. 152.
[167] *Milford Haven Port Authority v Unite the Union* [2010] EWCA Civ 400.
[168] Ibid., para. 15.
[169] Ibid., para. 17.

RMT v SERCO and *ASLEF v London & Birmingham Railway Ltd.*[170] In this judgment, the Court of Appeal revisited the notification requirements regarding identity of the employees involved in industrial action, which is also the subject of the 2010 RMT application to the European Court of Human Rights.[171] Small errors and the failure to keep absolutely accurate records will, it seems, no longer be fatal to the union's ability to take industrial action. Small failures in notice requirements, while not covered by the 'small accidental errors' provisions regarding balloting,[172] can be understood as linked to a *de minimis* principle. The figures must, as is stated in section 226A(2D) of TULRCA be '*as accurate as is reasonably practicable in the light of the information in the possession of the union at the time when it complies with the subsection*', but the creation of statutory protection in terms of balloting errors, should not preclude some allowance by the courts on minor errors regarding notification;[173] nor was the explanation of the figures to be unduly onerous.[174] It was also clarified that 'accidental' errors under section 238A of TULRCA need only be understood as 'unintentional' and not 'unavoidable'.[175]

All this was consistent with the understanding of Elias LJ that it has been established in 'a number of cases' that Article 11 of the ECHR protects a right to strike. On this basis, he commenced his judgment with a rejection of the view that there was any parliamentary intention that the interests of employers should be preferred. Rather, the statutory immunities had to be merely understood as the way in which the UK enables unions to take lawful industrial action. On this basis the legislation had to be '*construed in the normal way, without presumptions one way or the other*' as to the superiority of union or employer interests.[176] This case, notably, does not go so far as to do away with the *American Cyanamid* test, as has been proposed by some scholars,[177] but it does at least partially correct what had become a worrying trend.

This 'neutral approach', identified by RUTH DUKES,[178] remains uncertain in its ambit. *Metrobus* is still considered to be good authority for the view that the UK

---

[170] The joined cases of *RMT v SERCO* and *ASLEF v London & Birmingham Railway Ltd* [2011] EWCA Civ 226. See also R. DUKES, 'The Right to Strike under UK Law: Something more than a slogan?' (2011) 40 *ILJ* 302.

[171] TULRCA, s. 226A.

[172] TULRCA, s. 232B.

[173] The joined cases of *RMT v SERCO* and *ASLEF v London & Birmingham Railway Ltd* [2011] EWCA Civ 226, paras 86–7.

[174] Ibid., para. 103. Statement that an 'audit' had taken place was not positively and materially misleading and therefore could not fall foul of the statutory requirement.

[175] [2011] EWCA Civ 226, paras. 54–6.

[176] Ibid., para. 9.

[177] N. COUNTOURIS and M. FREEDLAND, *Injunctions, Cyanamid and the Corrosion of the Right to Strike in the UK*, UCL Working Paper, LRI WP 1/2010, UCL, London 2010.

[178] R. DUKES above n. 170, 310.

legislation regarding industrial conflict complies with Article 11 of the ECHR. However, whether in fact the UK courts do really comply with the European Court of Human Right's understanding of Article 11 depends very much on their interpretive approach to that legislation. The difficulty is that, while in the light of *Enerji Yapi-Yol Sen,* the UK courts may wish to adopt a stance which facilitates union (and worker) access to industrial action, the very wording of the statutory provisions (in terms of substantive and procedural preconditions for immunity in tort) militates against this. Smith LJ's view of parliamentary intent, citing that of Millett LJ some time ago,[179] is arguably too generous. Millett had observed that: *'Parliament's object in introducing the democratic requirement of a secret ballot is not to make life more difficult for trade unions by putting further obstacles in their way before they can call for industrial action with impunity but to ensure that such action should have the genuine support of the members [...] It would be astonishing if a right that was first conferred by Parliament in 1906, which has been enjoyed by trade unions ever since and which is today recognised as encompassing a fundamental human right should have been removed by Parliament [...]'* The problem however is that, while the ability to take industrial action has not been removed by statute, the legislation seems to go quite intentionally beyond what might be needed to ensure that industrial action is approved by its members. While such stringent statutory controls on industrial action remain, employers are likely to try to use these to their advantage.

7. LOOKING TO THE FUTURE

Successive UK governments have for some considerable period of time been prepared to continue a legislative system for regulating industrial conflict which remains in clear breach of ILO and other international human rights standards. It will be interesting to see whether, as the European Court of Human Rights comes to offer a more 'integrated approach' to the interpretation of the ECHR, this will be sustainable. There is no hint however of a more lenient legislative approach at the present juncture. If anything, the prospects tend in the opposite direction.

Rather than removing constraints on secondary action or protection from dismissal, the current Coalition government seems more interested in restricting recourse to industrial action. Certainly, the Coalition did not support a private members' bill concerning 'Lawful Industrial Action (Minor Errors)', which was designed to reduce the ease with which employers were gaining injunctions to

---

[179]   [2010] EWCA Civ 669, para. 153 citing *London Underground Ltd v National Union of Railwaymen, Maritime and Transport Staff* [1996] ICR 170.

prevent industrial action.[180] The current government appears more likely to be responsive to the CBI, which is currently calling for changes to the balloting process, introducing a majority threshold (40% of those eligible to vote) which would make it more difficult to take industrial action.[181] It is notable that Boris Johnson, the Conservative mayor of London, took up this call with enthusiasm.[182] The prospects for domestic legislative reform do not therefore look promising for trade unions or their members.

Moreover, the UK developments regarding availability of injunctive relief still do not assist UK unions which wish to organise strikes which may have EU free movement implications. It would still seem that the standard principles apply (the demonstration of only a *prima facie* case and determination on the basis of the balance of convenience), such that when an employer has any potential claim that their free movement entitlements are affected by industrial action, an injunction can still readily be issued.[183]

EU legislative reform has been contemplated. The Monti Report of 2010 proposed a provision modifying the operation of the Posted Workers Directive 96/71/EC so as to ensure that '*the posting of workers in the cross-border provision of services does not affect the right to take industrial action and the right to strike as it is protected by the European Charter of Fundamental Rights and in accordance with national law and practices which respect Community law*'.[184] However, the question of what national law and practice concerning industrial action would sufficiently respect EU law on this point remains a matter of controversy.[185] The Commission's proposed 'Monti II Regulation', published in March 2012, seeks to elaborate on the legitimate scope of union-led collective action in the context of posted work, but has met with a hostile reception from the UK TUC and the ETUC.[186] It may be that significant change will come from the judicial rather

---

[180]   Hansard, House of Commons Debate, 22.10.10, at col. 1258.

[181]   CBI, *Making Britain the Place to Work: An Employment Agenda for the New Government*, June 2010, 10.

[182]   See J. KIRKUP, Boris Johnson says Coalition "lily-livered" on strikes, *The Telegraph* 04.05.11.

[183]   See the facts of the British Airline Pilots Association (BALPA) dispute as set out in *Application by the British Air Line Pilots Association to the International Labour Organisation Committee of Experts on the Application of Conventions and Recommendations against the United Kingdom for breach of ILO Convention No. 87* drafted by John Hendy QC, available at: <www.balpa.org/Document-Library/Industrial-Issues/BALPA-ILO-Application-2009–01–26.aspx> accessed 31.10.2011.

[184]   M. MONTI, *A New Strategy for the Single Market*, European Commission, Brussels, 2010, p. 71.

[185]   On this point, see A. IOSSA, 'Protecting the Right to Collective Action and to Collective Bargaining: developments and new perspectives at European and international levels' in A. BUCKER and W. WARNECK (eds.), *Reconciling Fundamental Social Rights and Economic Freedoms after Viking, Laval and Rüffert*, Nomos, Baden-Baden 2011, p. 245.

[186]   Proposal for a Council Regulation on the exercise of the right to take collective action within the context of the freedom of establishment and the freedom to provide services Brussels,

than the legislative institutions, with the CJEU responding to developments in the jurisprudence of the European Court of Human Rights, and thereby redressing the balance.[187] However, yet again, there is little sign of this. For the time being, significant legal restrictions operate in respect of UK industrial action, not only by virtue of domestic common law and legislation, but also with reference to EU law.

21.3.2012 COM(2012) 130 final; see for ETUC response: www.etuc.org/a/9823, and for the TUC response: www.lcdtu.org/. For some of the reasons for this rejection, see K.D.Ewing, 'The Draft Monti II Regulation: An Inadequate Response to *Viking* and *Laval, The Institute of Employment Rights, IER Briefing, March 2012*.

[187] T. Novitz, 'The Impact of Viking and Laval: Contesting the social function and legal regulation of the right to strike' in E. Ales and T. Novitz (eds.), above n. 1 at p. 272; and K.D. Ewing and J. Hendy, 'The Dramatic Implications of *Demir and Baykara*' (2010), 39 *ILJ* 2.

CHAPTER 6

COLLECTIVE REPRESENTATION AND INFORMATION AND CONSULTATION

1. INTRODUCTION

Collective representation has experienced progressive and quiet change over the last two decades. One of the main drivers for this change has been the imposition of information and consultation requirements by the European Community (now European Union). Participation of workers through representatives is considered as central to the European Social Model.[1] The slow penetration and integration of European Directives concerned with the obligation to inform and consult the workforce has transformed the industrial relations landscape in the United Kingdom. From a system where trade unions were the only collective voice mainly through collective bargaining, the picture has evolved to dual representation where the information and consultation function can be exercised by either recognised trade unions under specific circumstances, or elected representatives. The result is a complex and patchy framework. As European Directives on information and consultation were enacted, UK governments added new layers of legislation without necessarily appreciating or considering the impact on industrial relations, trade unions and the coherence of the law in this field. Consultation, however, preceded any European input. Outside of the legislative framework, trade unions and other representatives had been consulted by employers on a number of matters and joint consultative committees or works councils have existed for a number of years.[2] The European influence has however been clearly significant[3] both in terms of inserting a new democratic function at a collective level in the workplace and a new channel of representation.

---

[1]   S. Laulom 'Towards New Synergies Through Workers' Representatives?' paper presented at *Before and After the Economic Crisis: What Implications for the 'European Social Model'?* Conference in honour of Brian Bercusson and Yota Kravaritou, European University Institute, October 2009, 1.

[2]   N. Millward, A. Bryson and J. Forth, *All Change at Work? British Employment Relations 1980–1998, as portrayed by the Workplace Industrial Relations Survey series*, Routledge, London 2000, from p. 108.

[3]   B. Bercusson, 'The European Social Model Comes to Britain' (2002) 31 *ILJ* 209.

In order to navigate through the current legislative maze, a chronological approach has been adopted. Information and consultation entered the national legal sphere originally in specific situations, primarily in relation to restructuring. The agenda moved to general obligations to inform and consult through works councils or equivalent channels. While considering in depth how such obligations were transposed in the national setting, the chapter will also analyse the impact of the growth of the obligation to inform and consult on collective representation. Additionally, some consideration will be given to the co-existence of collective bargaining and consultation.

2. INFORMATION AND CONSULTATION IN SPECIFIC SITUATIONS

Employers are required to inform and consult the workforce in a number of specific situations determined by statutes and regulations. This section will focus on collective redundancies, transfer of undertakings and health and safety. Where an employer considers training policies, needs and plans for the workforce and where pension plans are revised, a duty to inform and consult also arises, but these are left outside the remit of this book.[4]

2.1. COLLECTIVE REDUNDANCIES

Where multiple economic dismissals are planned, the employer must inform and consult the workforce representatives on a number of issues. The process can be understood as attempting to prevent or limit such termination of employment.[5] This obligation was imposed by the European Directive relating to collective redundancies.[6] The transposition into national law has given rise to a number of

---

[4] On training, TULRCA, s. 70B introduced by the Employment Relations Act 1999. See also *It's Time to Talk Training – How to develop a dialogue on skills at the workplace. Guidance on Good Practice from the CBI, TUC, BERR and DIUS (Department for Innovation, Universities and Skills)* (July 2008) available at <www.berr.govuk/files/file47079.pdf> accessed on 6.11.2011. On pension, Occupational Pension Schemes (Contracting Out) Regulations 1996, SI 1996/1172, reg. 4 and Occupational and Personal Pension Schemes (Consultation by Employers and Miscellaneous Amendments) Regulations 2006, SI 2006/349.

[5] As TULRCA, s. 188 requires consultation about ways to avoid dismissals, reduce the number of employees to be dismissed and mitigating the consequences of the dismissals. However, in practice it has been shown that trade unions' role has not been to reduce the number of redundancies but to ensure that when they took place, they were voluntary and that payment were as generous as possible. See S. DEAKIN and A. KOUKIADAKI, 'Capability Theory, Employee Voice and Corporate Restructuring: Evidence from UK Case Studies' (2012) *Comparative and Labor Law Policy Journal*, forthcoming, p. 1 of the paper.

[6] Council Directive 75/129/EEC of 17 February 1975 on the approximation of the laws of the Member States relating to collectives redundancies [1975] OJ L48/29, amended by Council

difficulties which are evidence of the tension existing between European traditions and the UK approach to employees' views and contributions to managerial decisions. The following sections highlight the uneasiness with which legislator and judiciary had to deal with concepts and mechanisms designed to enhance collective representation and employee representatives' input.

Before discussing the essence of the obligation, it is worth noting that the process is only triggered if a number of pre-conditions are fulfilled. Firstly, a threshold of 20 employees has to be met.[7] Small scale redundancies do not warrant collective consultation. Such thresholds are allowed by the Directive[8] but the original transposition in the UK did not mention numbers. This was subsequently added by a Conservative Government when reviewing the instrument.[9] This hurdle is secondly reinforced by a time constraint. The proposed redundancies must take place within 90 days.[10] This requirement restricts the protection offered by the collective consultation. Scenarios of economic dismissals occurring over a longer period of time are easily envisaged. Finally the exercise must take place in an establishment,[11] a term which is not defined in statute. The Court of Justice of the European Union (CJEU) indicated that the term must be construed widely notably to maximise the protection granted to employees.[12] This was not necessarily applied strictly in the UK context as employers tried to treat a unit artificially as an establishment to bypass the threshold of 20.[13]

2.1.1. Timing of information and consultation

The duty to consult arises where an employer 'proposes to dismiss'.[14] This general requirement is underpinned by the necessity to consult in good time. This is further explained by a timescale inserted in the legislation: if the employer proposes to dismiss 100 employees or more, the consultation should start 90 days before the dismissal takes effect and if the number of employees is less than 100, the time frame is reduced to 30 days.[15]

    Directive 92/56/EC of 24 June 1992 [1992] OJ L245/3 and consolidated in Council Directive 98/59/EC of 20 July 1998 [1998] OJ L225/16.

[7]   TULRCA, s. 188(1).

[8]   Art. 1(1)(a) (ii).

[9]   See M. HALL and P. EDWARDS, 'Reforming the Statutory Redundancy Consultation Procedure' (1999) 28 *ILJ* 299, 302.

[10]   TULRCA, s. 188(1).

[11]   TULRCA, s. 188(1).

[12]   Case C-449/93 *Rockfon A/S v Specialarbeiderforbundet i Danmark, acting for Nielsen* [1996] IRLR 168, Case C-270/05 *Athinaiki Chartopoiia AE v Panagiotidis* [2007] IRLR 284.

[13]   See contrasting decisions in *Mills and Allen Ltd v Bulwich* (2000) IRLB 648 and *MSF v Refuge Assurance plc and anor* [2002] IRLR 324.

[14]   TULRCA, s. 188(1).

[15]   TULRCA, s. 188(1A).

The legislative wording and timetable can be criticised because they do not correspond to the spirit of the Directive. The aim was to engage in meaningful consultation in order to consider alternatives to the redundancies and minimise the effects of the termination.[16] This aspiration did not sit well with a culture of industrial relations where business decisions belong solely to managerial prerogatives. This is evidenced by the discrepancy in the wording of the European Directive and national law. The Directive refers to consultation starting when the employer 'contemplates' redundancies[17] while TULRCA 1992 mentions 'proposes'. The different terminology raised questions about whether national law was in breach of the Directive as 'contemplates' suggests a much earlier stage than 'proposes'. The variation has been acknowledged by the judges who conceded that the statutory language denotes finality about the decision to dismiss whereas the Directive's wording opens the possibility for further discussions on the actual occurrence of any redundancies. For a long period of time, the British courts nevertheless refused to indicate that statutes should be rewritten or even to construe it in a fashion that would equate to 'contemplate'.

In *R v British Coal Corporation and Secretary of State for Trade and Industry ex p Vardy*[18] where the decisions to close pits had been taken without consultation of the unions, Glidewell LJ clearly stated that the obligation imposed by TULRCA is to consult on the carrying out of the redundancy programmes that management deems necessary. 'Proposes' suggests that the employer has already decided to make employees redundant. By contrast, the European Directive requests employers to consult when they are first envisaging that they may make employees redundant.[19] The language of the two texts is so different that TULRCA could not be interpreted as meaning the same thing as the Directive. Glidewell LJ notes that statutory construction of a term found in legislation that transposes a European Directive requires a purposive approach so that the meaning of the statute is as close as the interpretation given by the Court of Justice of the European Union.[20] However, at that time, the CJEU had not ruled on this matter. This reasoning was applied in *MSF v Refuge Assurance plc and anor.*[21] The European Court was eventually asked to interpret 'contemplates' and the timing of consultation in the case of *Junk v Kuhnel.*[22] The question arose as to whether an employee could be notified of his economic dismissal before the consultation had been completed. This was extremely relevant to the UK courts because TULRCA 1992 provides for a consultation timetable that

---

[16]   Council Directive 98/59/EC, Art. 2(1) and 2(2).
[17]   Art. 2(1).
[18]   [1993] IRLR 104.
[19]   Ibid. at [124].
[20]   Ibid. at [123].
[21]   [2002] IRLR 324.
[22]   Case C-188/03 [2005] IRLR 310.

counts backwards from the time the first dismissal takes effect.[23] Where an employer proposes to make 40 people redundant for example, and notifies the employee of the termination of their contract in 30 days, any consultation seems less effective on the possible alternatives measures as the decision appears as a fait accompli. This tension was captured by the CJEU which stated that

> 36. The case in which the employer 'is contemplating' collective redundancies and has drawn up a 'project' to that end corresponds to a situation in which no decision has yet been taken. By contrast, the notification to a worker that his or her contract of employment has been terminated is the expression of a decision to sever the employment relationship, and the actual cessation of that relationship on the expiry of the period of notice is no more than the effect of that decision.

> 37. Thus, the terms used by the Community legislature indicate that the obligations to consult and to notify arise prior to any decision by the employer to terminate contracts of employment.

> 38. Finally, this interpretation is confirmed, in regard to the procedure for consultation of workers' representatives, by the purpose of the directive, as set out in Article 2(2), which is to avoid terminations of contracts of employment or to reduce the number of such terminations. The achievement of that purpose would be jeopardised if the consultation of workers' representatives were to be subsequent to the employer's decision.

The message was clear: an employer could not notify employees of their economic dismissal until the consultation process had been concluded. The judgment led to statutory and judicial activity at national level. Firstly, the then government decided to review consultation provisions in relation to the obligation to notify the public authorities of the incoming redundancies. Such requirement is found in section 193 of TULRCA 1992 and was modified through the Collective Redundancies (Amendment) Regulations 2006.[24] Notice of redundancy must be given to the relevant government department at least 30 days before giving notice to terminate an employee's contract of employment (rather than before the actual dismissal date). However, this does not fully resolve the issue in relation to employee representatives. The government acknowledged that stakeholders were concerned about the lack of clarity surrounding the requirement of consultation 'in good time'.[25] In particular, there was lobby for clear statutory language that consultation be completed before any notice of redundancies had been issued. However, the government

---

[23] TULRCA, s. 188(1A).
[24] SI 2387/2006 – see further explanation in section 2.1.5.
[25] DTI, *Collective Redundancies; employers' duty to notify the Secretary of State – response to consultation* (September 2006).

still maintained that the current legislation could be interpreted in conformity with the Directive and without amending the current statute. It recognised that 'for greater coherence', further DTI guidance should be provided to explain how the law should be interpreted in light of *Junk* but it did not produce the relevant materials. It was therefore left to the courts to reconcile *Junk* with TULRCA 1992.

The second effect of the CJEU case law was felt in *Leicestershire County Council v Unison*.[26] The EAT had stated that 'proposal to dismiss' should be interpreted as less than a decision that dismissals are to be made and more than a possibility that they might occur. This was consistent with *Junk v Kuhnel* and the Court of Appeal did not interfere with such finding on technical grounds.[27] The question of timing and substance of consultation was further clarified in the case of *UK Coal Mining Ltd v National Union of Mineworkers (Northumberland Area) and another*.[28] In the situation of a closure of a colliery, the principal question was whether trade unions should have been consulted about the reasons for the closure.[29] If the answer was positive, the implications about the timing were significant as discussing managerial reasoning to arrive at a decision are clearly different to discussing the implications of the decision. The basis for the *ex parte Vardy* decision would not stand any longer and the duty to consult would arise prior to the making of the decision. The EAT followed that line of argument by indicating that consultation should be about avoiding the dismissals and therefore about the reasons for dismissals. This, in turn, involves discussing the reasons for the closure. The decision was another positive step towards complying with the European Directive and its interpretation by the CJEU without changing the wording of UK statute.

However, the most recent CJEU case has muddied the water in terms of what 'contemplates' means. In *Akavan Erityisalojen Keskusliitto AEK ry v Fujitsu Siemens Computers Oy*,[30] the closure of a plant in Finland triggered questions about the timing of information disclosure when the decision is made by a parent company. The CJEU took this opportunity to give guidance on the timing of consultation. It indicated that consultation does not start where redundancies are only a probability because premature triggering of the obligation could lead

---

26   [2006] IRLR 810.
27   The employer had tried to contest this interpretation of the statutory wording at the EAT. The argument was rejected because the point was not raised at the employment tribunal by the employer. The Court of Appeal did not allow the new argument to be put forward.
28   [2008] IRLR 4.
29   It appears that the false reason originally given by the employer to explain the closure had an impact on the final decision: trade unions were told that the closure was for health and safety reasons when it was subsequently announced that the rational was economic.
30   Case C-44/08 [2009] IRLR 944.

to unnecessary uncertainty for the workers. However, beginning consultation when the decision has been made is not conceivable either. The decision seems to validate the interpretation given in *Leicestershire County Council v Unison*. The Court of Appeal has, however, recently requested further clarification from the CJEU. In *USA v Nolan*,[31] a number of questions have been referred to the CJEU for interpretation as the question of *proposes* v *contemplates* re-emerged. The US government decided to close a military base in Hampshire. Mrs Nolan, representing a number of employees, considered that appropriate consultation had not taken place because the employer consulted after the decision had been taken and not about the reasons for closure. The breach of the law was principally based on *UK Coal Mining*. The ET and the EAT agreed with Mrs Nolan. Yet, armed with the *Akavan v Fujitsu* decision, the US government tried to argue that *UK Coal Mining* is no longer applicable and that they did not have to consult about the reasons for the closure. The consultation is about the application of the decision that was made. The Court of Appeal faced with the question of applying the Finnish case has asked for more explanation from the CJEU because it considered that *Fujitsu* is not clear as to the meaning of *contemplates*. It is therefore hoped that, when faced with a question directly relevant to the UK legal framework, the current conundrum will finally be resolved by the Court.

2.1.2.   *The procedural and substantial requirements of the information and consultation obligation*

The content and method of the obligation to inform and consult found in TURLCA 1992, section 188 reflect the wording of the Directive, although some essential requirements were originally left out and had to be included at a later stage after intervention of the CJEU.

Firstly, the consultation should focus upon ways to avoid the dismissals, to reduce the number of employees to be dismissed and to mitigate the consequences of the dismissals. Further, the consultation process must take place with a view to reaching an agreement.[32] The current text is the result of various amendments inserted progressively because the CJEU ruled that there were a number of shortfalls[33] in the UK original transposition of the Collective Redundancies Directive[34] (and the Acquired Rights Directive). The original legislation did not state that consultation with workers would take place *with a view to reaching an agreement* and did not ensure that consultation with workers

---

31   [2011] IRLR 40.
32   TULRCA, s. 188(2).
33   The others are analysed under the relevant headings below.
34   Case C-383/92 (collective redundancies) *Commission v UK* [1994] ECR I-2479.

covered means of avoiding redundancies or mitigating the consequences.[35] Such omission connoted the difficult application of a model where the rationale and content of management decisions had to be discussed and potentially changed. The subject matter of the consultation has raised difficult questions about how far the reasons for dismissals can be discussed. As was seen earlier, in a situation of closure, it was recently established that there is an obligation to consult over the reason for the decision to close the workplace even though statute does not expressly say so.[36] It can be implied from this decision that the consultation is therefore not anymore about the implementation of a decision but about the decision itself.

Secondly, the consultation process should be based on specific information to be provided to the representatives. The list is provided by statutes and includes the reasons for the dismissals, the people affected, the selection criteria, the proposed method to carry out the dismissals and to calculate redundancy payments.[37] This reflects the inventory found in the Directive.[38]

Statute does not explain further how the consultation process should unfold. In other areas of information and consultation, there is a more specific procedure where employee representatives are expected to reply to proposals and management should respond to the views expressed.[39] In a redundancies situation, the requirement is to consult with a view to reaching an agreement, which suggests a process in which proposals and counter-proposals are discussed. The CJEU has pointed out that the parties should try to reach an agreed solution.[40] The term 'consultation' is however not defined in English law. It is simply assumed that it is not 'negotiation' and that ultimately the decision remains with the employer. It does not necessarily follow that the process is pointless, provided that the employer can demonstrate a real attempt to comply with the procedure. From a trade union perspective, this could still lead to frustration as the end result remains and managerial power cannot be challenged. Case studies have shown over the years that consultation remains about the handling of job losses rather than the decision to proceed to

---

[35]   This was rectified by the Collective Redundancies and Transfer of Undertakings (Protection of Employment) (Amendment) Regulations 1995/2587, reg. 3(2).

[36]   *UK Coal Mining Ltd v National Union of Mineworkers (Northumberland Area) and another* [2008] IRLR 4.

[37]   TULRCA, s. 188(4).

[38]   Art. 2(3).

[39]   See for example Council Directive 02/14/EC of the European Parliament and of the Council of 11 March 2002, establishing a general framework for informing and consulting employees in the European Community [2002] OJ L80/29, Art. 4(4)(d) reproduced in the Information and Consultation of Employees Regulations 2004, reg. 20(4) (see section below).

[40]   Case C-44/08 *Junk v Kuhnel* [2005] IRLR 310.

restructuring.[41] However, a breach of the procedure could potentially harm the employer financially as will be seen in the section below.

2.1.3.   Representatives

The identity of the relevant counterparts to management when a duty to inform and consult arises has been controversial. The debate on this issue was sparked by the provisions that transposed the Collective Redundancies and the Acquired Rights Directives. They specified that recognised trade unions had to be informed and consulted. This was in line with the traditional industrial relations system. The European Commission was not satisfied that the Directives were fully implemented as there was no provision for workplaces where there were no recognised trade unions. As recognition or de-recognition was at the discretion of the employer, this potentially prevented many employees to be protected by the European measure. In 1994, the CJEU upheld the complaint in this regard, thus forcing the UK government to take appropriate steps to bring UK law into line with EU law. The instrument adopted by the UK government in response to the judgment was the Collective Redundancies and Transfer of Undertakings (Protection of Employment) (Amendment) Regulations 1995.[42] Appropriate representatives had to be informed and consulted. They were defined as either recognised trade unions or elected representatives. Such a system was strongly criticised by the unions. It allowed trade unions to be bypassed by elected representatives even when unions had managed to be recognised. Further, the election system was not detailed and could therefore potentially lead to abuse by employers.[43] Following criticisms raised by the trade union movement and also by the European Commission in respect of the 1995 Regulations, the Labour Government amended the obligations through new regulations in 1999.[44] The provisions now found in TULRCA 1992, section 188(1)(B) retained the dual channel representation to conform to the CJEU judgment, but returned to giving trade unions priority. Trade unions will therefore be informed and consulted on redundancy situations if they are recognised.[45] If this is not the case, the employer can chose between using existing employee representatives who had been appointed or elected by the workforce for other purposes than redundancy or the employer can elect such representatives.[46] If the employer has attempted elections but the affected employees fail to elect representatives, the employer is

---

41   S. Deakin and A. Koukiadaki, above n. 5, p. 20 of the paper.

42   SI 1995/2587, following case C-383/92, above nr. 34.

43   See *R v Secretary of State for Trade & Industry Ex parte Unison and others* [1996] IRLR 438 about the compatibility of the Regulations with the Collective Redundancies Directive.

44   The Collective Redundancies and Transfer of Undertakings (Protection of Employment) (Amendment) Regulations 1999, SI 1999/1925.

45   TULRCA, s. 188(1B)(a).

46   TULRCA, s. 188(1B)(b).

deemed to have fulfilled his/her obligations and is only required to inform the affected employees individually with the information that would be disclosed to the representatives.[47] Consultation is however non-existent. This is depriving employees of an important right. While apathy and employees' responsibility can be put forward as reasons for such a result, reality dictates that in non-organised workplaces and settings, employees may not feel comfortable or sufficiently equipped to put themselves forward as representatives. The process of election is minimalistically explained in statutes.[48] Employers are mainly required to conduct the election process fairly and to decide how many representatives are needed and their terms of office. The vote should be secret, as far as is 'reasonably practicable'.[49] Such elections are therefore not supervised by any external body, leaving room again for potential abuse.

European law created dual channel representation in the UK.[50] This aspect will be considered more fully below in relation to the impact on trade unions,[51] but it was through the requirements of transposing the Collective Redundancies and the Acquired Rights Directive that the process was initiated.

2.1.4. Enforcement and remedies

Where an employer fails to follow the requirements of information and consultation with the appropriate representatives, the relevant affected party can complain to an employment tribunal within a specific time frame.[52] If the complaint is upheld, the relevant employees are entitled to a protective award. Such award is effectively payment for the failure to abide by the statutory rules. The amount of the award is determined by reference to a protected period. In effect the sum to be paid to the affected employees varies from 1 to 90 days pay depending on what is deemed to be just and equitable by the tribunal, '*having regard to the seriousness of the employer's default in complying with the section 188 requirements*'.[53] The CJEU had found that the UK had failed to make provision for effective sanctions against employers who did not comply with the obligation to inform and consult employee representatives.[54] The length of the protected period remained at 90 days but the previous provisions, that allowed setting off the amount of the protective award against any other payment made

---

47   TULRCA, s. 188(7B).

48   TULRCA, s. 188A inserted in 1999.

49   TULRCA, s. 188A(1)(i).

50   P. DAVIES, 'A Challenge to Single Channel' (1994) 23 *ILJ* 272.

51   Also see chapter 1 for a discussion on the current picture of employee representation and rights and protection granted to all representatives.

52   TULRCA, s. 189.

53   TULRCA, s. 189(4)(b).

54   Case C-383/92, above n. 34.

by the employer to the employee for damages for breach of contract for example,[55] was removed. The judicial approach to the determination of remedies for non-compliance with the duty to consult has gone some way to fulfil the objective of acting as deterrent for employers. In *Susie Radin Ltd v GMB*,[56] the Court of Appeal explicitly indicated that non-compliance by the employer should be treated very seriously. It gave guidelines to the employment tribunal when determining the amount of the protective award and notably insisted that the purpose of the award is to sanction the employer and not to compensate the employees affected. This is a noteworthy statement considering that damages directly paid to employees have not been a traditional remedy for breach of collective labour law. It is all the more significant that such award is multiplied by the number of employees affected and that there is no ceiling to the weekly pay, as is the case for unfair dismissal or redundancy pay. Finally, the Court of Appeal guided the tribunals as to how to assess the length of the protected period. A proper approach in a case where there has been no consultation is to start with the maximum period and to reduce it only if there are mitigating circumstances justifying a reduction to an extent which the employment tribunal considers appropriate.[57] In the above case, the protective award was for the maximum 90 days' pay permitted by statute.[58] In a situation where the 30 days period applied because less than 100 employees were economically dismissed, the EAT took a very strict view that the length of the consultation period should not be linked to the amount of the award. In *Hutchins v Permacell Finesse Ltd*,[59] the EAT overturned the decision of the Employment Tribunal which had granted 30 days pay as protective award because the consultation period was 30 days. The court considered that the 90 days should still apply in line with the *Susie Radin* principle because no consultation had taken place. This positive outlook of the remedies available is perhaps counterbalanced by other decisions which interpreted statutes more narrowly. For example, if employees were not dismissed, they were not entitled to the award.[60] Further, only employees who are members of the trade union which brings an action will benefit from the award and not other employees who were made redundant but were not represented.[61] Similarly, where an individual successfully brings an action under section 188 (where there is no union or elected representatives), the award cannot be extended to all employees affected.[62]

---

[55]   Under Employment Protection Act 1975, s. 102.

[56]   [2004] IRLR 400.

[57]   Ibid. at [45].

[58]   TULRCA, s. 189(4).

[59]   [2008] All ER (D) 112.

[60]   See *Securicor Omega Express v GMB* [2004] IRLR 9 and *Hardy v Tourism South East* [2005] IRLR 242.

[61]   *TGWU v Brauer Coley Ltd* [2007] IRLR 207.

[62]   *Independent Insurance Co Ltd v Aspinall* [2011] IRLR 716.

An employer has a defence for lack of consultation. If it can be established that there were 'special circumstances' which rendered it not reasonably practicable for the employer to undertake its duty,[63] sanctions will not be applied. Such special circumstances are not defined in statutes and the employer still has to demonstrate that despite such circumstances, all reasonable steps had been taken to comply with the obligation. The defence is not found in the European Directive and has therefore been interpreted restrictively by the courts.[64] For example, insolvency cannot be regarded as special circumstances unless it occurs suddenly and unexpectedly.[65] Nevertheless, employers have the option to try to justify non-respect of the procedure where this was not envisaged by the Directive.

2.1.5. Notification to authorities

Following the requirements set out in the Directive, employers had to notify the competent public authority of multiple redundancies.[66] Section 193 TULRCA 1992 transposed this obligation into UK law, which had to be amended following the *Junk* judgment.[67] The section now provides that notice of redundancy must be given to the Secretary of State before giving notice to terminate employment contracts and at least 30 or 90 days (depending on the number of redundancies proposed) before the first dismissal takes effect (rather than before the actual dismissal date).

The duty to inform and consult introduced by European Directives was initially difficult to implement in the traditional industrial relations system. It certainly appears that with or without the influence of the CJEU, recently the national courts seem to have toughened their attitude in relation to timing of consultation, content of the obligation and applicable sanctions. There is an incremental fusion with the spirit of the Directive in relation to the process and aim of consultation. Such positive outlook is counterbalanced by two current developments. Firstly, the decision of the CJEU in *USA v Nolan* will shed some light on the meaning of *contemplates* as discussed above. In times of economic recession, judges may be mindful of not imposing what could be perceived as additional burden on employers. Secondly, at the time of writing, the current Coalition government is reviewing the consultation redundancy rules, specifically envisaging reducing the 90 days consultation period.[68] The rationale

---

63   TULRCA 1992, s. 188(7) and s. 189(6).
64   *Clarks of Hove Ltd v Bakers' Union* [1978] ICR 1076.
65   Ibid.
66   Art. 3.
67   Collective Redundancies (Amendment) Regulations 2006 SI 2387/2006. On the case of *Junk v Kuhnel* [2005] IRLR 310, see section 2.1.1. above on 'timing of information and consultation'.
68   BIS, Department for Business, Innovation and Skills, *Call for Evidence, Collective Redundancy Consultation Rules*, (URN 11/1371, November 2011).

given is the 'age' of the rules, the uncertainty created by the current statutory language in relation to timing of consultation and the negative effect on decision making.[69] Statutory intervention may therefore potentially dilute or weaken the current framework.

2.2. TRANSFER OF UNDERTAKINGS

The duty to inform and consult in transfer of undertakings situations is essentially similar to the one found in collective redundancies. This stems from the source of the obligation which is also European[70] and it was enacted at a similar time under the same Social Action Programme. However, while the redundancy Directive was transposed under a Labour government, the Acquired Rights Directive was reluctantly implemented by a Conservative administration in 1981 in the Transfer of Undertaking (Protection of Employment) Regulations.[71] The regulations were subsequently amended in 2006 to reflect the changes brought by the 1998 Acquired Rights Directive.

The identity of employee representatives and their method of selection is the same as for collective redundancies. TUPE 1981 mirrored the requirements of the collective redundancies provisions: only recognised trade unions would be informed and consulted. This led to the same shortfalls in terms of employees' protection and reach of the right to inform and consult. The CJEU therefore condemned the UK simultaneously and required the UK to change the law for transfer of undertakings. The governments adjusted the provisions at the same times (1995 and 1999)[72] and the regime now found in TUPE 2006, Regulations 13 and 14 require employers to consult recognised trade unions if they exist or appropriate representatives in the same fashion than in TULRCA 1992, section 188.

The process and timing of information and consultation, as well as the remedies available differ slightly from the requirements in collective redundancies and there are therefore discussed further below.

---

69 Ibid., at 8.
70 Council Directive 77/187/EEC of 14 February 1977 on the approximation of the laws of the Member States relating to the safeguarding of the employees' rights in the event of transfers of undertakings, businesses or parts of businesses [1977] OJ L61/26 (the 'Acquired Rights Directive'). This Directive was amended by Council Directive 98/50/EC of 29 June 1998 [1998] OJ L210/88 and now codified in Council Directive 01/23/EC [2001] OJ L82/16.
71 Originally in the Transfer Of Undertakings (Protection of Employment) Regulations 1981, regs. 10–12, now in Transfer Of Undertakings (Protection of Employment) Regulations 2006, regs. 13–16.
72 See 2.1.3 'Representatives' above.

2.2.1. Timing, substance and process

The procedure for informing and consulting the affected employees through their representatives is partly similar to the redundancy system but varies in other aspects. It is a wide-ranging duty as the 'affected employees' are not necessarily only employees who transfer from an employer to another but any employees affected by the changes in the transferee and transferor undertakings.[73] As with economic dismissals, the type of information to be provided to the representatives is listed in the regulations and cover the following: the fact that the transfer will take place, its date and the reasons for it; the legal, economic and social implications of the transfer for the affected employees and the measures that the transferor or the transferee envisages to take in relation to the affected employees.[74] Similarly, the subject of consultation is found in the statutory provisions. In transfer situations, consultation only covers the last item of information provided: the measures that the employer envisages to take.[75] If no measures are envisaged, no consultation will take place. The statutory language is not clear and could potentially lead to confusion on the scope of the duty to consult. The word 'measure' is not defined and it is not necessarily easy to distinguish this category with the 'legal, economic and social implications of the transfer'. In the case where a transfer leads to employees having to commute to another location for example, would the financial compensation offered to transferred employees for additional travelling cost be considered as economic implications or measures? The notions are not explained in statutes or in the government guidance.[76] In *IPCS v Secretary of State for Defence*, it was held that 'measure' should be interpreted widely and includes steps, actions or arrangements.[77] A recent example shows that where an employer argues that changes beneficial to employees are simply administrative implications which do not warrant consultation because they are not measures, the EAT is prepared to evaluate the proposed changes and find the employer in breach of its consultation duty.[78] In that case, changes of the payment dates and to annual leave were considered as measures. However, the test applied to consider whether there is legal, social or economic implications and measures to be envisaged has been interpreted as subjective by the Court of Appeal. An employer who genuinely believes that there is no implication for the workforce

---

73 TUPE 2006, reg. 13(1).

74 TUPE 2006, reg. 13 (2).

75 TUPE 2006, reg. 13(6).

76 Department for Business, Innovation and Skills (BIS), *Employment Rights on the transfer of an undertaking. A guide to the 2006 TUPE Regulations for employers, employees and their representatives*, June 2009.

77 [1987] IRLR 373. Also see P. LORBER, 'Information and Consultation' in C. BOURN (Ed.) *The Transfer of Undertakings in the Public Sector*, Ashgate Dartmouth, 1999, p. 215.

78 *Todd v Strain and ors* [2011] IRLR 11.

does not have to consult the representatives.[79] Despite the risk that employers could potentially exempt themselves from the obligation to consult by simply stating that they had thought that the law did not apply, the Court of Appeal considered that as long as the employer discloses what he perceived to be in compliance with his legal requirements, he does not have to ensure the accuracy of this perception. The consequence of this case could be damaging to the consultation process. An objective test would put employee representatives in a less uncertain situation.

The consultation should take place with a view to 'seeking' an agreement. The language is slightly different than in the redundancy situation where the consultation must be with a view to 'reaching' an agreement. While this may denote a slightly weaker obligation, TUPE defines the consultation process in more detail than the redundancy provisions. The employer must consider representation made by the employee representatives, respond to them and if the proposals are rejected, the employer must give reasons for its decision.[80]

The information obligation is to take place 'long enough before the transfer' to enable the employer to consult the appropriate representatives.[81] Further, if the transferee envisages measures to take place, the information about such measures should be provided to the transferor at such time that will enable the transferor to perform its duties.[82] There is therefore a vague requirement and a potential difficulty in determining what is 'long enough' and what is a reasonable time for a transferee to pass on the relevant information to the transferor. A specific timetable for consultation is missing in the regulations. However, if representations have to be made by the employee side and reasons for accepting or rejecting such representations have to be given, a reasonable amount of time will have to be set aside for the consultation. Such flexibility could be helpful, in particular in complex cases, but it could also lead to uncertainty for the parties involved. The case law has however recently specified that consultation is not envisaged after the transfer between affected employees and the transferee.[83]

2.2.2. Remedies

Where the employer fails to fulfil the duty to inform and consult adequately or where there are issues about the employee representations, the remedies and actions to be taken are similar but not identical to what is found in the redundancy statutory provisions. The same parties can complain to an

---

[79]   *Royal Mail Group v Communication Workers Union* [2009] EWCA Civ 1045.
[80]   TUPE 2006, reg. 13(7).
[81]   TUPE 2006, reg. 13(2).
[82]   TUPE 2006, reg. 13(4).
[83]   *Amicus v City Building (Glasgow) LPP* [2009] IRLR 253.

employment tribunal and obtain declaration and compensation.[84] In case of the tribunal finding in favour of the complainant, the appropriate compensation is expressed in weeks rather than days and cannot exceed thirteen weeks.[85] The amount is to be determined according to what is viewed as just and equitable considering the seriousness of the failure to comply with the obligation. The judiciary coherently followed the guidance given by the Court of Appeal for failure to inform and consult in redundancy situation.[86] The nature of the remedy is not compensatory but punitive.[87] In *Cable Realisations Ltd v GMB*,[88] it was held that the size of the protective award should reflect the justice of the case.

The defence of 'special circumstances' is also available to employers to justify the inadequate information and consultation.[89] This exemption is also absent from the Acquired Rights Directive. As an exception, this defence should also be interpreted restrictively in transfer situations, in line with the collective redundancy approach.[90]

2.3. HEALTH AND SAFETY

The duty imposed upon employers to inform and consult with employees' representatives also arises in the field of health and safety. Unlike the measures discussed above, this obligation existed in UK law prior to initiatives being adopted at European level.[91] In the 1970s, the trade unions managed to put pressure on the government to introduce state intervention in this field.[92] The Safety Representatives and Safety Committee Regulations 1977 (SRSC) allowed trade unions to appoint safety representatives and to request the establishment of a safety committee in workplaces where they were recognised.[93] The representatives were entitled to exercise a number of functions such as consultation with management on health and safety matters, investigation of potential hazards and dangerous occurrence, examination of the causes of accidents, investigation of complaints by employees relating to health and safety, etc.[94]

---

[84]   TUPE 2006, regs. 15 and 16.
[85]   TUPE 2006, reg. 16(3).
[86]   See above 2.1.4. 'Enforcement and remedies', *Susie Radin Ltd v GMB* [2004] IRLR 400.
[87]   *Sweetin v Coral Racing* [2006] IRLR 252.
[88]   [2010] IRLR 42.
[89]   TUPE 2006, reg. 13(9).
[90]   See 2.1.4 above.
[91]   Health and Safety at Work etc. Act 1974, s. 2(6), and the accompanying Regulations, the Safety Representatives and Safety Committee Regulations 1977 (SI 1977/500).
[92]   D. Walters and T. Nichols, *Worker Representation and Workplace Health and Safety*, Palgrave Macmillan, 2007, p. 14.
[93]   SRSC 1977, reg. 3 for employee representatives and reg. 9 for safety committee.
[94]   SRSC 1977, reg. 4(1).

When the proposal for a Directive on the introduction of measures to encourage improvements in the health and safety of workers at work was put to the Member States of the European Community in 1989, there was no attempt to oppose the legislation by the UK.[95] Indeed, the national legislation only required minor adjustments to comply with the European standards. The relevant regulations are the Management of Health and Safety at Work Regulations 1992,[96] amended by the 1999 Regulations.[97] For example, a new regulation 4A in SRSC 1977 defined further the process of consultation: consultation should take place in good time and be related to a list of items found in the regulations, such as introduction of new measures that may affect the health and safety of employees, or the health and safety training envisaged by the employer.

In response to the decision of the CJEU in *European Commission v UK*,[98] the Health and Safety (Consultation with Employees) Regulations 1996 (HSCE)[99] extended the right of consultation to non-unionised workplaces. The regulatory solution partially mirrored what had been offered for the redundancy and transfer of undertakings consultation processes. Where unions were not recognised and had not appointed safety representatives, employers could either consult the employees directly or organise elections for employee representatives (named differently to the 1977 Regulations and known as 'employee representatives safety').[100] The HSCE do not include any rules on the organisation of the elections. An employer can simply choose whether to consult employees directly or through elected representatives. The choice left to employers for the identity of safety representatives where unions are not recognised is highly undesirable. First, this system is not in line with what exists in other information and consultation scenarios. As was seen in the previous section, the Labour government redressed partly the situation for redundancy and transfer situations where elections are the method preferred where there is no recognised trade union. Direct consultation is only permitted where the elections are unsuccessful, but this has not been done in respect of health and safety, making HSCE highly anomalous. Furthermore, the system limits the effectiveness of the consultation process and reach. Individuals, without collective support, are less likely to become involved and to challenge management. As a result, significant part of the workforce will not have a voice on health and safety matters. This is significant when research has shown that

---

[95] Council Directive 89/391/EEC of 12 June 1989 on the introduction of measures to encourage improvements in the safety and health of workers at work [1989] OJ L183/1.

[96] SI 1992/2051.

[97] SI 1999/3242.

[98] Discussed in 2.1.3.

[99] SI 1996/1513.

[100] HSCE 1996, reg. 4.

accident prevention is more likely in places where there are organised systems of health and safety representation.[101]

Other criticisms have been raised concerning the efficiency of the regulatory framework. They relate principally to the lack of coverage of the 1977 Regulations, in particular because of the decline in trade union recognition, and to the limited effectiveness of the representatives under HSCE, in terms of their function and the remedies available.[102] There is also an understandable wish for a rationalisation of the legislative framework that is fragmented and also reflects the layering of regulations in response to European requirements.[103] It is complex and counterproductive to have two sets of regulations, the 1977 and 1996 statutory instruments, one or the other applying depending on whether there are recognised trade unions or not. There have been a number of developments in this area, but the regulatory system has yet to be amended.

Since 1999, the Health and Safety Commission (HSC) has attempted to introduce measures to improve consultation of workers on health and safety matters.[104] Currently, this aim is expressed in a 'Collective Declaration on Worker Involvement'[105] which was the first output of A Strategy for Workplace Health and Safety on Great Britain to 2010 and beyond.[106] The latest development has been a consultation on worker involvement.[107] However, these initiatives have failed to materialise in legislative proposals that would address the shortcomings highlighted above.[108]

Finally, any breach of the regulations constitutes an offence.[109] As a result, the health and safety inspectors can intervene by issuing improvement notices. There are also specific provisions in the 1977 and 1996 Regulations which allow employee representatives to paid time off to exercise their functions and have access to training. Any complaint relating to these aspects would come under the employment tribunal jurisdiction.[110]

Information and consultation are available to employees and their representatives but through a fragmented system. This contrasted with the situation in a number of other European Member States where a general duty to

---

[101] D. Walters and T. Nichols, above n. 92, chapter 2.
[102] See P. James and D. Walters, 'Worker Representation in Health and Safety: Options for Regulatory Reform' (2002) 33 IRJ 141.
[103] D. Walters and T. Nichols, above n. 92, p. 152.
[104] See P. James and D. Walters, Health and Safety Revitalised or Reversed, Institute of Employment Rights, London 2004.
[105] <www.hse.govuk/involvement/hscdeclaration.pdf> accessed 1.11.2011.
[106] <www.hse.govuk/aboutus/strategiesandplans/strategy.htm> accessed 1.11.2011.
[107] <www.hse.govuk/consult/condocs/cd207.htm> accessed 1.11.2011.
[108] See D. Walters and T. Nichols, above n. 92, p. 157.
[109] Health and Safety Act 1974, s. 33(1)(c).
[110] SI 1977/500 and SI 1996/1513, reg. 7.

inform and consult workers on changes in the workplace existed. European Law came 'to the rescue' by requiring all Member States to have general systems of information and consultation in place.

3. THE GENERAL OBLIGATION TO INFORM AND CONSULT EMPLOYEE REPRESENTATIVES

Two European directives required undertakings to have information and consultation bodies or channels. Chronologically, a first instrument targeted multinationals which operated in at least two Member States of the European Union. The 1994 European Works Council Directive aimed at creating transnational bodies that would discuss issues that affected the workforce in more than one country. This was subsequently supplemented by a 2002 Directive that tackled national undertakings and required Member States to ensure that companies of a certain size informed and consulted representatives on matters that have an impact on the workforce.[111] Both instruments were mainly procedural and left Member States with a wide discretion in implementing the obligation to inform and consult. For the UK, these were significant developments as a statutory general duty to inform and consult on economic and social changes was a novelty. It therefore required careful consideration of transposition in relation to the scope of the duty, its content and its enforcement. This section considers first the obligation to inform and consult for national undertakings before analysing the situation of multinationals.

3.1. INFORMATION AND CONSULTATION IN UNDERTAKINGS OF MORE THAN 50 EMPLOYEES[112]

The Information and Consultation of Employees Regulations 2004[113] transposed the 2002 Informing and Consulting of Employees Directive. Undertakings employing more than fifty employees are required to set information and consultation arrangements whereby employee representatives can discuss issues

---

[111] Council Directive 94/45/EC of 22 September 1994 on the establishment of a European Works Council or a procedure in Community-scale undertakings for the purposes of informing and consulting employees [1994] OJ L254/64 and Council Directive 02/14/EC of the European Parliament and of the Council of 11 March 2002, establishing a general framework for informing and consulting employees in the European Community [2002] OJ L80/29. For the latter, see B. BERCUSSON, 'The European Social Model Comes to Britain' (2002) 31 *ILJ* 209.

[112] This section draws in parts on an earlier paper by P. LORBER, 'Implementing the Information and Consultation Directive in Great Britain: a new voice at work?' (2006) 22 *International Journal of Comparative Labour Law and Industrial Relations (IJCLLIR)* 231.

[113] SI 2004/3426.

that affect the workforce. The government was keen to maximise flexibility for businesses and to avoid disrupting trade union arrangements on consultation.[114] It therefore associated the national social partners to the process and concluded a tripartite agreement on the objective of the implementation and the main elements of the regulations. This was the first time that such approach had been taken in relation to implementation of European measures.[115] The regulations are primarily procedural. They could have built on a number of familiar concepts used in other pieces of legislation, such as consultation, but the government chose to transpose the directive verbatim, to exploit the flexibility left to the parties and as a result, has limited the right to information and consultation. This is evidenced by the scope of the regulations, the establishment and extent of the obligation to inform and consult, the choice of representatives and the enforcement mechanisms.

3.1.1. Scope

The regulations apply to undertakings with 50 or more employees.[116] The government opted for this formula rather than the other option provided by the directive which entitled Member States to cover establishments with 20 employees or more. The scope chosen by the government was to avoid burdening small businesses.[117] The consequence however was the exclusion of a great majority of companies as it was reported that 97% of them employed less than 50.[118]

The regulations apply to employees and they provide the relevant formula for counting the number of employees.[119] Controversially, employees who do not work full-time may only be counted as half employees.[120] This is a hurdle to trigger the right to information and consultation as well as potentially a discriminatory practice towards part-time employees.[121]

---

[114]　P. Lorber, 'National Works Council: Opening the door on a whole new era in the United Kingdom employment relations?' (2003) 19 *IJCLLIR* 297, 311.

[115]　P. Lorber, (2006) above n. 112, 233. See also M. Hall, 'EU Regulation and the UK Employee Consultation Framework' (2010) 31 *Economic and Industrial Democracy* 55, 60.

[116]　This is the case since April 2008. The government had operated a transitional implementation of the European measure. This option was allowed by Art. 10 of the Directive for member states which did not have permanent statutory bodies for information and consultation purposes. This affected the UK and Ireland.

[117]　BERR, *High Performance Workplaces: Informing and consulting employees. Consultation document*, July 2003, para. 2.32.

[118]　Ibid., Annex C.

[119]　Reg. 4.

[120]　Reg. 4(3).

[121]　Such practice may be caught by the principle of equal treatment between part time and full time workers protected by the Part –Time Workers (Prevention of Less Favourable Treatment) Regulations 2000 SI 2000/1551.

3.1.2. Establishment and functioning of information and consultation bodies

Management of an undertaking that fulfils ICER criteria has to consider setting up an information and consultation body or channel. The word 'consider' is used because there is no *de facto* obligation. The government followed the directive's lead and left it to the affected parties to engage in setting up the relevant system. Such formula leaves a legal vacuum as inaction from either the employee or the employer side translates into the non-application of the legal obligation. If management wishes to take the risk that employees will not request the establishment of an information and consultation body or channel, they may not be subject to the regulations and can effectively 'get away' from having to inform and consult the workforce on measures that affect the employees. The tactic is perhaps not so risky considering that their workforce is less likely to be aware of the regulations. Even with knowledge, it is uncertain whether employees would try to trigger the negotiations of information and consultation arrangements, firstly because of the need to find support from others (see below) and secondly they may not feel as confident or well-equipped to approach an employer to make such a request. An early assessment of the impact of the regulations suggests that employers' strategy of betting on employees' apathy had paid off.[122] Further, even trade unions did not necessarily engage with triggering the formation of new consultation bodies, by fear of undermining consultation and/or negotiation arrangements that had been carefully set up.[123]

The regulations do not impose a model of information and consultation. Prior to the regulations, and despite the lack of statutory intervention, management had experienced information and consultation bodies, while trade unions had negotiated with some employers consultative mechanisms.[124] The intention was therefore not to upset existing systems, either historically created by management or negotiated with trade unions. However, there are safeguards to prevent employers from imposing a system and as a counterpart, employees have to show support for the setting up of information and consultation mechanisms. The regulations therefore offer a number of options to management. The overall picture is that companies that have information and consultation mechanisms, prior to an employees' request to establish such mechanisms, will be outside the regulatory framework. Provided certain conditions are fulfilled,[125] companies

---

[122]   M. HALL, 'A Cool Response to the ICE Regulations: Employers and Trade Unions Responses to the new legal framework for information and consultation' (2006) 37 *IRJ* 456, 466 and 470.

[123]   Ibid., 467.

[124]   B. KERSLEY, C. ALPIN, J. FORTH, A. BRYSON, H. BEWLEY, G. DIX and S. OXENBRIDGE, *Inside the Workplace Findings from the 2004 Workplace Employment Relations Survey*, Routledge, London 2006, p. 126.

[125]   According to reg. 8, the agreement must be in writing; cover all the employees of the undertaking; set out how the employer will give information to the employees and their

can chose how and when they talk to their workforce. In such situation, there are no checks and balances as the enforcement mechanisms do not apply to what has been referred to as pre-existing agreement (PEA), potentially leaving the workforce without remedy if there is a breach.[126]

For undertakings that are not in this situation, negotiations, triggered by employer or employees, can take place to reach an agreement on the provisions of information and consultation. Conditions have to be fulfilled in relation to the proportion of the workforce that can make such request as one employee or existing employee representatives cannot kickstart the process.[127] Once the employee request or employer notification is registered, specific representatives have to be appointed or elected in order to negotiate the agreement.[128] Successful negotiations allow method and content of information and consultation to be agreed between parties, again without a steer from the regulations except for a time limit on the length of the negotiations[129] and for procedural guarantees.[130]

An additional scenario can lead to information and consultation being negotiated, if a PEA is called into question by the workforce. This situation was envisaged to allow employees to challenge a procedure or policy that would have been 'imposed' by the employer or that employees would like to see improve.[131] However strict conditions are also applied for such a challenge in order to avoid well-established mechanisms to be altered or to allow what are regarded as vexatious requests to disrupt agreed processes. If the request comes from more than 40% of the workforce, the employer will have to negotiate a new agreement. If the request represents less than 40% of the employees (but more than 10%), the employer can organise a ballot seeking to endorse the employees' request. A result in favour of the employees forces the employer to negotiate, but the result of the votes is subject to a qualified majority which imposes a high threshold for the workforce.[132]

---

representatives and seek their views on such information. Finally, the agreement must have been approved by the employees.

[126] Similarly, individual employees can find it difficult to enforce collective agreements through their individual contracts, see chapter 3.

[127] 10% of the workforce with a minimum of 25 employees and a maximum of 2500 according to reg. 7(2) and (3).

[128] Reg. 14(1) and (2).

[129] Employer and negotiating representatives must reach an agreement within six months. However, the employer and a majority of the negotiating representatives can extend, without limit, the length of the negotiations. Reg. 14(3) and (5).

[130] Agreements must be in writing and dated, cover all employees and set out the circumstances in which the employees will be informed and consulted. Finally, agreements must be endorsed by the employer and the employees. Reg. 16(1).

[131] For an example where pre-existing agreements with trade unions were challenged by an individual see *Stewart v Moray Council* [2006] IRLR 592.

[132] Reg. 8(6) which requires 40% of the employees employed in the undertaking and the majority of those voting to have voted in favour of endorsing the request.

It is only if negotiations fail or if an employer does not respond to an employee request that a statutory model is imposed upon the employer.[133] In this case, the regulations dictate how employee representatives are elected[134] and how information and consultation should take place.[135] Employee representatives should be *informed* of the recent and probable development of the undertaking's or the establishment's activities and economic situation. They should be *informed and consulted* on the situation, structure and probable development of employment within the undertaking and on any anticipatory measures envisaged, in particular where there is a threat to employment, and on decisions likely to lead to substantial changes in work organisation or in contractual relations, including collective redundancies and transfer of undertakings. Information must be given at such time, in such fashion and with such content as are appropriate to enable employees' representatives to conduct an adequate study, and, where necessary, prepare for consultation. Consultation is defined as an *'exchange of views and establishment of dialogue between the employees' representatives and the employer'*. Further, consultation shall take place while ensuring that the timing, method and content are appropriate; in such a way as to enable employees' representatives to meet with the employer and obtain a response, and the reasons for that response, to any opinion they might formulate; and with a view to reaching an agreement on decisions within the scope of the employer's powers likely to lead to substantial changes in work organisation or in contractual relations. The obligation is much more detailed than in any of the other cases of information and consultation. While the statutory model has been used as a template for negotiating agreements,[136] recalcitrant employers have been ordered by the CAC to follow such procedure when they fail to respond to employees' request.[137]

Overall, the regulations give priority to procedure and legitimacy. They also encourage negotiations. They however fail to give a substantial right to information and consultation. The lack of benchmark or minimum requirements shows the lack of commitment to the right. There is a further weakening of the involvement of the employees because of the provisions on confidential information. An employer may refuse completely to provide some information if it is believed that it could be prejudicial or seriously harm the functioning of the undertaking.[138] Further, the employer can request the recipient of the

---

133   Reg. 18.
134   Reg. 19.
135   Reg. 20.
136   M. HALL, S. HUTCHINSON, J. PURCELL, M. TERRY, J. PARKER, *Information and Consultation under ICE Regulations: Evidence from Longitudinal Case Studies*, BIS, Employment Relations Research Series No117, 10/1380, December 2010, p. 6.
137   *Amicus v Macmillan Publishers* [2007] IRLR 885.
138   Reg. 26.

information to keep it confidential.[139] On both accounts, the employer's decision can be challenged before the Central Arbitration Committee (CAC), but this is a further hurdle for employees and their representatives.[140]

3.1.3. Employee representatives

Considering the difficult application of previous directives on information and consultation in relation to the identity of employee representatives and considering the more rather positive attitude of the Labour government towards unions when it came to giving them a collective voice,[141] there was an expectation that unions would be given priority as employee representatives in the context of information and consultation. However, the government chose to privilege what they considered as democracy over established industrial relations.[142] In most instances where employee representatives are called upon, the regulations specify that they have to be elected or appointed by the workforce. The latter form of selection suggests that democracy is not truly understood as having constant resort to elections. As a result, recognised trade unions cannot claim an automatic right to being consulted, unless they stand for election or ask to be appointed or a PEA applies. For example, the standard information and consultation provisions, where applicable, require employee representatives to be elected[143] and do not mention trade unions. Similarly, in situations where there is an attempt to negotiate an agreement, negotiating representatives have to be appointed or elected according to certain criteria.[144] There are however inconsistencies within the regulations as the elections organised for employee representatives under the standard information and consultation are regulated by a much more detailed process, including the appointment of a ballot supervisor for example.[145] This does not apply to negotiating representatives but no justification was put forward for this difference in treatment.

Furthermore, little right is given to employee representatives as a whole. For example, they cannot request the start of negotiations for the establishment of

---

[139] Reg. 25.

[140] The CAC also has jurisdiction for disputes concerning the disclosure of information for the purpose of collective bargaining. See chapter 3.

[141] This was evidenced in the first few years of their new mandate by the introduction of the statutory recognition procedure for the purpose of collective bargaining (see chapter 3) and by the changes in TULRCA 1992 and TUPE 1981 aimed at allowing trade unions to be informed and consulted on collective redundancies and transfer of undertakings when they were recognised (see above 2.1.3.).

[142] P. Davies and C. Kilpatrick, 'UK Worker Representation After Single Channel' (2004) 33 ILJ 121.

[143] ICER, reg. 19.

[144] ICER, reg. 14(1) and (2).

[145] ICER, sched. 2.

information and consultation mechanisms. This is a serious disadvantage for the application of the regulations as employees have to gather the relevant number of signatures (10% of the workforce) instead of being able to rely on established and legitimate representatives when they are recognised in the workplace.

The choice of representatives and the mechanisms whereby they are selected have been criticised on a number of fronts.[146] Firstly, the regulations allow for direct participation of employees rather than collective representation. In case of negotiated agreements, the agreement can provide for information and consultation directly with the workforce instead of appointing or electing representatives.[147] This has been deemed possibly in breach of the directive which specifically refers to communication via representatives.[148] The regulatory choice reflects pressure by employers who prefer direct communication with the workforce.[149] Secondly, trade unions who are experienced representatives are deprived of an essential new function. This is potentially damaging to their organisation which would benefit from this role. As collective bargaining coverage and recognition keeps declining, performing information and consultation task would re-inforce industrial relations. Some case studies have shown that introduction or revision of information and consultation arrangements have 'created new sources of influence for trade unions'.[150] However, recent research shows that trade unions have been ambivalent towards the information and consultation function. Originally, there were fearful of management using the regulations to replace union voice and functions and some of those fear seem to have materialised in some instances.[151] They have not necessarily sought to create new bodies or to take part in the consultative committees, 'evidencing a remarkable lack of enthusiasm for making use of the new statutory procedures'.[152] Other studies provide mixed pictures where unions recognised for collective bargaining have worked with employee forum in situations of restructuring but have also competed.[153] Thirdly, multiplying the ways employee representatives are selected depending on the regulations that are engaged is disadvantageous to employers who may have to deal with different sets of counterparts. Fourthly, the impact on the effectiveness of the regulations

---

[146] See P. DAVIES and C. KILPATRICK, above n. 142.

[147] ICER, reg. 16.

[148] See P. LORBER (2006) above n. 112, 248–249.

[149] See for example, P.J. GOLLAN and A. WILKINSON, 'Implications of the EU Information and Consultation Directive and the Regulations in the UK – prospects for the future of employee representation' (2007) 18 *The International Journal of Human Resource Management* 1145, 1155.

[150] S. DEAKIN and A. KOUKIADAKI, above n. 5, p. 21 of the paper.

[151] C.F. WRIGHT, 'What role for trade unions in future workplace relations', (ACAS Future of Workplace Relations Discussion paper series, September 2011), p. 5.

[152] See M. HALL (2010), above n. 115, 63.

[153] S. DEAKIN and A. KOUKIADAKI, above n. 5, p. 18 of the paper.

and on a significant engagement in information and consultation could be damaging. Non-union representatives may not be appropriately skilled or trained to undertake the function. The regulations do not provide for training of the employee representatives. Finally, it has been shown that '*unions continue to be the most effective mechanisms for representing workers' interests and that non-union mechanisms produce limited benefits for management in terms of productivity*'.[154] Case studies have shown that most information and consultation bodies are elected, but that some bodies are hybrid, being constituted of union representatives and elected representatives of non-union employees.[155]

3.1.4.   Enforcement and remedies

ICER entrust two institutions to deal with complaints about the establishment and operation of the information and consultation bodies. The Central Arbitration Committee (CAC) adjudicates on most issues.[156] For example, if the employer fails to provide information about the number of employees employed in the undertaking for the purpose of finding if the workforce is larger than 50, a complaint can be brought before the CAC.[157] This is also the case if there is a dispute about election of representatives[158] or the operation of a negotiated agreement or of the standard information and consultation provisions.[159]

The sanctions that can be imposed by the CAC are declarations that the complaint is well-founded, followed by orders which aim to rectify the situation. For example, if the employer breaches the negotiated agreement by not disclosing the relevant information, the CAC can order the employer to do so within a specified time frame.[160] The remedies for employees and their representatives are therefore effective as they force the employer to respect their agreement or the regulations. This is in contrast with the other obligations to inform and consult which focus on financial compensation or punishment for the breach of the law.

The Employment Appeal Tribunal is the second body entrusted with enforcing the regulations. Firstly, it plays the role of appellate court to the CAC decisions. Secondly it is tasked to apply sanctions which are not orders. It is the court that can impose financial penalty for breach of negotiated agreement or of the standard provisions. In this case, the CAC must first declare that there has been

---

[154]   C.F. WRIGHT, above n. 151, p. 4.
[155]   See M. HALL, S. HUTCHISON. J. PURCELL, M. TERRY, J. PARKER (2010), above n. 136, 8.
[156]   All the decisions relation to ICER 2004 are listed on the CAC website at www.cac.govuk/ and see CAC Annual Report 2010–11 at 10.
[157]   ICER, reg. 6.
[158]   Reg. 15.
[159]   Reg. 22.
[160]   Reg. 22(4).

a breach. Armed with such a declaration, the complainant can go to the EAT and ask for a penalty notice to be issued.[161] This sanction is effectively a fine that is paid to the Secretary of State. It cannot exceed £75,000 and the amount is determined by the EAT considering a number of factors such as the gravity of the failure, the reason for it, etc.,[162] although the current case law indicates that each case is fact-specific when it comes to determining the overall amount.[163]

The nature of the EAT sanction is also unusual when compared to the protective award available for other information and consultation obligations. While the courts have indicated that the award is a punitive sanction against an employer breaching the law in redundancy and transfer,[164] the penalty notice seems to be in the same spirit. However, employees are not the beneficiaries in the case of ICER. There is no compensation but a fine that goes to the state. The amount is limited to £75,000 which is not only a maximum but compares favourably for the employer to the penalty of up to 90 days salary per employee affected by breach of information and consultation in a collective redundancy situation. Further, in a case of a serious breach, the EAT considered that £55,000 was enough to 'deter others from adopting [...] a wholly cavalier attitude to their obligations'[165] even if in redundancy situation, any lack of information and consultation warrants to start with the maximum 90 days of protective award. These aspects could weaken the significance of the regulations. The sanctions could be viewed as not significantly effective or deterrent. This is further evidenced by two other considerations. Firstly, a CAC order can never suspend or prevent a decision from being made even if information and consultation have not adequately taken place.[166] Secondly, the employer can avoid the penalty notice if it can establish that the failure to inform and consult resulted from a reason beyond its control or that there are some other reasonable excuse.[167] This defence is much wider than the one provided in redundancy and transfer legislation. It also does not appear in the Directive.

3.1.5. Assessment

The introduction of ICER was seen as a potential new voice for the workforce and the opportunity to involve more employee representatives in decision making. As Deakin and Koukiadaki highlight, the legislation provided

---

[161] Reg. 22(6).
[162] Reg. 23(3).
[163] *Darnton v Bournemouth University* UKEAT /0391/09/RN at [12] and *Brown v G4 Security* UKEAT/0526/09/RN at [23].
[164] See *Susie Radin Ltd v GMB* [2004] IRLR 400 and *Sweetin v Coral Racing* [2006] IRLR 252, discussed in sections 2.1.4. and 2.2.2.
[165] *Amicus v MacMillan publishers Ltd* [2007] IRLR 885 at [25].
[166] ICER, reg. 22(9).
[167] ICER, reg. 22(7).

'*information and consultation rights which did not depend on trade union recognition or membership [...], it opened up the possibility for a more integrative form of employee participation in firm level decision-making than that associated with collective bargaining, with its assumption of a clear separation of worker and employer interests*'.[168] Examination of the regulations shows that there are many hurdles for establishing the relevant communication channels. The incentives to do so are also limited as the obligation is rather weak in terms of substance, while the remedies are not fully adequate to deter employers. Such evaluation has further been underpinned by the number of agreements reported to be in existence under the regulations and the attitude of employers, trade unions and employees towards the purpose of the instrument. HALL reports that employers took a 'risk assessment' approach rather than a 'compliance' approach in view of employees' apathy.[169] It is also suggested that revisions of existing systems or creation of new bodies are less legislation driven than management-driven. For example, information and consultation committees were created outside the legislative framework.[170] Further, management is the main architect and influence in the design of the bodies and channels. Employees are not reported to trigger the regulations and trade unions have not been active in promoting this kind of dialogue.[171] However, other studies show that trade unions have influenced the content of agreements where established structures were already in place.[172] Finally, as the process is said to be management-driven, two types of bodies have emerged according to the researchers. One type of information and consultation structure will appear to be anticipatory and ready to discuss operational and managerial decisions before they are finalised with the representatives. Such bodies are reported to be dynamic, pro-active and fully embracing the idea that information and consultation can be beneficial to the undertaking. They also seem to play a very positive role in restructuring.[173] The second type of bodies is much more information-driven and allows employees to see the 'bigger picture' without having a real participatory role.[174] Research has also shown that some of the unions' fears towards ICER have been materialised. Some employers introduced or reviewed information and consultation mechanisms to stop union recognition claims.[175] These findings suggest that there are good practices that should be communicated widely but that employees

---

[168]   S. DEAKIN and A. KOUKIADAKI, above n. 5, p. 4 of the paper.
[169]   M. HALL (2006), above n. 122.
[170]   See M. HALL, S. HUTCHISON. J. PURCELL, M. TERRY, J. PARKER (2010), above n. 136, 2.
[171]   Ibid., 5.
[172]   S. DEAKIN and A. KOUKIADAKI, above n. 5, p. 9 of the paper.
[173]   Ibid., pp. 15–16.
[174]   M. HALL, S. HUTCHISON. J. PURCELL, M. TERRY, J. PARKER (2010), above n. 136, 6.
[175]   Examples were found in the retail sector where there was a strong union presence but no union recognised. S. DEAKIN and A. KOUKIADAKI, above n. 5, p. 14 of the paper or see J. PURCELL and M. HALL, *The effect of the Information and Consultation Directive on industrial relations in the EU Member States five years after its transposition: the UK*, European

and their representatives should take a more engaged attitude to make the process more widespread and effective. It is also advanced that trade unions should be given a more prominent statutory role as representative to avoid the law being used as a tool to prevent unions to enter the workplace.

The national obligation to inform and consult is complemented by a transnational duty.

3.2. EUROPEAN WORKS COUNCILS IN MULTINATIONALS

Employers were first exposed to an obligation to involve representatives in discussions on economic, financial and social developments when the European Works Council Directive was adopted in 1994.[176] It pre-dates ICER and only applies to multinationals. It required the establishment of European works councils (EWC) which would be informed and consulted on transnational matters that affected the workforce. The Transnational Information and Consultation of Employees Regulations 1999[177] are the implementing measure. They indicate what companies are caught by the obligations; how to establish an EWC; its function and the enforcement mechanisms and remedies.

While there are many similarities between ICER and TICER in terms of aims, mechanisms and substance, there are also noticeable differences. They can be explained by the fact the Information and Consultation Directive did not mirror exactly the European Works Council Directive. Further, the UK government did not replicate some of the provisions found in TICER into ICER for reasons which are not always clear. This has led to some inconsistencies that will be highlighted below but which ultimately add to the fragmented and incoherent nature of the legal framework.

Industrial Relations Observatory online, <www.eurofound.europa.eu/eiro/studies/tn1009029s/uk1009029q.htm> accessed 3.11.2011.

[176] Council Directive 94/45/EC of 22 September 1994 on the establishment of a European Works Council or a procedure in Community-scale undertakings and Community-scale groups of undertakings for the purposes of informing and consulting employees [1994] OJ L254/64.

[177] SI 1999/3323. The Regulations transposed Council Directive 97/74/EC extending, to the United Kingdom of Great Britain and Northern Ireland, Directive 95/45/EC on the establishment of a European Works Council or a procedure in Community-scale undertakings and Community-scale groups of undertakings for the purposes of informing and consulting employees [1997] OJ L10/22. The specific Directive directed at the United Kingdom was the result of the Labour government signing up to Directives which had been adopted during the opt-out period of 1992–1997 when the previous Conservative government had agreed not to be part of the European social chapter in the Maastricht Treaty.

3.2.1. Scope and application of the Regulations

The obligation to create an EWC applies to Community-scale undertakings or Community-scale groups of undertakings. They are defined by the regulations as companies that employ at least 1000 employees over the territories of the Member States of the European Union and at least 150 employees in each of at least two Member States.[178] Where the central management is located in the UK, the law applicable to the EWC will be TICER 1999[179] and it is the responsibility of that undertaking to establish the EWC. However, a multinational headquartered outside the European Union may still fulfil the threshold and TICER may apply if the multinational has nominated the UK operation as its headquarters or in absence of nomination, if the UK undertaking has the largest workforce in the EU.[180]

The regulations provide a mechanism to count the number of employees[181] and a procedure to complain if management does not provide the information on employees' number and repartition in the multinational.[182] Most of the CJEU case law on EWC has so far been focused on the disclosure of information to the workforce where employees or their representatives try to ascertain if their company qualifies for the establishment of an EWC.[183]

As of November 2011, there were just under 1,000 active EWC across the EU, with just under 120 from UK headquartered companies.[184] These figures place the UK just behind the US and German multinationals. The government estimates that 265 companies headquartered in this country could potentially be caught with 43% having a EWC or equivalent procedure set up.[185]

3.2.2. Establishment and functioning of EWCs

The EWC Directive and TICER gave wide discretion and freedom to companies to establish their European information and consultation forum. As with ICER, the emphasis was on procedure rather than substance, encouraging

---

[178] TICER 1999, reg. 2(1).

[179] Reg. 4.

[180] TICER, reg. 5(1).

[181] Reg. 6.

[182] Reg. 8.

[183] See Case C-62/99 *Betriebsrat der Bofrost v Bofrost* [2001] IRLR 403; Case C-440/00 *Gesamtbetriebsrat der Kuhne & Hagel v Kuhne & Nagel* [2004] IRLR 332; Case C-349/01 *Betriebsrat der Firma ADS Anker v ADS Anker* [2004] 3 CMLR 299.

[184] See Worker Participation.eu, Facts and Figures (service of the European Trade Union Institute) at <www.worker-participation.eu/European-Works-Councils/Facts-Figures> accessed 2.02.2012. Examples of UK companies reported to have EWC are Barclays or Rolls Royce.

[185] BIS, *Impact Assessment on the Recast EWC Directive* (April 2010).

multinationals to put in place systems adapted to their own circumstances but ensuring that there would be communications and exchanges on matters that affected the workforce beyond their own frontiers. Three options were offered to companies. One was the same opt out from the regulations as under ICER. If companies had an agreement that fulfilled certain conditions, TICER would not apply. The differences with ICER were twofold. Firstly, pre-existing agreements only had to fulfil three conditions to be valid: covering the entire workforce; providing information and consultation on transnational matters and be in place before the implementation of the Directive in national law.[186] The latter condition explains the second difference. The pre-existing agreements are no longer a valid choice for undertakings as they had to be in place before TICER came into force (in December 1999). Such a deadline meant that there was an incentive for companies to conclude agreements and the figures show that there was a significant increase in EWC around that time.[187] In ICER, such deadline does not exist since the pre-existing agreement must pre-date an employees' request. This would explain the risk assessment strategy applied by employers. In this respect, TICER was more conducive to establishing information and consultation mechanisms and to complying with the law.

The second route opened to undertakings for the establishment of European Works Council is the negotiation of an agreement according to the procedure laid out in TICER. This remains a flexible option because the parties do not have to apply a specific model but simply abide by the rules which stipulate how the EWC should be set up. The process is similar to ICER as either the employer or employees request the start of negotiations for the EWC agreement.[188] The differences are again twofold. Firstly, employee representatives can approach management while in ICER only employees can do so.[189] This means that in organised workplaces, trade unions can take an active role and take away the burden placed upon individual employees. A high and qualified threshold remains however when employees or their representatives initiate the process. The request must come from at least 100 employees or their representatives, provided they come from at least two undertakings located in two different Member States.[190] This constitutes a second difference with ICER and is explained by the transitional nature of the EWC. The additional condition presupposes either links between trade unions from different countries or, if the workforce is not organised, communications between employees across borders when they do not necessarily speak the same language. The need for transnational collaboration to engage management in establishing EWCs has

---

[186] TICER, reg. 44.
[187] See Worker Participation.eu, Facts and Figures, above n. 184.
[188] TICER, reg. 9.
[189] Reg. 9(1).
[190] Reg. 9(2).

therefore been identified as a hurdle and as one of the reasons for the slowing down in negotiating EWC agreements.[191]

Once the request has been made, the principle of appointing negotiating representatives remains, but a Special Negotiating Body (SNB) must be established for the life of the negotiations.[192] The sole purpose of this body is to determine with central management the scope, composition, functions and terms of office of a EWC, by written agreement.[193] The composition of the SNB must reflect the location of the workforce throughout the Member States. Each country where the undertaking operates must be represented according to the legal framework of each national representative. A French representative would be appointed according to the French labour code or a Spanish worker according to the Spanish legislation. The UK members are elected according to a detailed process laid down in the regulations.[194] The exception to the holding of a ballot is if a consultative committee exists already in the undertaking. In this case, the consultative committee nominates from its number the UK members of the SNB.[195] The reference to consultative committee is unusual because such bodies did not exist statutorily at the time that TICER was drafted. Research shows that equivalent bodies which perform information and consultation function were operational in 14% of workplaces in 2004 and were in decline.[196] This is a small fraction but it is valuable that TICER recognised industrial relations realities. It is anticipated that such structures may develop with the effect of ICER 2004. However, it has been seen that the impact of the national information and consultation regulations has been limited.[197] The next Workplace Employment Relations Survey due in 2012–2013[198] should help shedding some light on whether consultative committees will increase because of ICER. Assuming the presence of national information and consultation bodies is also beneficial to a comprehensive system of participation in multinationals with layers of democratic bodies effective at all levels of the organisation and liaising with each other. TICER defines a consultative committee as a body whose function includes the carrying out of information and consultation free from management interference. It must represent all UK employees and members must have all

---

[191]   P. LORBER, 'Worker Participation and Industrial Democracy: Strengthening Information and Consultation' in E. ALES, T. JASPERS, P. LORBER, C. SACHS-DURAND, U. WRENDELING-SCHROEDER (eds.), *Fundamental Social Rights in Europe: Challenges and Opportunities*, Intersentia, 2009, p. 138–139.
[192]   TICER, regs. 11–15.
[193]   Reg. 11.
[194]   Regs. 13 and 14.
[195]   TICER, reg. 15.
[196]   B. KERSLEY, C. ALPIN, J. FORTH, A. BRYSON, H. BEWLEY, G. DIX AND S. OXENBRIDGE, above n. 124, p. 126.
[197]   See 3.1.5. above.
[198]   See <www.bis.gov.uk/policies/employment-matters/research/wers> accessed 2.11.2011.

been elected.[199] The last condition further limits the use of existing representative channels if members of the consultative committee had been appointed by trade unions for example. However, it is reported that 57% of consultative committees have their members elected.

Management and the SNB must reach an agreement that will stipulate the function of the forum, the composition of the EWC, the venue and frequency of meetings, the financial and materials resources allocated to the EWC and the duration of the agreement.[200] This list is more comprehensive than in ICER where more freedom is given to the parties.[201]

If an agreement cannot be reached, or if the employer does not respond to an employees' request, a model EWC is imposed upon the multinational.[202] The details of the functioning of the EWC and of its membership are found in the subsidiary requirement. The differences between the standard information and consultation arrangements in ICER and TICER are primarily about the consultation process. The latter includes the necessity to meet once a year to discuss transnational matters only.[203] The ICE Regulations are more specific in relation to timing of the process, meeting with management, responses to representatives and consultation with a view to reaching an agreement.[204] This makes the EWC process weaker. However, some of those aspects have been improved by the recast EWC Directive[205] which came into force in June 2011 in national law (see below).

As with ICER, the information and consultation obligation can be limited where the employer labels the information as confidential. The provisions are identical.[206]

3.2.3. Employee representatives

The inconsistencies discussed in relation to ICER and the other body of law relevant to information and consultation[207] when it comes to employee representatives is further complicated with TICER. While ICER does not refer to

---

[199]   TICER, reg. 15(4).
[200]   Reg. 17.
[201]   Compare with ICER 2004, reg. 16.
[202]   TICER, Reg. 18.
[203]   TICER, sched, paras. 6 and 7.
[204]   See section 3.1.2.
[205]   Directive 2009/38/EC of the European Parliament and of the Council of 6 May 2009 on the establishment of a European Works Council or a procedure in Community scale undertakings and Community scale groups of undertakings for the purposes of informing and consulting employees (Recast) [2009] OJ L122/28.
[206]   TICER, regs. 23–24.
[207]   For redundancies, transfer of undertaking or health and safety.

trade unions at all, TICER seem more attuned to existing channels of communication without giving full priority to trade unions where they are recognised. This is more positive than ICER but again confuses matters from the perspective of employers and trade unions or employees who wish to engage and participate in information and consultation machineries. The discrepancies are all the more puzzling in that the same government implemented both sets of Directives. It has already been noted that TICER gives some role to existing consultative bodies which represent the workforce and allow employee representatives to approach the employer to request negotiation of an EWC agreement. Further, the standard EWC can be composed of UK members who are trade union representatives if the trade union is recognised.[208] In this case, such representatives can be selected or appointed to represent the UK workforce on the EWC. This is on condition that all UK employees are represented by such trade unions, which may not always happen, especially where some trade unions represent one category of workers but not others. Where trade unions or other employee representatives do not represent the whole workforce, elections have to be organised according to the rules found in the subsidiary requirements.

3.2.4. *Enforcement and remedies*

The enforcement mechanisms also bear some resemblance to ICER as the CAC and EAT are the bodies involved in adjudicating disputes. However, the role of the EAT was more complex than in ICER where it is the 'financial' enforcer of the CAC decision in addition to being a court of appeal.[209] In TICER, CAC and EAT shared the competence of dealing with disputes at the first level. For example, the CAC arbitrates in relation to election of employee representatives if there is a complaint about the ballot arrangements[210] or about whether a consultative committee fulfils the criteria of the definition given by the regulations.[211] However, the EAT had jurisdiction to hear a dispute about the non-establishment of a EWC[212] or about the operation of the EWC under a negotiated agreement or under the statutory model found in the subsidiary requirements.[213] This was unusual and caused some difficulties to the EAT when a case came before it on the operation of the P&O EWC agreement.[214] This inconsistency has been remedied following the implementation of the recast EWC Directive as will be seen below.

---

[208]   TICER, sched. Para. 3.
[209]   See section above 3.1.4.
[210]   TICER, reg. 13(4).
[211]   Reg. 15(7).
[212]   Reg. 20.
[213]   Reg. 21.
[214]   *P&O European Forum (European Works Council) v The Peninsular &Oriental Steam Navigation Company* (EAT) unreported, transcript provided as part of a case study: The agreement to establish a European Works Council for Dubai Ports World www. euroworkscouncil.net as discussed in P. LORBER, 'The EWC in domestic case law – United

The remedies keep the same as ICER. Originally both the CAC and EAT could make orders to remedy a situation such as change to the arrangements of a ballot or an order for management to comply with the terms of the EWC agreement. However, the CAC is now the only body using such remedy following the changes made by the government in 2010 (see below). The EAT may issue a penalty notice within exactly the same parameters as for ICER.[215] The similarities were such that the maximum for the penalty notice was also £75,000 originally. Clearly there should have been a different tariff as undertakings with 50 employees do not have the same means as multinationals. This has also been amended by the transposition of the recast Directive. The same defence (as in ICER) is available to an employer who can argue that failure to establish an EWC (or to enter into appropriate information and consultation) was for reasons beyond central's management control or some other reasonable excuse.[216]

3.2.5. Recast Directive and changes to TICER 1999

The European Works Council Directive was updated in 2009 via a recast directive.[217] This was the result of a long process where European trade unions and management could not agree on how to proceed after the European Commission had initiated the revision process.[218] The recast was a modernisation of the Directive and it pursued several aims: the effectiveness of employees' transnational information and consultation rights; the increase of the number of EWCs; the resolution of some of the practical problems encountered when applying the Directive; the lessening of the legal uncertainty raised by some provisions or the lack of provisions; the facilitating of the liaising between national and transnational levels of information and consultation.[219] The intentions translated into a number of changes which involved a more precise definition of the process of information and consultation for coherence between all European information and consultation Directives;[220] a more specific definition of what constitutes 'transnational';[221] provisions to cater for changes in the structure of the multinationals (such as mergers or selling of some of the

---

Kingdom' in F. DORSSEMONT and T. BLANK (eds.) *The Recast of the European Works Council Directive*, Intersentia, 2010, p. 213.

[215] TICER, reg. 21 for example and 22 on the penalties.

[216] Reg. 21(7).

[217] Council Directive 2009/38/EC above n. 205.

[218] Envisaged in the original Directive 94/45/EC at art. 15. For comments on the process for revision, see R. JAGODZINSKI, 'Review, revision or recast? The quest for an amended EWC Directive' in F. DORSSEMONT and T. BLANK (eds.), *The Recast of the European Works Council Directive*, Intersentia, 2010, p. 293 or P. LORBER, 'Reviewing the European Works Council Directive: European Progress and United Kingdom Perspective', (2004) 33 *ILJ* 191.

[219] Council Directive 2009/38/ EC, above n. 205, preamble, recital 7th.

[220] Ibid. Art. 2(f) and (g).

[221] Art. 1(4).

establishments located in a country) which would warrant changes in the EWC agreement;[222] the inclusion of a more positive role for employee representatives[223] and a requirement for EWC agreement to explain the link between national information and consultation channels and EWCs.[224] Weaknesses remain because the emphasis continues to be on procedure and flexibility rather than the imposition of minimum standards on all undertakings meeting the 1,000 employee threshold. A noticeable effort has however been made to consolidate and link information and consultation measures at European level.[225]

The Recast Directive was quickly transposed in national law by the Labour government. Regulations of 2010[226] modified TICER 1999 accordingly and came into force in June and October 2011. The regulations mainly copy what was found in the recast Directive but the following changes are of interest. Firstly, the process of information and consultation is more clearly defined and in line with what is found in ICER 2004.[227] Secondly, if the EWC agreement does not make reference to the relationship between EWC and national information and consultation body, when circumstances arise that may lead to substantial changes in work organisation or contractual relations, the process of information and consultation with both bodies must be linked and start within reasonable time of each other.[228] Thirdly, the maximum amount of penalty notice that may be awarded by the EAT has increased from £75,000 to £100,000.[229] Whilst this is an improvement, it remains minimal for multinationals.[230] Some of the jurisdictions given originally to the EAT as a 'court of first instance' have been moved to the CAC to rectify what was a highly unusual system of resolution of dispute.[231] The EAT can still issue a penalty notice but will not adjudicate on issues regarding the operation of the EWC. Fourthly, management is now under an obligation to provide EWC members with '*the means required to fulfil its duties to represent collectively the interests of the employee*',[232] but this explicitly excludes a requirement to give time off to representatives to exercise such duties.[233] In addition, employee representatives negotiating an EWC or sitting on an EWC are entitled to necessary training, paid by central management, in order

---

[222] Art. 13.

[223] Art. 10.

[224] Art. 12.

[225] For an evaluation of the changes brought by the Directive, P. LORBER, above n. 191; S. LAULOM, 'The Flawed Revision of the European Works Council Directive' (2010) 39 *ILJ* 202.

[226] SI 2010/1088.

[227] TICER, reg. 18A.

[228] Reg. 19E.

[229] Reg. 22.

[230] TICER, new reg. 19B inserted by reg. 11 TICE amendments Regulations 2010 and TICER 1999 reg. 25 as amended by reg. 16 of TICE amendments Regulations 2010.

[231] Regs. 21 and 22 as amended by regs. 12, 13 and 14 TICE amendments Regulations 2010.

[232] Reg. 19A.

[233] TICER, new reg. 19A inserted by reg. 11 TICE amendments Regulations 2010.

to fulfil effectively their functions.[234] The government has also published guidance on the new regulations;[235] although not binding, they can be considered by the enforcement bodies.

4. CONCLUSION

European Law has heavily influenced the UK system of industrial relations by inserting a new dimension to collective representation. Collective bargaining has been the traditional way of defending workers and their interest in the workplace. Information, consultation and participation have taken a significant place on the statutory book and there was therefore an expectation that this additional voice would also be heard. This should be viewed as a positive intervention of EU law as it furthers industrial democracy. However, the current system can be criticised on two accounts. Firstly, it is fragmented and appears as a patchwork of implementing regulations. Evidence is found in the different ways workers' representatives are designated, in the diverse definitions of information and consultations, and in the varying remedies available. Similarly, links between the various rules are not systematically clear or well-thought of. For example, while information and consultation bodies under ICER could deal with restructuring considering the information they receive, the regulations require that TULRCA obligation on redundancy consultation should still be adhered to.[236] Ideally, a consolidation of the current legal framework should be undertaken to help clarity and effectiveness of the information and consultation mechanisms. The Equality Act 2010 shows that assimilation and clarification of multiple laws with the same goal is achievable. A reform of the information and consultation legal framework would limit the burden on employers to juggle a set of regulations and acts. This may also strengthen trade unions' roles and rights. As the success of the system relies significantly on the strength of the national system of representation, it is paramount that trade unions engage with the law and the opportunities it offers and that the rules facilitate such engagement. As discovered with ICER and TICER the law has not been helpful and UK trade unions remain ambivalent towards the system. Recent research shows that trade unions should not be too wary of the information and consultation bodies as they have not encroached upon traditional collective bargaining machinery. The potential of the regulations should be more embraced as in some cases they have proved effective even in hybrid structures where non-

---

[234] Reg. 19B.
[235] See <www.bis.govuk/assets/biscore/employment-matters/docs/10–888-transnational-information-consultation-Regulations-2010-guidance.pdf> accessed 3.11.2011.
[236] ICER 2004, reg. 20(5).

union representatives work alongside trade union activists.[237] There are dangers for unions if management takes the lead but use of the legal framework could be more beneficial than inertia.

Secondly, the idea that workers' representatives should regularly participate in managerial decisions that might affect their livelihoods is an objective which has not yet been fully achieved. There are signs that inroads are created by the judiciary via interpretation of the duty to consult in redundancy situations. If the CJEU indicates that employee representatives have to be consulted before the decision is made, this may pave the way to the workers' representatives being able to influence decision making. However, ultimately, it is the actors who must take the lead. As seen with ICER, pro-participation management is key to an effective system where employee voice makes a difference. A stronger and more coherent regulatory system would however help a more widespread takeup of procedures which should be considered as routine for industrial relations practices.

---

[237]   See M. HALL, S. HUTCHISON. J. PURCELL, M. TERRY, J. PARKER (2010), above n. 136, 5.